Dangerous Ideas on Campus

Dangerous Ideas on Campus

Sex, Conspiracy, and Academic Freedom in the Age of JFK

MATTHEW C. EHRLICH

UNIVERSITY OF ILLINOIS PRESS
Urbana, Chicago, and Springfield

© 2021 by the Board of Trustees
of the University of Illinois
All rights reserved
1 2 3 4 5 C P 5 4 3 2 1
♾ This book is printed on acid-free paper.

Publication supported by a grant from the
Winton U. Solberg US History Subvention Fund

Library of Congress Cataloging-in-Publication Data
Names: Ehrlich, Matthew C., 1962– author.
Title: Dangerous ideas on campus : sex, conspiracy, and academic
    freedom in the age of JFK / Matthew C. Ehrlich.
Description: Urbana : University of Illinois Press, [2021] |
    Includes bibliographical references and index.
Identifiers: LCCN 2021020091 (print) | LCCN 2021020092
    (ebook) | ISBN 9780252044199 (cloth) | ISBN 9780252086243
    (paperback) | ISBN 9780252053153 (ebook)
Subjects: LCSH: Academic freedom—United States—History—
    20th century. | College students—Sexual behavior—United
    States—20th century. | Freedom of speech—United States—
    History—20th century. | Universities and colleges—United
    States—Sociological aspects—20th century.
Classification: LCC LC72.2 .E37 2021 (print) | LCC LC72.2 (ebook) |
    DDC 371.1/04—dc23
LC record available at https://lccn.loc.gov/2021020091
LC ebook record available at https://lccn.loc.gov/2021020092

Contents

Acknowledgments vii
Introduction: Little Explosions 1
1 Tidal Wave 17
2 Sex Ritualized 39
3 Seriously Prejudicial 63
4 Storm Coming 87
5 International Vermin 111
6 Ungloriously Wrong 135
Conclusion: Yeast and Ferment 159
Notes 175
Index 207

Acknowledgments

Thanks to William Maher and the rest of the staff of the University of Illinois at Urbana-Champaign Archives for generous helpings of time and assistance. An incomplete list of those individuals who responded to my many questions and requests includes Susanne Belovari, Cara Setsu Bertram, Katherine Majewski, Katie Nichols, Jameatris Rimkus, Linda Stahnke Stepp, and Ellen Swain.

For additional assistance with research and with obtaining images, thanks to Sherrie Bowser, Karla Gerdes, Shalini Smith, and the rest of the staff of the Champaign County Historical Archives; Ryan Ross of the University of Illinois Alumni Association; the staff of the History, Philosophy, and Newspaper Library at the University of Illinois; the staff of the Wisconsin Historical Society; the staff of the Chicago History Museum Research Center; and the staff of the Decatur Public Library in Illinois.

A number of individuals who lived through the events related in this book were kind enough to submit to my questions by phone, email, or in person. Thanks to Rich Archbold, Lew Collens, Eden Martin, Philip Martin, Jim Nowlan, Karen Lucas Petitte, and Ron Szoke. Thanks as well to Chris Czurylo Craven, David Krohne, Christopher Stoner, and the late Betsy Shirah.

Daniel Nasset of the University of Illinois Press (UIP) shepherded this book as well as most of my previous books for UIP. Many other individuals at UIP have helped me over the years; an incomplete list includes Angela Burton, Margo Chaney, Kevin Cunningham, Jennifer Fisher, Heather Gernenz, Ellie

Hinton, Dustin Hubbart, Denise Peeler, Ami Reitmeier, Tad Ringo, Michael Roux, Mariah Schaefer, and Roberta Sparenburg. Thanks also to two anonymous reviewers and to the UIP faculty board for helpful suggestions on the first draft of this project. Geof Garvey copyedited the final manuscript. Hans-Joerg Tiede of the American Association of University Professors kindly shared with me a manuscript of his own that had yet to be published.

My brother Paul Stephen Ehrlich assisted me with genealogical research. You can find P. S. Ehrlich's literary efforts at skeeterkitefly.com.

ns on Campus

INTRODUCTION

Little Explosions

> The only power that should prevail in university life is the merit of an idea—an idea openly advanced and opened to free debate by all concerned.
>
> —David D. Henry, University of Illinois president, in a 1969 commencement address

> [Revilo] Oliver and [Leo] Koch in one decade are more than one institution should bear!
>
> —David D. Henry, University of Illinois president, in a 1964 private letter[1]

These are challenging times for American higher education. Even before the COVID-19 pandemic descended upon the United States in 2020, public universities had experienced years of declining funding, leading to tuition hikes and growing fears of pernicious influence from the private sector. Campuses have felt increasing pressures to fight sexual assault and harassment. And they face charges of pandering to "snowflake" students and suppressing free speech (especially but not exclusively among conservatives), even as white supremacist propaganda targets colleges.[2] In such a climate, it is tempting to look wistfully to the past when seemingly funding was more secure, students were less fragile, and academic freedom was more respected.

History indicates, however, that things were not always so rosy. Witness the University of Illinois at Urbana-Champaign (U of I) in 1960, a time when the "silent generation" of college students was routinely viewed as being apathetic, if not spoiled. The university was facing a freeze on building funds and uncertain prospects for voter approval of a bond issue that was needed to accommodate the impending surge of boomer generation enrollees. That March, U of I biology professor Leo Koch wrote a letter to the *Daily Illini* student newspaper condoning premarital sex among young people. The subsequent public uproar was partly fomented by a onetime communist turned right-wing minister. Ultimately Koch was fired, and the university was censured by the American Association of University Professors. Four years later, in 1964—amid growing student political awareness fueled by the civil rights movement and the Cold War—U of I classics professor Revilo Oliver published an article charging that the communists had assassinated President John F. Kennedy as part of a planned takeover of the United States. Oliver had stirred controversy before with white supremacist remarks, and his wife had charged that the U of I was unfairly targeting him for his views. Now, just as in the Koch case, many people called for Oliver's firing. This time, though, the university defended the professor's freedom to speak: an action wholeheartedly supported by *Daily Illini* editor Roger Ebert, among others.

This book will use the Koch and Oliver cases to help us think about academic freedom, free speech, the legacy of the 1960s, and the roiling debates over sex and politics that have persisted to this day both on and off campus. The mission of universities always has been to nurture ideas and critical thinking, as U of I president David D. Henry indicated in his 1969 commencement address. But when those ideas seem dangerous or irresponsible enough to arouse public condemnation, academic freedom controversies erupt, to the consternation of college administrators such as Henry. The Koch and Oliver cases both emerged from a time and place not ordinarily seen as rife with dissent (the idealistic John F. Kennedy era at a traditionally conservative midwestern university). They signaled a significant shift in the understanding of academic freedom, as Oliver benefited from more liberal protections that the Koch case helped encourage. The two cases also embodied the stark oppositions over beliefs and values that continue to divide our society. Though polar opposites in their political views, Koch and Oliver were in many ways mirror images of each other in their roles as campus gadflies and public provocateurs. Even today, some of what Koch espoused retains its power to goad, just as most of what Oliver espoused retains its power to disturb.

Thinking about Academic Freedom

At first glance, it may be surprising that Koch and Oliver ever created so much controversy. The ideas that premarital sex is permissible and that a conspiracy underlay President Kennedy's 1963 assassination hardly seem shocking now, if public opinion polls are any indication. Even six decades ago, it was widely understood that many unmarried people had sex, just as many people believed virtually from the day of Kennedy's murder that a conspiracy had killed him.[3] (Oliver's own conspiracy theory prompted the Warren Commission that was investigating the assassination to subpoena him for a deposition.)

Yet the public rhetoric surrounding sex was very different in 1960 from what it is today. "The middle-class culture of respectability so widely endorsed in mid-twentieth-century America provided a clear set of rules about sexual behavior," writes historian Beth Bailey. "At its heart was a simple stricture: no sex outside of marriage." When Leo Koch asserted in the student newspaper that "there is no valid reason why sexual intercourse should not be condoned among those sufficiently mature to engage in it without social consequences," he outraged many members of the public. As for John F. Kennedy, the grief over his assassination still was fresh when Revilo Oliver wrote of him, "So long as there are Americans, his memory will be cherished with distaste." Historian Susan J. Douglas wryly observes that the public did not know during Kennedy's presidency that "it was impossible for him to keep his fly zipped within a fifty-mile radius of rustling pettipants." He was widely seen as an inspirational figure, especially among the young. "Never for one minute did I think JFK was talking only to boys," Douglas recalls. "He was talking to me as well. The spirit of the times invited, even urged, girls to try to change the world too."[4] For Oliver to attack the late president just weeks after his violent death seemed beyond the pale.

Koch and Oliver provoked anger with more than just their words about sex or Kennedy. Koch acknowledged that at times he could be "stubborn, irascible, or domineering"; he also was a regular and caustic critic of organized religion. By the start of 1960, he already had irked his U of I superiors enough that they had given him a terminal contract set to expire the following year. His letter to the *Daily Illini* that condoned premarital sex also condemned what Koch called "the hypocritical and downright inhumane moral standards engendered by a Christian code of ethics which was already decrepit in the days of Queen Victoria."[5] As for Oliver, his views of the late president were mild compared with his views on people of color and Jews. By 1964, he already had been quoted as calling Cuba "an island largely populated by mongrels" and Africa a continent inhabited by "mangy cannibal[s]." In the summer of that year, he would brand the three young civil-rights workers who had just been murdered in Mississippi "cockroaches." Two years later, in 1966, he would tell a political rally that it was pointless to hold a "beatific vision" in which "all the Bolsheviks or all of the Illuminati or all the Jews were vaporized at dawn tomorrow."[6] Oliver made all those remarks while still employed as a U of I professor.

Oliver and Koch exemplify the conflicts that regularly develop over academic freedom, which can seem an arcane or confusing concept. Stanley Fish argues that academic freedom has been viewed according to multiple schools of thought. They range from the "it's just a job" school, whereby "academics are not free in any special sense to do anything but their jobs," to the "critique" and "revolution" schools, whereby academic freedom protects dissent and supports the struggle for systemic change both inside and outside the academy.[7]

The most widely recognized model of academic freedom has been that promoted by the American Association of University Professors (AAUP). Matthew W. Finkin and Robert C. Post succinctly define this model: "In essence, academic freedom consists of the freedom to pursue the scholarly profession according to the standards of that profession." More specifically, faculty members possess freedom of research and publication, freedom of teaching, freedom of "intramural" speech (the freedom to criticize their own colleges), and freedom of "extramural" speech—the freedom as citizens to comment on public affairs via such means as speeches, articles, letters to the editor, and social media. University president Patricia McGuire has summarized the freedoms as the "ability to conduct research freely, publish whatever we choose, teach as we must, and speak openly without fear."[8]

Professional standards are central to this model, with faculty being the ones judging how well their peers are doing their jobs. "There is a fundamental distinction between holding faculty accountable to professional norms and holding them accountable to public opinion," Finkin and Post write. "The former exemplifies academic freedom; the latter undermines it." For Henry Reichman, free speech is a "liberal democratic value," whereas academic freedom is "largely a meritocratic value." Rather than being evaluated in a public marketplace of ideas in which anyone might participate, faculty should be evaluated by fellow academics—particularly those in the same field or discipline—and those faculty should decide what qualifies as meritorious. To be sure, fellow professionals may not always be fair or impartial, as Joan Wallach Scott acknowledges: "The devastating review, the charges of incomplete research, mockery by one's elders can bring an end to a promising academic career, especially one that engages in a critique of disciplinary premises." Nonetheless, Scott argues that faculty autonomy remains essential to avoid transforming the university "from a place where ideas are contested, debated, and exchanged to one in which vigilant risk managers allow consumers to influence what can and cannot be said."[9]

That model of academic freedom has endured from the AAUP's founding in 1915. Its influence can be seen in David Henry's 1969 commencement address in which he said that "the only power that should prevail in university life is the merit of an idea," as presumably judged by individuals who are thoroughly versed in the norms of university life and professionally competent to judge merit. Yet two questions have persisted over the years. First, to what extent does professional responsibility accompany professional freedom? Second, what happens when other powers threaten to prevail in university life, as, for example, when public opinion is passionately aroused by "extramural" speech and when "consumers"—students, parents, and taxpayers—assert that such expression is dangerous or harmful?

The notion that faculty should exercise responsibility as well as freedom is an old one. John K. Wilson traces its roots to what he calls a "gentleman scientist" interpretation of academic freedom that stressed "propriety and obligations": the obligation to conduct oneself as a "gentleman" (or, presumably, as a "lady") and to "conform to the behavioral rules and moral standards" of one's university. Although the strict emphasis on conformity and rules has lessened over time, an ideal of reasoned decorum in university life has remained. When David Henry delivered his 1969 address during a time of widespread campus protests over Vietnam, he invoked that ideal by insisting "upon reason, upon respect for the views of others and their right to express them, upon intellectual humility.... Arrogance of opinion, bullhorn shout-downs, and confrontations are foreign to the university tradition and if pursued destroy the academic freedom essential to an effective university." Matthew Finkin and Robert Post vigorously extol faculty freedom, but they also emphasize the need for professional restraint: "On any plausible account, the production of knowledge requires not merely the negative liberty to speculate free from censorship but also an affirmative commitment to the virtues of reason, fairness, and accuracy."[10]

John Wilson rejects what he sees as an overemphasis on professional niceties. He says that academic freedom should be seen as "the individual right of a professor to express dissenting views" as opposed to the "collective right of the faculty to determine professional standards"; it is not "a kind of property belonging to an elite academic class of tenured professors." That viewpoint—representing what Wilson calls a "liberty model" of academic freedom—is consistent with a libertarian interpretation of free speech and the First Amendment. It is epitomized by such landmark US Supreme Court decisions as 1964's *Times v. Sullivan* (which asserted that "debate on public issues should be uninhibited, robust, and wide-open") and 1971's *Cohen v. California* (which declared that "the state has no right to cleanse public debate to the point where it is grammatically palatable to the most squeamish among us"). A liberty model of academic freedom embraces passionate political debate among students and faculty without fear of censure. It also puts a premium on protecting unconstrained extramural expression, for, as Wilson notes, "the history of academic freedom cases is overwhelmingly a record of extramural utterances, where professors speak on controversial issues outside of their academic work."[11]

Indeed, faculty political expression that challenges prevailing orthodoxy always has risked a backlash. The anticommunism of the 1940s and 1950s "silenced an entire generation of radical intellectuals," according to historian Ellen W. Schrecker. Today, some conservatives in the humanities and social sciences charge that their academic freedom is being threatened, with one professor going as far as to claim that conservatives are "the most discriminated-against higher education employees"; meanwhile, private donors have endowed centers to further conservative thought on what they see as left-leaning campuses.[12] Controversies over extramural expression have continued to rock colleges and universities. Decades after the Leo Koch academic freedom case, the U of I once again landed on the AAUP censure list after it denied a tenured professorship in 2014 to Steven Salaita, who had posted angry tweets about Israel. The U of I said that Salaita's speech was "uncivil" and hence disqualified him for the faculty position that the university already had offered to him.[13]

A particular flashpoint over the years has been campus speech that seems utterly removed from any semblance of reason, fairness, or accuracy, as, for example, when Revilo Oliver called people "mongrels," "cannibals," and "cockroaches" while musing about their hypothetical vaporization. (Steven Salaita vigorously denied claims that his tweets had denigrated Jews; in contrast, Oliver's extramural expression was unambiguously anti-Semitic, as well as being racist.)[14] Recent controversies have erupted when outside speakers have come to universities to promote white nationalism or to attack gays, lesbians, and transgender people. Several scholars have challenged First Amendment absolutism and unquestioning acceptance of the idea that, as John Durham Peters has described it, "righteous citizens steel themselves by learning to live with the thought they hate." On the contrary, according to Mari J. Matsuda, "Tolerance of hate speech is not tolerance borne by the community at large. Rather, it is a psychic tax imposed on those least able to pay." Responding to conservative scorn of "snowflake" students who protest campus speech that they regard as hateful and discriminatory, Ulrich Baer praises the students for "strengthening rather than severing the link of free speech and equality that is fundamental to our democracy" and also for opposing speakers who seek to exercise "raw power" through "a weaponized conception of free speech" that threatens the university's "central purpose of advancing knowledge and respecting the truth."[15]

Henry Reichman harbors no sympathy for those sorts of speakers, but he still defends their right to appear on campuses. He approvingly quotes from a 1994 AAUP statement on university speech: "An institution of higher learning fails to fulfill its mission if it asserts the power to proscribe ideas—and racial or ethnic slurs, sexist epithets, or homophobic insults almost always express ideas, however repugnant." But Reichman also supports the rights of individuals to "object to and protest" such ideas, arguing that "threats to academic freedom from politicians, trustees, and corporatizing administrators appear much more ominous than efforts by impassioned sophomores to silence outside provocateurs." (As for conservatives who assert that their political expression is being squelched, Reichman says that "the conservative political movement for campus 'free speech' is aimed mainly at the freedom only of certain speakers," and he adds that many conservatives "are not only hypocritically silent when leftists are assaulted; they participate in the assault.")[16]

Joan Wallach Scott similarly warns of the chilling effect on academic freedom that can be imposed by the powers that be. Much as Reichman does, she distinguishes academic freedom from free speech: "Free speech makes no distinction about quality; academic freedom does." And contrary to John Wilson, who sees academic freedom as an individual right rather than a collective right, Scott reasserts the importance of collective professional oversight, saying that it should take precedence over vague or self-serving notions of academic responsibility or civility: "Academic freedom protects those whose thinking challenges orthodoxy; at the same time, the legitimacy of the challenge—the proof that the critic is not a madman or a crank—is secured by membership in a disciplinary community based upon shared commitment to certain methods, standards, and beliefs."[17]

All these tensions lay at the heart of the Koch and Oliver cases: academic freedom versus free speech, faculty freedom versus faculty responsibility, individual liberty versus equal rights, and the power exerted by ideas versus the power exerted by campus overseers and public opinion. Higher education historian John R. Thelin has argued that it is "crucial to have informed discussions about changes in academic freedom and campus speech over time" in order to put current debates over those issues into proper context.[18] By examining the Koch and Oliver cases in detail and the individuals caught up in them, we can better understand what truly is at stake in controversies over such things as extramural expression, and we can see how the two cases shaped the national debate over such expression. (The Koch case would contribute to mounting student dissatisfaction at the University of California in Berkeley that culminated in the 1964 Free Speech Movement.)[19] The cases also help us recognize the difficulties in balancing competing demands and values while trying to determine who may be "a madman or a crank." They show that academic freedom has in fact protected conservative speech—even speech from the extreme right. Finally, the two cases help us appreciate a vitally important era in US history and higher education, as well as the many parallels between that era and today.

Thinking about College in the Age of JFK

The current state of higher education is frequently compared unfavorably with the higher education of the past. For example, Joan Wallach Scott argues that critical thinking "has been severely compromised as the mission of the university, replaced by an emphasis on vocational preparation, on the comfort and security of students, on the avoidance of controversy lest students, parents, trustees, legislators, and donors find offense." The implication is that things used to be significantly better. Education professor David F. Labaree suggests that many "professors and administrators grieve for the good old days of the midcentury university and spin fantasies of recapturing them."[20]

People also hold nostalgia for the era corresponding with John F. Kennedy's presidency. Historian Brian Ward notes a widespread sense that "there was a 'good' early 1960s" full of idealism, affluence, and political consensus, followed by "a 'bad' 1960s" full of disillusionment, decay, and political factionalism. Kennedy's 1963 assassination is often cited as a turning point at which optimism began giving way to disenchantment.[21] Some people hold a contrary viewpoint: the early 1960s were "repressed and repressive" when it came to such things as sex, while the "sexual revolution" of the succeeding years was liberating, just as the political upheaval of those years "gave birth to a new America, a nation more open to new peoples, new ideas, new norms, and new, if conflicting, articulations of America itself."[22]

There is some truth to popular notions about the 1960s, but the era was more complex than might be realized. The decade did in many ways mark a high point for universities. Historians have called it "the most dynamic period in the long history of American higher education," characterized by "the 'three P's' of prosperity, prestige, and popularity." David Henry, U of I president from 1955 to 1971, recalled it as a time when the idea that "educated men and women are the chief resource of America became an article of faith, a faith widely shared, even when the relationship of higher education to the health and prosperity of the nation was not measurable in specific terms." But, as University of California president Clark Kerr observed, "The past had its own troubles." Among those troubles was the ongoing difficulty of "convincing the public, legislatures, and donors that growth was occurring and required adequate funding." As Kerr also noted, there always has been a "'normalcy' of a sort in the continuing struggles of colleges and universities to survive and improve while being threatened by diverse external forces."[23]

For David Labaree, the historical norm—to which we have reverted in the twenty-first century—has been for Americans to see higher education "as a distinctly private good" that should be supported primarily by individual consumers. The 1960s were part of a postwar aberration during which "Americans went through an intense but brief infatuation with higher education as a public good. Somehow college was going to help save us from the communist menace and the looming threat of nuclear war." The Soviet launch of the Sputnik satellite in 1957 and the ongoing Cold War prompted a surge in federal funding and foundation support for research, much of it related to defense. So strong were the connections among higher education, the military, and private industry that John Thelin argues that they constituted a "military-industrial-educational complex."[24]

Thelin's choice of label points to the dangers of viewing the 1960s too heavily in terms of rupture or revolution. The pejorative label "military-industrial complex" had been coined by President Dwight Eisenhower, and many social activists would invoke that same label during the Kennedy and Lyndon Johnson administrations. According to Brian Ward, that is just one indication that "the transition from the aged Ike to the youthful JFK, like that from the nominally conservative, sober, and ascetic 1950s to a liberal, hopped-up, and innovative 1960s, was neither as dramatic, nor as unequivocal as once believed." Ward also cautions about drawing too sharp a contrast between the Kennedy years and the turbulent years that followed, noting that the early 1960s were marked by dramatic developments related to civil rights, the Cold War, domestic politics, feminism, environmentalism, and popular culture: "It seems more perverse than productive to isolate the latter part of the decade when so many of the themes, events, trends, organizations, personalities, and legal frameworks that shaped the entire period were established well before Kennedy's assassination." Likewise, Beth Bailey asserts that the "sexual revolution" was as much evolutionary as revolutionary, coming about "less through pitched battles and overt cultural warfare than through negotiation and compromise" over many years and across the whole swath of America, including its supposedly straitlaced heartland.[25]

What about the college students of the 1960s? Were they made of sterner and more idealistic stuff than the students of today? They did display "hope, optimism, and self-confidence," as Michael V. Metz recalled (he himself was a 1960s college student and antiwar activist at the U of I). But that was not the whole story, if scholarly studies and news coverage from the time are any indication. One study at the start of the decade called students "politically disinterested, apathetic, and conservative." A 1963 *Saturday Evening Post* article remarked that for "a surprisingly large number, college has become a time of confusion, misery, frustration and failure," and *Mademoiselle* posed a poignant question the following year: "Are American college students rapidly 'cracking up'? Or are they instead being coddled?" At the U of I, dean of women Miriam Shelden somberly observed that "young people have lost their belief in tomorrow."[26]

Such fretful comments remind us that being young always has been stressful and that the older generation always has looked askance at the younger generation. They also highlight the anxieties of the first half of the 1960s. Consider the continuous threat of nuclear annihilation that ironically was helping boost investment in higher education. "What's the use?" the *Saturday Evening Post* quoted one Ivy Leaguer as saying. "We're all going to be blown up soon anyhow." Miriam Shelden said that students' lost belief in the future was driving them "to seek security in intimate relationships, to seek to belong to someone." The desire for intimacy raised thorny issues related to gender and sex. "Was I supposed to be an American—individualistic, competitive, aggressive, achievement-oriented, tough, independent?" Susan J. Douglas recalled of her youth. "Or was I supposed to be a girl—nurturing, self-abnegating, passive, dependent, primarily concerned with the well-being of others, and completely indifferent to personal success?" When it came to sex, Beth Bailey observes, "Young people were not sexually pure; rather, most engaged in a series of sexual skirmishes. 'Nice girls' said no; boys kept pushing." Pressures on young women to shun sexual intercourse before marriage still permitted a "whole variety of other sexual acts" just short of intercourse.[27]

Anxieties over both public and private affairs shook complacency and began prompting questions about why things were the way they were. Students wondered whether higher education's growing emphasis on research was coming at the expense of undergraduate teaching. They asked why universities continued to commit so heavily to the principle of in loco parentis, acting as surrogate parents whose philosophy seemingly could be summed up in a single admonition: *Don't*.[28] Students also became increasingly interested in politics and in social movements, with the conservative Young Americans for Freedom and the left-liberal Students for a Democratic Society both forming in 1960. According to sociologist Rebecca E. Klatch, "A parallel process of disillusionment provoked the involvement of young people at either end of the political spectrum." That process was not limited to colleges with a history of pronounced political activism. U of I graduate Roger Ebert wrote in 1967 that it had extended to his own campus: "Civil rights was the issue which first awoke the 'apathetic' campus, but once the lid was off Pandora's Box, the causes and the issues were many. Some University students joined peace demonstrations and others joined the Peace Corps, [while] some split off into vociferous liberal and conservative factions."[29]

The ferment of the time is a key reason why John Thelin argues that the early 1960s deserve as much attention as the latter part of the decade in studies of higher education history; he also notes that the concerns of that era foreshadowed many of today's concerns.[30] Beyond their relevance to academic freedom and campus speech, the Koch and Oliver cases relate to other enduring issues on campus and elsewhere.

One such issue is sex. Certainly campus sex mores have changed from the Kennedy years, as increased tolerance of nonheterosexual identities and numerous studies of so-called "hookup culture" attest. For such observers as Hanna Rosin, that culture's destigmatizing of casual sex has been empowering. "Young women are more in control of their sexual destinies than ever before," Rosin writes, adding that "what makes it stand out is the new power women have to ward off men if they want to." In her own study of campus sex, Vanessa Grigoriadis is less sanguine. She shares numerous graphic anecdotes of sexual assault, along with statistics indicating that 20 percent of female students have been victims of such assaults. She also notes that universities have compiled a mixed record in complying with federal mandates to combat rape culture. Yet Grigoriadis is optimistic, saying that college students have been leading the way "in a nationwide process of rewriting the rules of consensual and nonconsensual sex, overcoming deeply ingrained attitudes and making men respect women and their bodies."[31]

Leo Koch's 1960 letter—which extolled the virtues of a "mutually satisfactory sexual experience" for young people—in many ways foreshadowed today's more liberalized campus culture. It also highlights what perhaps has not changed over the years. Koch wrote his letter in response to a *Daily Illini* column written by two male students under the headline "Sex Ritualized." The column lamented the social pressures on undergraduates to conform to prescribed gender roles and see young women as "only female sex units." Many decades later, Donna Freitas would argue in her book *Consent on Campus* that things have not changed much: "It is just as much a culture of sexual oppression, repression, and problematic, stereotypical gender norms and expectations." The one real change is "instead of prescribing that young adults, especially young women, should not be having sex (before marriage), hookup culture prescribes that they *should*, even *must*, be having sex or something is wrong with them."[32]

If the Koch case anticipated current debates and divisions over sex, both the Koch and Oliver cases anticipated current debates and divisions over politics. Leo Koch and Revilo Oliver could not have been more different in their views. Koch was an avowed secular humanist who invoked John Dewey in his class lectures: "John Dewey wrote that 'God is the active relationship between the actual and the ideal,' but he did not insist that the word God was necessary." Oliver saw Dewey's philosophical pragmatism as the essence of communism: "The communist is the perfect pragmatist, a nihilist. He denies the existence of absolute truth. He repudiates and hates the traditions and culture of the past. ... Intellectually speaking, he is a beast—of the lowest and most dangerous kind."[33] Koch associated with such liberals as Harry Tiebout, a U of I philosophy professor who advised the campus NAACP chapter and backed local civil rights campaigns. Oliver associated with such anticommunists as Ira Latimer, a Chicago minister who would launch a campaign aided by Oliver's wife that targeted the likes of Tiebout and Koch and whipped up public furor after Koch published his letter on sex.

If anything, the two men seemed to take the left-right divide to its logical extreme: Koch would promote nudism, cofound the Sexual Freedom League, join the antiwar movement, go to the Woodstock festival, and retire to live off the land; Oliver would befriend William F. Buckley Jr., contribute to *National Review*, cofound the John Birch Society with Robert Welch, break with Buckley and Welch over his vocal anti-Semitism, and embrace neo-Nazism. Even if they were outliers, the two men still typified the opposing camps that would do battle in the "culture wars," which, according to historian Andrew Hartman, has "pitted liberal, progressive, and secular Americans against their conservative, traditional, and religious counterparts." Hartman traces those wars to the legacy of the 1960s and its challenges to long-standing social norms: "Whereas the Left considered post-sixties American culture a closer approximation of its ideal form, the Right considered it an abomination."[34] The culture wars continue to be fought today, representing bitter rifts that already were well established by the era of Koch and Oliver.

Oliver also presaged controversies over white supremacist speakers and propaganda on campuses. In George Hawley's overview of today's so-called "alt-right" movement, Hawley writes that the movement has distanced itself from predecessors whom it regards as having been ineffectual; it derisively labels those predecessors as "White Nationalism 1.0." Even so, Oliver has been described as "one of the most important figures in the development of American white nationalism."[35] Oliver's ideas closely align with those of such contemporary alt-right icons as Richard Spencer. (When Spencer spoke at Auburn University in 2017 after the university tried and failed to block his appearance, he said that a "black cloud" hung over the heads of White people, and he called individuals who protested his talk "communist scum.") Oliver's anti-Semitism also aligns with that of white nationalists of both the present and the past: the man who shot and killed a guard at the Holocaust Museum in Washington, DC, in 2009 had written a book dedicated to Oliver and others of his kind. Finally, Oliver's conspiracy-mindedness—which extended well beyond the John F. Kennedy assassination—is echoed by the conspiracy-mindedness of today. Political scientist Thomas Milan Konda characterizes it as a mind-set that long has mistrusted "expertise, policy makers, literary icons, [and] even scientists," while it also has been tied to "right-wing and authoritarian politics."[36]

Plan of Procedure

The protagonists in academic freedom controversies can be caricatured as rabid radicals, craven cowards, or maligned martyrs, according to one's perspective. This book will draw on university archives, personal papers, and memoirs to help us see the key players in the Koch and Oliver cases as more fully human and as the richly textured (and often richly eccentric) characters who always have populated college campuses. Doing so is not intended to elicit unwarranted sympathy for them; it will be argued here that U of I administrators and trustees were clearly wrong to fire Koch, and although they were right to retain Oliver, his viewpoints were clearly abhorrent. In the case of white supremacists such as Oliver, it is important not to normalize or rationalize their worldviews. It is also important to avoid false equivalence in assessing Koch and Oliver. Koch's attitudes toward sex as expressed in his 1960 letter have become comparatively mainstream today, while Oliver's virulent attitudes toward Jews and African Americans remain on the extremist fringes of political discourse, even though the far right keeps trying to make those views seem more acceptable.[37]

Regardless, it is helpful to understand what shaped both professors and why their public speech would prove so nettlesome to the likes of U of I president David Henry. For example, Henry had a strict religious upbringing and would see himself as having been "a missionary all my life"; Oliver was raised within a central Illinois clan so fractious and litigious that a newspaper would half-seriously suggest that an "evil genius has been following the footsteps of this ill-fated family."[38] To evoke the tenor of the early 1960s, the book will draw on news stories, oral histories, and interviews with U of I students from that time.

Chapter 1, "Tidal Wave," begins with a review of the postwar history of the U of I and the controversies that had erupted over administrators and professors who had been deemed to be too liberal. The chapter also looks at the so-called silent generation of college students and the U of I's efforts under David Henry to upgrade facilities in anticipation of the tidal wave of baby boomers then making their way through elementary and secondary school. In 1958, Illinois voters defeated a university bond measure; in 1960, the U of I vigorously mounted a new campaign to pass a bond issue that the university believed was critically important to its future. In the meantime, Ira Latimer was mounting a campaign of his own. He was a former communist and civil-rights activist who had executed an about-face in becoming an archconservative Baptist minister. Unhappy over the scathing criticism that he had received from some people at the U of I, Latimer worked with Revilo Oliver and Oliver's wife Grace to expose purported subversives on campus. In short order, a prime target emerged in Leo Koch.

Chapter 2, "Sex Ritualized," reviews Leo Koch's life and career to 1960. He had arrived at the U of I in 1955, and after tensions had developed with his division heads, they had informed him that his contract would not be renewed after it expired in 1961. Perhaps feeling that he now had nothing to lose, Koch ramped up his criticisms of religion and society through letters to the *Daily Illini* student newspaper and other local papers. The letter that would get him fired focused primarily on sex, and this second chapter also examines the campus sex mores and gender relations of that era, including the practice of in loco parentis and the double standard faced by women students. After the *Daily Illini* published its "Sex Ritualized" guest commentary in March 1960 questioning women's objectification, Koch wrote an impassioned response arguing that traditional codes of morality and sexual conduct were outmoded; he also emphatically told the *Daily Illini* editor that he wanted his response published. It appeared in the newspaper just as thousands of high schoolers and their family members were arriving on the U of I campus for a statewide basketball tournament. Koch was immediately asked by a colleague—only semijokingly—if he planned to submit his resignation right away or wait until later.

Chapter 3, "Seriously Prejudicial," reveals how the uproar triggered by Koch's letter quickly took his fate out of his own hands. Two U of I trustees wrote to President Henry to object to Koch, and then letters from the public began pouring in, especially after Ira Latimer circulated a letter to parents of female students in which he blasted Koch and the U of I's campaign for the bond issue (which eventually would pass after Koch's dismissal). News media across the country also weighed in on the case. The U of I's academic freedom committee issued a report saying that Koch had acted irresponsibly but should not be fired. Yet Koch's own unit recommended dismissal—saying that his conduct had been "seriously prejudicial" to the university—and President Henry concurred, prompting students to protest and hang Henry in effigy. After a formal hearing, the Board of Trustees voted to confirm Koch's termination. The AAUP's subsequent investigation of the case revealed a deep divide within the organization over the issue of faculty responsibility. The AAUP finally decided in 1963 to censure the U of I, which responded by revising its statutes and enhancing its academic freedom provisions.

Chapter 4, "Storm Coming," begins with John F. Kennedy's campaign visit to the U of I campus in October 1960, at which he quoted from a letter written by Abraham Lincoln one hundred years earlier on the eve of the Civil War: "I see the storm coming." In fact, the JFK years witnessed the U of I transforming from a comparatively placid place into one that was much more politically active, if not turbulent. The chapter reviews the development of both liberal student groups and conservative student groups on campus. It also looks at growing concerns about issues that included civil rights and the Cold War, with the 1962 Cuban missile crisis provoking particular worries. In addition, students questioned campus disciplinary procedures and limits on free expression. Roger Ebert often placed himself and the *Daily Illini* at the heart of such debates in his role as the student newspaper's editor during the 1963–64 school year. In November 1963 the U of I was shocked along with the rest of the world by Kennedy's assassination. During the subsequent holiday break, Revilo Oliver began work on his idiosyncratic interpretation of the president's murder.

Chapter 5, "International Vermin," examines Revilo Oliver's checkered family background and his lengthy connection to the U of I, first as a student in the late 1920s and then as a faculty member in the following decade. He would not display a pronounced preoccupation with politics until the 1950s, when he joined the editorial staff of William F. Buckley Jr.'s new magazine *National Review*, participated in antifluoridation campaigns in Illinois, and helped Robert Welch found the John Birch Society. The rise of the so-called "radical right" captured the attention of the news media plus such intellectuals as Richard Hofstadter and Daniel Bell; in response, many conservatives resented what they regarded as the patronizing dismissal of their interests and concerns. By the early 1960s, Oliver had become more avowedly racist and anti-Semitic in his public pronouncements (which excoriated so-called "international vermin"); those pronouncements alienated Buckley and alarmed U of I administrators.

The climax would come in early 1964 when Oliver published his attack on the late John F. Kennedy in *American Opinion*, the John Birch Society magazine.

Chapter 6, "Ungloriously Wrong," relates the fallout from Oliver's article. Once again there were angry letters from the public, along with news stories and editorials across the country commenting on Oliver. Roger Ebert wrote his own commentaries in the *Daily Illini* condemning the professor's article but also vigorously supporting Oliver's right to speak his mind. The response of U of I administrators and trustees would be markedly different from the way that they had handled the Koch case four years previously. President Henry sought faculty input, and the campus academic freedom committee defended what it called Oliver's right to be "ungloriously wrong," adding that he should be judged by fellow academics rather than by public opinion. Henry then announced that no disciplinary action would be taken, and the Board of Trustees agreed. Oliver's department head would fail to persuade him to temper his speeches and writings, which grew ever more virulent while his scholarly output diminished. Oliver broke with the John Birch Society after its leader decided that he had grown too extreme. Meanwhile, student activism steadily increased from 1964 into 1965 at the U of I and elsewhere, as students headed south for Freedom Summer, the Free Speech Movement emerged in Berkeley, and US involvement escalated in Vietnam.

The conclusion, "Yeast and Ferment," revisits the role of universities as places where new and challenging ideas are continually brewed: a process once described by U of I dean of women Miriam Shelden as being one of "yeast and ferment." The discussion will consider the implications of the Koch and Oliver cases for higher education's handling of issues related to sex, politics, and academic freedom.

In the *Daily Illini* in 1964, student Robert Jung approvingly wrote that ideas "can cause all kinds of little explosions down deep where people really live."[39] What follows is a case study about explosive ideas and the ongoing battle to ignite, spread, contain, or extinguish them.

CHAPTER 1

Tidal Wave

The University of Illinois as of the mid-twentieth century was an unlikely candidate to trigger a national furor over academic freedom and sex. Michael V. Metz has characterized the U of I during those years as a "staid institution, seeking notoriety in academics and athletics—certainly not in political activism or loosening of social mores." Its academic reputation rested heavily on science, engineering, and agriculture. A 1950 history of the university concluded with a lengthy summary of achievements, starting with the U of I's success in "combating the Hessian fly, the chinch bug, oat smut, flag smut, bitter rot, apple scab, and other enemies of farmers and orchardists in Illinois." That same history declared that although the U of I's contributions in nonscientific fields were perhaps not quite so renowned, the university was committed to achieving across-the-board excellence: "When an institution is aware of its sources of strength and weakness, when it is intensely active in the study of its own problems, and when it is suffused with eagerness to meet the commands placed upon it by the citizens who support it, only the foolhardy could say that it is not growing in prestige and service."[1]

By 1950, the University of Illinois was becoming intensely aware of the problem of trying to cultivate academic prestige while trying to meet citizen demands. Four years earlier, it had made George Stoddard its president. His hiring was intended to address concerns that the U of I lacked strong leadership and was burdened with "conservative and sometimes reactionary senior professors and administrators," as an external evaluation of the university had put it. Stoddard quoted a fellow university president in speaking of the U of I as a "sleeping giant which is awakening," but his efforts to bestir the institution provoked resistance. He hired Howard Bowen in 1947 to become dean of the College of Commerce and Business Administration. Bowen had come from the East, and he tried to revitalize the college through dozens of new hires. In May 1950 a longtime economics professor resigned, triggering insinuations from Champaign-Urbana's *News-Gazette* newspaper that the college was importing professors with "leftist and ultra liberal ideas" (such as Keynesian economics) into the upstanding "black dirt country" of central Illinois. The departing professor fueled the controversy by ominously alluding to "pale pinkos" on the faculty: "and great reds from little pinkos grow." Bowen finally was forced to resign at year's end, followed by an exodus of many of commerce's top faculty members.[2]

The Bowen affair corresponded with the onset of McCarthyism and a grim era in American higher education. It was a time, as one 1950s overview of academic freedom glumly noted, when political opportunists claimed "that our colleges and universities are overrun with communists, undermined by them, infected by them.... The fact that these charges are false and utterly misleading does not concern [the ones making the charges]. Their appeal is to prejudice, not to intelligence." The universities' response was shamefully inadequate, according to historian Ellen W. Schrecker: "The academy did not fight McCarthyism. It contributed to it." Schrecker charged that "the failure to protect academic freedom eroded the academy's moral integrity."[3]

At the University of Illinois, President George Stoddard faced the unenviable task of being a liberal who tried to be "both actively anticommunist and actively anti-McCarthy at the same time," according to another historian.[4] Stoddard proclaimed that "Communism comes after us like a mad dog on a leash; our choice is running or resisting." The university security office said that it kept tabs on any "statement or action termed even slightly subversive or 'pink'" (although dean of students Fred Turner would tell an investigator for the Broyles commission—an Illinois legislative group probing alleged subversion—that he believed that there were no longer any "Pink or Red organizations" at the U of I). Under Stoddard's watch, the university also fired at least four faculty members for their political associations. In addition, the Illinois legislature in 1947 enacted the Clabaugh Act (named after its sponsor, a Republican state lawmaker from Champaign). The U of I already had a ban dating back to 1890 against using its buildings and grounds for political purposes. The Clabaugh Act went further, declaring that because "the universities of America have been the breeding ground of a series of invidious communist-inspired organizations which have sought to instill in the hearts of American youth contempt and hatred for ideals to which the people of this great nation have been dedicated," the U of I would forthwith be prohibited from allowing its facilities to be used by "any subversive, seditious, and un-American organization."[5]

On the other hand, when another Republican state lawmaker charged in August 1950 that the U of I was harboring "fifty reds, pinks, and socialists" on its faculty, a thoroughly annoyed George Stoddard sent the lawmaker a blank list to be filled in with the names of the purported offenders (he received no list in return). Stoddard also condemned the Broyles commission, and in 1953 he gave a speech saying that "paranoid persons, acting on their own initiative and at times with the support of gullible agencies, are indicting practically the whole United States!" Soon thereafter, the U of I Board of Trustees—led by former Illinois football great Red Grange—ousted the president.[6]

Stoddard's dismissal may have had less to do with his politics than it did with his occasional abrasiveness and frayed relationships with the trustees, one of whom complained that Stoddard had "seemed as if he liked nothing better than to get into a big fight" and that the university had experienced "one controversy after another since he came here." Yet his firing angered some faculty, and the *Daily Illini* student newspaper editorialized that Stoddard had been "completely out of place in the choking atmosphere of conservatism and bigotry in the community, the legislature, and the state as a whole." Stoddard's interim replacement, Lloyd Morey, raised no hackles (his death several years later would come while he was delivering an impassioned anticommunist talk in Champaign to the Daughters of the American Revolution).[7] In the meantime, the U of I searched for a new permanent president. The person the university finally found would prove in many ways to be the temperamental opposite of Stoddard.

David D. Henry and the "Silent Generation"

By his own admission, David Dodds Henry was never an imposing figure. "Certainly, I am not 'charismatic' in any way," he wrote in his memoirs. "I have been submerged in my work so completely that I have often felt that I have no personality or personal interest to others apart from career." He had been born in Pennsylvania in 1905 and raised in a former farmhouse with a fundamentalist Christian upbringing that included time spent in a Baptist school. By age twenty-six, he had earned a doctorate in English from Pennsylvania State University. "My youthful idealism, nurtured in religious orthodoxy, was sustained

David Dodds Henry, University of Illinois president from 1955 to 1971. He saw himself as a missionary for social betterment through education. (Courtesy of the University of Illinois Archives, Photographic Subject File, RS 39/2/20)

in the study of the humanities," wrote Henry. "Application of the humanities to human affairs supplemented the religious impulses, and thus I came to view the place of educational opportunity in the scheme of things—to believe that as minds are liberated, free choice becomes more meaningful." The slight, bespectacled professor became a proselytizer for social improvement through education: "In some ways, I have been a missionary all my life."[8]

Henry steadily climbed the higher education career ladder, becoming president of Wayne State University in Detroit in 1945 and then executive vice chancellor of New York University in 1952. Two years after Henry took the New York

University post, a search committee contacted him about the U of I presidency. Word of his candidacy quickly leaked, prompting someone in Detroit to send U of I trustees a letter that attacked Henry as being soft on communism. (Henry would blame the letter on a person who was unhappy over a family member having been passed over for an administrative position at Wayne State.) After an Illinois contingent traveled to Michigan to investigate the allegations against Henry, he angrily withdrew his name from consideration for the presidency. "The general faculty reaction [at Illinois], while not particularly partial to my appointment, relished the stand that I took and interpreted it as a 'slap' at the trustees," Henry recalled. Negative press coverage ensued against the university. Chastened, the trustees asked Henry to reconsider, and he became U of I president in 1955.[9]

Henry's timing in assuming his new position was in some ways propitious. Despite the McCarthyesque attack on Henry from Detroit, Joseph McCarthy himself had been formally condemned by his fellow US senators in 1954, and the worst of the anticommunist fervor on college campuses was subsiding, albeit not after having exacted a significant toll. ("All was quiet on the academic front," Ellen Schrecker would write, for "McCarthyism had silenced an entire generation of radical intellectuals.") Fully aware of lingering "unease and uncertainty" at the U of I after the turmoil of the Stoddard years and the contentious search for a new president, Henry sought to assume a comparatively low profile on campus: "I had the feeling that if I could get into the job quietly and unobtrusively, it would be better for all concerned." And "quiet and unobtrusive" seemed to align well with the mood of the student body, not just at Illinois but elsewhere too. "Youth today is waiting for the hand of fate to fall on its shoulders, meanwhile working fairly hard and saying almost nothing," *Time* magazine had opined in 1951. "The most startling fact about the younger generation is its silence."[10]

The "silent generation"—born during the years roughly spanning the onset of the Great Depression to the end of World War II—often has been remembered for its apparent complacency and its contrast with the rambunctious baby boom generation that would follow it. As is true of sweeping generalizations about any generation, the "silent" label is misleading and incomplete; Martin Luther King Jr., Gloria Steinem, Elvis Presley, and Abbie Hoffman all were born between 1929 and 1945.[11] Still, the label has endured. As children, according to Gail Sheehy, members of the silent cohort "were so good: drying dishes for their mothers by hand (before dishwashers), hanging up clothes with pins (before clothes dryers), and washing the family car long before they were allowed to drive it." As college students, according to William Manchester, they "were in bondage from the outset, as committed to the American way as any medieval youth off for the monastery."[12]

Sheehy and Manchester weighed in on the silent generation long after it had left college and moved on to full-fledged adulthood, but pundits of the 1950s and early 1960s already had expressed similar and often cutting assessments: Young people were "grave and fatalistic." They were "living a life of quiet desperation." They were "apathetic, silent, conformist, indifferent, confused." They were "slack on liberty" and ignorant of democratic principles.[13] In 1957 political scientist Philip E. Jacob published a study indicating that "American college students today tend to think alike, feel alike and believe alike," with their university education apparently doing little to shape their values one way or the other. Jacob used italics to underscore his key points: the students were "*gloriously contented*" and "*self-centered*," prepared to "conform to the economic status quo and to receive ample rewards for dutiful and productive effort." Perhaps behind their contented façades, the students actually were quietly desperate—but, if so, they did not blame their universities. According to another academic study, "the vast majority [of students] say that 'the colleges are doing a good job'; that 'most of what I am learning in college is very worthwhile.'"[14]

In his 1958 book *The Unsilent Generation*, political scientist Otto Butz noted that campuses had changed from the Depression years when economic upheaval and the Spanish Civil War were hot-button issues. He wrote (in words that would seem ironic a decade later during the Vietnam era) that students no longer demonstrated their commitments "by signing long petitions, by parading about with placards, or by fighting in somebody else's civil war." The pronounced lack of social criticism had an upside; it "helped to make American society as internally secure as it is," even though it also could encourage smugness and a tendency to take too much for granted. Regardless, Butz expressed confidence that contemporary students represented "*both* ambitious future businessmen, professionals, and administrators *and* determined, aware, and introspective young intellectuals."[15]

In fact, some students were showing that they were more intellectually aware and self-critical than much of the older generation gave them credit for. Writing in the *Daily Illini* in 1955, U of I student Bob Perlongo took his classmates to task for their apparent apathy toward the US Senate censure of Joseph McCarthy and the recent announcement of David Henry's appointment as U of I president; the student body seemed far more concerned with popular culture and the doings of campus fraternities and sororities. Perlongo attached his own moniker to his peers—the "hollow generation"—while telling them, "You are being lulled to sleep and you are being made indifferent." He hoped that the "anti-intellectual

Black Plague that is lulling our generation into a kind of mental stupor" would be eradicated while "the hollowness is filled in with some real values." Perlongo also worked in a swipe at his elders: "Maybe our generation watched the one that preceded it too closely. The people of that generation did not set a good example for us.... The generation before us was a negative one."[16]

Other young people would echo that criticism in the years that followed. "We're called the silent generation, but can you really blame us? We've studied under those who often make a fetish of silence," one college student said. Robb K. Burlage, a former editor of the *Daily Texan* student newspaper in Austin, agreed. He wrote in 1959 that "big" education had taken root in the United States: "And because bigness begets bureaucracy, conformism, discretion, the giant academic communities which today dominate American higher education are harboring teachers and administrators who deserve the appellation 'silent generation' as much as the students for whom the phrase was invented." Burlage noted that state universities in particular were facing increasing pressure from business and industry to serve private interests, resulting in "a greater need than ever for university administrators and teachers who are dedicated to a renaissance of freedom—and controversy—on the campus."[17]

In short, the seeds for critique and dissent already were being planted, even among some young people who displayed no overt disquiet. According to college administrator Edward D. Eddy, "Beneath the student's studied pretense of indifference and apathy lies an unfashionable but searching desire for meaning in all that he does." Even if higher education was not fostering critical thinking to the extent that some critics believed that it should, the *New York Times* suggested that "modern educational methods" (presumably of the sort introduced by John Dewey and his peers) were encouraging the young "to question and to doubt the black-and-white rightness and wrongness of any issue and to see everything as 'relative.'" That is, students were ready to challenge the status quo. Political scientist Philip Jacob argued in 1957 that the reduced influence of "the Puritan heritage on which the major value assumptions of American society have rested" had portentous implications for the future: "Perhaps these students are the forerunners of a major cultural and ethical revolution, the unconscious ushers of an essentially secular (though nominally religious), self-oriented (though group-conforming) society."[18]

That "revolution" would come to pass, possibly sooner than Jacob had anticipated, and it would be led in no small part by the students whom he had found to be homogeneous and docile. "As they turned out, the Silents were not silent at all," Gail Sheehy would write many years later. "Members of this generation were, in fact, the pathbreakers for much of the 1960s-era 'raised consciousness'—in music and film, civil rights and women's rights, and multicultural sensibility—for which Boomers too often claim credit."[19]

Of course, nobody knew how the future would play out as of 1955, when David Henry assumed the U of I presidency to confront a host of daunting challenges. "There are many problems which need immediate and forceful attention," the *Daily Illini* editorialized at the start of Henry's tenure. "The outlook is a pessimistic one. But we have confidence in David Henry. He is an optimist."[20]

The Baby Boom and the 1960 Bond Issue

Henry would agree with the student newspaper's characterization of him, or at least with the idea that he habitually took things in stride. "I was fortunate to be sustained by good health, energy, and a phlegmatic temperament," he wrote in his memoirs. He seemed to pride himself on harboring no delusions of grandeur: "The 'full-steam ahead' approach receives public acclaim and the 'knight on the charging horse' is a heroic figure, but in the political world, the heroic figure is not always the successful one." Rather than seeking slam-dunk triumphs, he would try to build consensus and work toward what he called "a succession of partial victories."[21]

As the *Daily Illini* had indicated, the U of I system (which included an undergraduate campus and a medical center in Chicago in addition to the Champaign-Urbana campus) faced numerous problems when Henry took office. The Chicago campus at Navy Pier on the shoreline of Lake Michigan was deteriorating, and it needed to be moved to a new, permanent location that had yet to be determined. There was also the ongoing concern of enhancing the U of I's academic standing. According to Henry, Illinois was widely viewed "as an 'open admissions' institution with low academic standards, a place where superior students were not attracted and one where admission standards were minimal." That in turn pointed to another problem: the university's image. Although the U of I did hold significant room for improvement, Henry believed that its reputation for mediocrity was undeserved, and he sought to strengthen its public relations outreach along with its ties to important constituencies that included the Illinois legislature. Speaking in the capital city of Springfield in 1957, Henry asserted that the "potential of the University will be realized only when every citizen, individually and personally, feels some kinship with its work and has some understanding of its significance to all the people of the state."[22]

A sobering reality added urgency to the U of I's efforts: the baby boomers were coming. The demand for higher education already had increased dramatically. By 1955, 40 percent of Illinois high schoolers were choosing to attend college, in comparison with only 15 percent in 1940. The state's birthrate had skyrocketed as well—almost 203,000 babies had been born in 1951, up from a little more than 141,000 in 1945. And in the not-too-distant future, those babies would reach college age. Enrollment at the U of I was projected to reach 38,000 by 1972, more than double what it had been in 1954. One observer described the oncoming surge of students across the country as an "avalanche"; more widely, it was referred to as the "tidal wave." (David Henry later would regret this label, saying that the "connotation of disaster was hardly appropriate.")[23]

Many reasons were given for the heightened interest in a university education. The business world wanted more advanced skills from its workforce. The veterans who had gone to college on the GI Bill in the immediate postwar years were encouraging other young people to attend. The 1957 launch of Sputnik stirred fears that the Soviet Union was overtaking the United States in science and technology, increasing demand for training in those fields. Whatever the reasons, colleges and universities gained a cachet they had never before had. "Families sought higher education for their children because it provided opportunities for better life prospects, a relative advantage in economic opportunities, social status, and cultural distinction," writes historian Roger L. Geiger. Long into the 1960s, according to one student of the day, college represented "the hopes and dreams of a lot of young people, myself included, who saw higher education as the gateway to the American dream."[24]

In theory, that all should have added up to an unalloyed blessing for the U of I. In reality, as David Henry recalled it, the U of I and other universities "grimly took stock of the requirements for new space, new equipment, and additional personnel." The fact was that there never had been adequate space. To accommodate returning veterans and their families just after World War II, the U of I had built temporary housing on the far southeast and southwest corners of the Champaign-Urbana campus in developments called Illini Village and the Parade Ground Units (the latter name referring to the housing units' location on the onetime campus parade grounds). One history of the university would refer to the developments as "cardboard villages." Women students were put up in similar temporary housing labeled "T-Dorms," which had the disadvantages of being far from campus and possessing "comparatively thin walls," as the *Daily Illini* put it. Even with the T-Dorms, there still was a chronic shortage of housing for women, and many prospective female students—as many as four hundred during a school term—were turned away from the U of I as a result.[25]

The space crunch extended to educational facilities, with classes shifted to evenings and weekends when those were the only times that the classes could find an open place to meet. The School of Social Work moved into a converted house, and art students adapted a former grocery into a studio. Speech classes met in a dilapidated building that was so cold in the winter that students had wear mittens while taking notes. Other classes doubled up on rooms—literally so, with two classes meeting simultaneously at opposite ends of a room—and English instructors tripled or quadrupled up on desks, staking claim to individual corners and drawers as office space. The College of Education became a poster child of sorts in graphically demonstrating the lack of adequate facilities. A photo feature in the *Daily Illini* showed how the college was scattered across thirty campus buildings that included a former fraternity house, a "glorified barn," a "run-down barracks," and one of the parade ground units in which students were said to be "'all shook up' as a pile driver hammers incessantly."[26]

Adding to the general sense of decrepitude was the demise of the U of I's elms. The campus had been home to approximately two thousand of the stately trees, some of them dating back to the 1870s when the university was still in its infancy. The elms formed a majestic cathedral-like arch over the main quadrangle's west footpath that generations of students referred to as the Broadwalk. Beginning soon after World War II and then accelerating with sickening speed, Dutch elm disease and another disease called phloem necrosis struck the trees. The most famous of the elms, dubbed "Ma-Wan-Da," stood eighty feet tall and shaded the Illini Union's terrace with its 110-foot spread. University workers tried to save it with sulfa, DDT, fertilizer, and a custom-designed drainage system. Nothing worked, and in the summer of 1958 the tree was cut down, a fate met by almost all the U of I's other elms. By the end of the 1950s, the campus was scarred by hundreds of stumps.[27]

Constructing new buildings and planting new trees would cost money, which was hard to come by even though times were relatively prosperous and higher education was enjoying heightened prestige. "Competition [for funds] was severe," David Henry would recall. "Increasing population created demands for financial assistance in other areas of public service—new facilities and services for health care, recreation, social service, and elementary-secondary education; for new highways and public utilities; and other operations." The Illinois legislature routinely gave the U of I far less money than it requested in state appropriations. For example, the U of I asked for more than $35 million in 1957, but it received only a little more than $14 million in response.[28]

Even so, Henry saw Illinois governor William Stratton as an important ally (he later praised Stratton as "the most farsighted governor whom I encountered in my years of public service in Michigan, New York, and Illinois").[29] The Republican governor put forward a bond issue referendum to go before Illinois voters in 1958. If passed, the bond issue would give the U of I $86 million in building funds. The university campaigned vigorously for the measure, which received more yes votes than no votes—yet it still failed. The Illinois constitution mandated that in order for the referendum to pass, it had to be approved by a majority of the people who voted in state legislative races. That meant that if someone voted for a legislative candidate but did not vote at all on the bond question, it was the same as voting against the bond question. Unfortunately for the U of I, almost seven hundred thousand Illinois voters had done precisely that, not marking their ballots either way on the bond question. Henry summed up the university's reaction: "It is both ironic and tragic that the fate of our universities should be determined by those not voting!"[30]

The U of I persevered. It overcame determined opposition from Champaign-Urbana landlords in gaining state funding for the construction of new student residence halls. The landlords had argued that state-subsidized student housing represented unfair competition, overlooking the fact that some of the private housing that they had been renting to students was substandard or exorbitantly priced. The U of I also used student fees to help pay for a large addition to the Illini Union, a new student services center, and a new arena named Assembly Hall, which resembled a giant flying saucer. (During the 1958 bond issue campaign, some Illinois Democrats had questioned whether the U of I would use part of the money to "build a sports palace"; as it turned out, the university was able to build one anyway.) To restore its landscape, the university began planting four thousand new trees that included a mix of oaks, maples, and honey locusts to prevent a recurrence of the catastrophe that had befallen the monoculture of campus elms.[31]

Those were only partial victories, as David Henry might have described them. In an effort to balance the state budget, Governor Stratton froze some $15 million in university building funds from the summer of 1959 until the following year. The freeze set off a "chain reaction," as reported by the *Daily Illini*. The withheld money delayed completion of the utility and power-plant improvements that were necessary to provide heat, electricity, and sewer service to the Illini Union addition, the new student services center, and Assembly Hall, among other projects. Consequently construction on those projects also had to be delayed. In addition, a planned increase in office space was put on hold; that, in turn, threatened to force the university to restrict enrollment, because the new space was needed to accommodate additional staff to handle the anticipated increase in new students. On top of everything else, a nationwide steel strike and strikes by local craft unions would add to the delays. And after the failure of the 1958 bond issue, there still was not nearly enough money to fund the amount of construction that the U of I would require in order to meet future needs.[32]

Thus a new bond issue referendum was placed on the 1960 Illinois ballot. David Henry recalled that he "regarded the bond issue, regardless of the outcome, as an unusual opportunity to take to the people of Illinois an account of the University's accomplishments, its potential, and its needs."[33] In other words, it was the perfect chance to show the state's citizens—especially those citizens who had seen no reason to vote on the 1958 bond question—that the U of I directly related to them and mattered to their collective future. The bond issue campaign would test the effectiveness of the public outreach that Henry had made a priority upon becoming U of I president five years previously.

The university waged its campaign on multiple fronts. It won endorsements for the bond issue not only from incumbent governor William Stratton but also from his Democratic opponent in the 1960 gubernatorial race, Otto Kerner. The U of I began what it called a "low-pressure mail campaign" asking its staff members to contribute money toward publicizing the need for the bonds. (The university also formed the Committee on Bond Issue Interpretation, which was tasked in part with calling on staff members who did not respond to the mail appeal, suggesting that the campaign may not have been 100 percent low-pressure. Still, the bond issue campaign would be funded entirely through private rather than state funds.) The student senate announced its support, and U of I students placed pro-bond-issue bumper stickers on the cars of people who wanted the stickers; in addition, they joined students from other Illinois public universities (which also would benefit from the bond issue) in organizing an Olympic-style torch marathon that would carry a "flame for higher education" across the state. Mailings were sent to eighty thousand alumni soliciting money and votes, and the U of I's Moms Association and Dads Association were enlisted as well. The two associations asked their members to "telephone at least five close friends," to write letters to the editor, and to talk up the referendum "at social gatherings, club meetings, service club luncheons and similar events."[34]

The bond campaign appealed to self-interest and reason. Some citizens had objected to the 1958 bond issue because they thought that it would have automatically allocated an unfair share of money to the U of I at the expense of other state universities. The 1960 bond issue contained no preset allocations; the money that it raised would go into the state treasury, and each state university could make its case to the legislature to get the funds that it needed. In response to critics who asked why the universities needed so many new buildings, the bond campaigners pointed to what the baby boom already had wrought: "Look about your own community where your school boards have had to build additions, new schools, then more new schools to provide facilities to teach these youngsters. As they are graduated from high school more than 50 percent will go on to a college or university—if they can be admitted." As for people who did not understand the need to act as quickly as possible, the U of I responded that even if the bond issue passed, it still would take three to four years to complete new campus buildings. "Sophomore, junior and senior students in our high schools will seek admission before we can add any new educational facilities," said Joseph Begando, an assistant to President Henry, in a talk to the Champaign Rotary Club. "We cannot fail to start now, for the onrushing wave of students is clearly visible on the educational horizon. Urgency is now upon us."[35]

The campaign also appealed to sentiment. The most prominent bond issue opponent was the Illinois Agricultural Association; it campaigned against both the 1958 and the 1960 referendums on the grounds that they could lead to the imposition of a statewide property tax to pay off the bonds. Bond supporters responded with a flier featuring a drawing of a little boy kneeling in a cornfield

One of the promotions for the 1960 Illinois higher education bond issue. The University of Illinois made passage of the bond issue a top priority. (Courtesy of the University of Illinois Archives, Dean's Subject File, RS 41/2/31)

and watching someone (presumably his farmer father) work the newly sprouted corn plants with a hoe. "Good crops spring from fertilized and tended land—great thoughts from enriched and disciplined minds," the accompanying copy said. "Nourish the mind, and the harvest can be bountiful beyond all measure, for the mind contains the most precious of all seeds—the ideas that shape our world. . . . Young minds, too, need cultivating." Along with sentiment, there were appeals to guilt. One newsletter included a photo of angelic-looking fourth graders peering up at the camera. "The picture on the left shows a group of college freshmen of 1969," the caption read. "If the Bond Issue fails, some of them will be denied a college education. Pick out the ones that should be denied an opportunity to go to college."[36]

If all else failed, there was always Cold War–inspired fear to exploit. Along with pictures of overcrowded college classrooms and deteriorating university buildings, a pro-bond-issue slide show included an image of Soviet leader Nikita Khrushchev. "The nation has been concerned, and rightfully so, by what appear to be the rapid advances made by Russia in scientific discoveries and education of scientists," the narration said. "Whatever lag there has been in the United States will be made greater if research facilities essential to these activities are not made available." A pro-bond newsletter published a particularly pointed quote from an Illinois attorney: "Cuba should be sufficient warning of the grave peril in which we stand. Should we fail our responsibilities to our college youth today, it could be the downfall of our country. Should our enemies ever conquer us, all of the side issues now being raised to defeat the Universities Bond Issue will have become moot."[37]

The bond issue campaign was launched in the fall of 1959. By the following March, the U of I had reason to be cautiously optimistic about the prospects for success. Even the Illinois Agricultural Association agreed that higher education needed more funds and buildings; its objections concerned the proposed means by which the money was to be raised. But one Illinoisan was about to raise far more serious objections: ones that would cut to the heart of the university's mission while preying on fear to a degree well beyond anything employed by the U of I's supporters.

Ira Latimer and the Fear of Subversion

Ira Latimer would spend his life wandering far and wide in his travels, his vocations, and his politics. His beginnings were conventional enough, having been born in Ohio in 1906 and then graduating from Ohio State University in 1926. Over the next nine years, however, Latimer continued his studies at a succession of far-flung schools—the Chicago Theological Seminary, the University of Paris, the University of Vienna, and the University of Chicago—while returning to Ohio State long enough to earn a master's degree. He also traveled to China to teach at a Christian college there, as well as to Memphis, Tennessee, to teach at an African American college. Deciding that he wanted to become a lawyer, Latimer attended both DePaul University and the Chicago-Kent College of Law, only to be dropped from both programs because of what later was described as "poor scholarship." He eventually did earn a degree from the John Marshall Law School in Chicago in 1953.[38]

Along the way, Latimer worked as a tour guide, real-estate broker, and court clerk; his *Who's Who in the Midwest* biography listed his occupation as sociologist,

Ira Latimer in 1940, at about the time that he was supporting student pacifists at the University of Illinois. Latimer's politics would veer sharply to the right in subsequent decades.

and he became an ordained Baptist minister. From 1936 to 1955, he led an organization called the Chicago Civil Liberties Committee that became active in left-leaning causes. Latimer visited the U of I in the spring of 1940 to support campus pacifists who were opposing US involvement in the war that was then raging in Europe. He called for criminal charges to be filed against local police for their treatment of the pacifists. Latimer's visit sparked rumors that the pacifist group was controlled by communists, and that in turn prompted U of I president Arthur Willard to travel to Springfield to mollify state lawmakers who feared that the whole university was soft on communism. In 1945 Latimer backed a Champaign-Urbana group led by Vashti McCollum that was fighting the teaching of religious classes in Illinois public schools during school hours; the year after that, he returned to the U of I to speak to a campus group about the evils of racism.[39]

Latimer's work in civil liberties had allied him with both socialists and communists (much as critics back in 1940 had charged, even if their worst fears had been exaggerated). By 1945, he had become a communist himself, although he later would say that this association lasted only a couple of years. Latimer's politics and personality sometimes provoked clashes with people in authority. He tried to get a certificate in 1949 to teach in Chicago's public schools, but he was turned down for not meeting the standards of "character, scholarship, and general fitness"; it was observed that Latimer had once been threatened with a "punch in the nose" for refusing to leave a state legislative hearing in Springfield, and on another occasion, he had been ordered out of the Chicago police commissioner's office. Latimer's subsequent lawsuit against the board of education failed. Then, in 1950, Latimer posed as a United Nations representative in a ruse to raise the UN flag over Chicago city hall. In an editorial commenting on the incident, the archconservative *Chicago Tribune* charged that Latimer's civil liberties efforts once had been underwritten by communists, and now they were being underwritten through Latimer's association with a lawyer who represented mobsters. The *Tribune* concluded that Latimer was an all-too-appropriate representative of UN internationalists who were "activated solely by the motive of tearing down the Constitution of the United States."[40]

In 1954—the year after he earned his law degree—Latimer formally renounced communism and sought admission to the Illinois bar after having passed the bar examination on his fourth try. As what had happened when he applied for his teacher's certification, he was informed that he lacked the "candor, veracity, integrity and responsibility" that were necessary to practice law. Latimer's appeal of that decision would drag on into 1957. He claimed that fifty Chicago attorneys were communists (much as, a few years earlier, an Illinois lawmaker had charged that fifty U of I faculty were communists). The appeal finally made it to the Illinois Supreme Court, which ruled against Latimer. The court said that he had engaged in "intimidation calculated to compel the granting of a certificate of good moral fiber and fitness, irrespective of [his] qualifications." The court also summarized that effort at intimidation: everyone who opposed Latimer "was accused of being a Communist," whereas Latimer himself said that he "was being persecuted because of his present anti-Communist leanings and activities." Moreover, he had made false oaths in previous litigation in which he had been embroiled, claiming never to have been a communist when in fact he had been one.[41]

The Latimer case occasioned comment in *National Review*, the conservative magazine that William F. Buckley Jr. had founded in 1955. Reacting to Latimer's having been denied admission to the bar, the magazine said that "a good many people, in Illinois and out over the country as well, have yet to hear a sensible answer to the question: Why?" According to the magazine, part of the answer seemed to be that the committee that had denied his admission was "openly hostile to Latimer, badgered him, asked him innumerable loaded questions, and unabashedly took cognizance of hearsay evidence." *National Review* also noted that Latimer's list of fifty purportedly communist lawyers never had been made public, and the magazine suggested that the list ought to be investigated to determine whether in fact it had been "Communist influence that blocked his path to admission to the bar."[42]

It is unknown how the obscure case of a would-be lawyer in Illinois received notice in a national periodical. But it reflected how anticommunism represented what one academic study of the day called the "distinctive doctrine of the Right Wing, and the great cause that binds disparate groups into an impressive contemporary movement" that continued to thrive even after Joseph McCarthy passed from the scene. Onetime communists turned anticommunists were especially prized spokespersons for the political right, and Buckley and *National Review* gave the conservative movement cohesion and a distinctive voice. Buckley was friends with U of I classics professor Revilo Oliver, who was a contributor to *National Review*; Oliver and his wife Grace also became acquainted with Latimer sometime after Latimer renounced communism.[43] Possibly the U of I professor helped bring the case to *National Review*'s attention.

Latimer doubled down on his conservatism after he was rejected for the bar. He became an advocate for small businesses and antiunion efforts while representing himself as a spokesperson for a Chicago organization called the Institute of Economic Policy. He also doubled down on his religion, sometimes referring to himself as Reverend Latimer. In attacking secular humanism, Latimer charged that the "most logical humanist is a Communist," and he warned against "modern pagans" who were threatening to squelch "the last generation of free Americans." His views were consistent with other conservatives who excoriated such humanists as John Dewey and the progressive educational methods that seemed to be making young people question the status quo. A 1960 study spoke of the "contention of right wingers that 'Progressive Education is Reeducation,'" as well as of their conviction that "the godless, treasonable, obscene and illiterate curriculum which they find in present-day American schools has enabled the communists to control Russia and will serve them equally well here."[44]

As of the start of 1960, though, Latimer's animus did not appear to extend to the U of I. His daughter was enrolled as a freshman there, and although she had to wait to move into a residence hall because of the ongoing shortage of women's housing on campus, she and her father were able to spend a few days in early February at the Urbana home of Revilo and Grace Oliver. Latimer also used that visit to address a group called the Champaign-Urbana Anti-Communist League that was led by Howard Barham, a member of the Champaign park board and the American Legion. The local newspapers publicized Latimer's talk in advance, and about forty people attended; the papers also covered the talk itself. "You're in a war—the worst war of any," Latimer told the group. He claimed that some forty communist-front groups were operating in Champaign-Urbana without any effective opposition: "They have penetrated every mass institution and organization."[45]

The same day that Latimer spoke, a letter from a U of I law professor appeared in the *Champaign-Urbana Courier*. Victor Stone was a civil-liberties advocate and a member of the U of I's academic freedom committee. He said that he was writing the *Courier* to correct what he described as "false billing" in the publicity for Latimer's talk. Latimer had been described as a lawyer even though he had been denied admission to the bar (Stone quoted at length from the Illinois Supreme Court's ruling against him). Latimer also had been called the "former executive secretary of the Civil Liberties Union"; that label incorrectly implied that he had been an officer of the ACLU, of which Stone was a proud member. "The Champaign-Urbana sponsors of Latimer owe the community an explanation of the false credentials used in advertising their meeting, and also a little more candor in the future," Stone wrote in conclusion. He sent a virtually identical letter to Champaign-Urbana's *News-Gazette* newspaper, which published it a few days later.[46]

Latimer already had begun following up on his Champaign-Urbana visit by sending Howard Barham detailed plans for a "pilot project in the country" that would aggressively target leftism. The project would "teach Organization and Ideas" so that it could "penetrate and take over any Organization and use it for the Cause of God and Freedom.... God's help is all that can save us from Soviet conquest from within and without." Now, with Stone's criticism of him having been published, Latimer asked Grace and Revilo Oliver to send him a "who's who of Leftists-Liberals—names, addresses, interlocking Organizational activities—and past associations with Liberal Leftist regimes" at the U of I, with an eye toward uncovering how those individuals had managed to "silence or neutralize the whole faculty." He also asked for anything that the Olivers could scrounge up on a host of campus organizations: the NAACP, the ACLU, the American Association of University Professors, B'nai B'rith, and even the Wesley Foundation affiliated with the United Methodist church (Latimer had heard of a liberal-tinged talk being delivered there). He said that he needed the material "*as soon as* possible—so I can work on Patterns, and deductions of my own."[47]

In the meantime, Howard Barham wrote a letter to the editor in response to Victor Stone. The letter implied that Latimer's bar application had been squelched by a group that included "the Illinois Supreme Court, Chicago Bar Association, National Lawyer's [sic] Guild, Cook County Bar Association (Negro), [and] Decalogue Society (Jewish Bar Association)." The explicit references to organizations' affiliations with Jews and African Americans seemed intended to undermine their credibility. The letter also quoted from congressional testimony claiming that "the main function of the ACLU is to attempt to protect the Communists in their advocacy of force and violence to overthrow the government, replacing the American flag and erecting a Soviet Government." Ira Latimer sent the Champaign-Urbana newspapers his own response to Stone: communist-infiltrated groups had denied him his law license; the ACLU was communistic as well. Latimer offered to debate Stone at "any time, any place, no holds barred of course," adding that if the professor "misstates the facts as grossly to his students as he does to your readers there is a serious question whether he should be continued to be paid by our tax monies."[48]

The back-and-forth volley of letters to the editor continued through February and into March. U of I graduate student R. D. Mikesell addressed a needling note to members of the Anti-Communist League: "Did you know that there is a genuine Fascist organization right here in this city? If you don't already know them, do; they hate Communists with a vengeance. They also hate Negroes, Jews, and progressive ideas, such as national mental health programs (for obvious reasons). You should find that you have a lot in common with them. I will give you their names if you would be kind enough to write me for them."[49] Meanwhile, the Anti-Communist League brought another speaker to town, Herbert

Philbrick, a former undercover agent for the Federal Bureau of Investigation. He told his audience at Champaign High School that communists had changed their tactics: "Instead of going to cell meetings now, they go to PTA meetings." Philbrick also charged that a phone campaign had tried to discourage people from attending his Champaign talk, and he asked why the U of I did not invite anticommunists such as himself to campus.[50]

Ira Latimer grew more agitated in his correspondence. He urged friends in Champaign-Urbana to "recruit some professors and graduate students as fast as possible who can take up the typewriter and do battle in the press columns where the comrades have selected a field they are expert in." He also directed Howard Barham to make elaborate arrangements for a return speaking engagement in Champaign-Urbana—Latimer should make his speech while local dignitaries sat on stage beside him; anticommunist literature should be procured and sold; a robust turnout that included sympathetic, right-thinking U of I professors should be generated. Barham sent Latimer a protesting note in return: "I do not have anybody that will sell, collect or s[i]t on a stage. Now how in the He— can I do this all by myself." Latimer apologized, telling Barham, "There is only so much energy and this winter has about gotten me down several times. That is the unvarnished truth."[51]

One reason for Latimer's funk may have been the dismal dossier that he had been meticulously compiling on the U of I with the help of his Champaign-Urbana allies. It contained clippings (marked "Subversive Material") written by the likes of Victor Stone, fliers on such organizations as the university YMCA (which had sponsored a "USSR Night," complete with folk music), and index cards with detailed notes on individual faculty and students. The cards included such easy targets as Edward Yellin, an engineering doctoral student and ex-communist who, in March 1960, was on trial for contempt of Congress after he refused to name his past associates. (The U of I, after briefly suspending Yellin, quickly reinstated him and restored his graduate fellowship, and eventually the US Supreme Court overturned his contempt conviction.)[52] There also were multiple cards on philosophy professor Harry Tiebout, who maintained ties to a long list of liberal organizations.

Yet the index cards also extended to some of the most prominent figures on campus: Jack Peltason, who later would serve as U of I chancellor; Norman Graebner, a history professor revered by multitudes of students; associate provost Royden Dangerfield (whose card characterized him as a "most wily, clever intriguer"); dean of women Miriam Shelden; and even President Henry himself (said to be a "friend of leftist-defender"). A few cards contained scurrilous sexual gossip about faculty and staff and their family members. Back in

1945, a Jewish newspaper in Chicago had heaped praise upon Latimer ("If ever a man fought for the rights of the people, it's Ira Latimer"); now, fifteen years later, Latimer's U of I dossier was flecked with derogatory references to African Americans and Jews.[53] The "patterns" that he had said he was looking for had led him to deduce that communists controlled the Champaign-Urbana Ministerial Association, the Illini Christian Fellowship, and the Baha'i Student Foundation (plus the local PTA, much as Herbert Philbrick had warned). And that was not all—Latimer believed that a veritable tidal wave of communist influence had engulfed not only the nation's schools and universities, but also the media, the unions, most of the churches, and the government's judicial, legislative, and executive branches all the way up to the White House.

Compounding Latimer's worries was an odd letter that he received from the U of I scholarship office during the second week of March: somehow the university had formed the impression that his daughter had not enrolled for the spring term, and it was threatening to withdraw her scholarship as a consequence. Latimer immediately replied that he had paid his daughter's tuition by check and that she was now living in a university residence hall. He also asked the president of the U of I Dads Association (of which Latimer had become a member) to investigate, saying that if there were no records of his daughter's enrollment, "there is most certainly something RADICALLY wrong." Grace Oliver had sent Latimer a note a few weeks earlier complaining about what she said was an ongoing "smear campaign" aimed at her husband Revilo because of his anticommunist activities. Now Latimer suspected that he and his family were being similarly targeted as part of the same overarching pattern of conspiracy. There was the "phony form letter" from the scholarship office, the "Letters to the Editor 'debate' in which the Reds got steamed up" while comparing him and his friends to Hitler, and so forth.[54]

Only days later, Latimer would be confronted with something that must have represented to him both the worst possible confirmation of his suspicions and the best possible weapon to brandish in his crusade against evil. It would prompt Latimer to write a three-page single-spaced letter that would be sent to the parents of hundreds of women students at the U of I. The letter repeated what he had written earlier: "something is terribly wrong in the University of Illinois." An individual at the university, displaying the "standard operating procedure of the Communist conspiracy," had staged "an audacious attempt to subvert the religious and moral foundations of America." That act of perfidy raised the urgent question of why the university was "currently using the taxpayers' money to finance a propaganda campaign to wheedle those taxpayers into assuming at the coming election the additional burden of a bond issue of

$195,000,000." And it raised grave doubts about the future, for the ultimate victims would be "the students, both men and women, who are being demoralized to produce a generation that will not even know that when it loses liberty and personal integrity, it has lost all chance to find meaning and joy in life."[55]

The person whose actions would inspire this screed against the university was already in Latimer's dossier for being a humanist and rabble-rouser. As it happened, he also already had one foot out the U of I's door.

CHAPTER 2

Sex Ritualized

In 1963—after he had taken up nudism, but before he cofounded the Sexual Freedom League—Leo Koch decided that he wanted to try LSD. He prepared an autobiography for the International Foundation for Advanced Study, a small organization in the San Francisco Bay Area that was testing LSD's effects on personal creativity and well-being. The autobiography outlined Koch's reasons for wanting to take the drug, with him hoping that "perhaps the LSD experience may help me to integrate my 'scientific humanism' with the best thought of 'religions'." The autobiography also gave Koch a chance to reflect on everything that had led up to the defining event of his life: his writing of a letter to the editor that had gotten him fired from the University of Illinois and forever branded him as "the Sex Prof."[1]

The Making of a Gadfly

Leo Koch (pronounced "Cook") found his scandalous reputation to be ironic, noting that people who met him without knowing his background "undoubtedly think of me as an ordinary person. I suspect this is because of my crew haircut, my ordinary features and [my] somewhat less than average height." His early life had been similarly unremarkable. Koch was born in 1916 in North Dakota to a Roman Catholic family; his mother was especially devout, and Koch would say of her in 1963, "She still prays for me." The family moved to Petaluma,

California, when Koch was thirteen, at about the same time that he fell under the influence of a rebellious older brother: "Through him I became a skeptic and pursued unorthodox as well as politically radical ideas." Unorthodox or not—and despite some disciplinary problems before he left parochial school for public school—Koch did well academically, juggling school and work before graduating from the University of California in 1941. While at Berkeley, Koch became president of the Student Workers Federation and attended meetings of other leftist student organizations. He then served in the US Navy during World War II, experiencing what he described as "growing resentment and antagonism between me and my commanding officer" that ended only when the officer was relieved of command. After the war, Koch returned to college on the GI Bill, became expert in bryology (the study of mosses), and earned a doctorate from the University of Michigan in 1950.[2]

By that time, Koch already was on his second marriage. He had wedded his first wife in 1940, but they lived together for only a week, long enough to conceive what would be his first child. Koch lived with his second wife Shirley for three years before they married in 1944; they would have three children of their own by the time that Koch completed his doctorate. Between 1951 and 1954, he taught biology at Bakersfield College in California. "I quickly decided that questions of values and philosophy were equally as important as questions of fact and began to incorporate them in my classes," Koch recalled of his time there. "I was promptly informed by the college president that nonconformist views of teaching were not acceptable. I could reform or be asked to leave at the end of my third year. I decided to leave." A one-year appointment at Tulane University in New Orleans followed. "My brusque independence and inconsideration for my administrative superior were duly noted, and I was not asked to remain there," Koch said. He acknowledged that those professional setbacks, plus the ones still to come, could be interpreted as either "my attempt to retain integrity and self-respect," or else "my 'immaturity' in not adjusting to society and in not 'playing the game.'" (He also acknowledged that his ego had "never suffered from lack of strength," and that at times in his life he had displayed "persistence bordering into irrational stubbornness.")[3]

In March 1955, while Koch was still at Tulane, the University of Illinois contacted him about a position teaching biology in its Division of General Studies (DGS). The DGS was part of a short-lived movement in US universities to promote interdisciplinary undergraduate education in liberal arts and sciences. The general studies movement had reached its peak right after the war, but it began to wane in the 1950s, undermined at Illinois and elsewhere by charges that it lacked the rigor of traditional academic departments and disciplines.[4]

Nevertheless, the U of I saw Koch as a potential fit in a program that emphasized teaching science to nonmajors and that also stressed teaching over research. Koch immediately expressed interest in the U of I position, saying that "the relationship of science to society, and the implications of scientific method for the individual, seem to me to be the most important aspects of general education." Nothing that Illinois may have learned about Koch's past faculty appointments deterred the university from hiring him as an assistant professor of biology starting in the fall of 1955. He received a two-year appointment paying him $5,300 dollars annually, with reappointment contingent on performance.[5]

Koch's subsequent experiences at the U of I would be summarized in a 1960 memorandum jointly written by James McCrimmon (head of the Division of

Leo Koch at about the time of his hiring by the University of Illinois in 1955. Tensions soon would develop between him and his unit heads. (Courtesy of the University of Illinois Archives, Administrative and Personnel Actions File, RS 2/15/10)

General Studies) and Otto Kugler (head of biological sciences in DGS). After an uneventful first year, Koch's second year was marked by conflicts over unauthorized requisitions for supplies. Although Kugler believed that Koch's teaching record warranted reappointing him for a second term from 1957 to 1959, he received no merit pay increase. Koch responded that he would seek employment elsewhere, and the U of I did nothing to dissuade him from doing just that; still, he remained at Illinois.

Soon new clashes developed. McCrimmon and Kugler thought that Koch was deliberately circumventing established procedures for securing travel and research funds related to a grant he had received to study California mosses. Differences were patched up enough that Koch was again reappointed for 1959 to 1961, but Kugler informed Koch that his contract would not be renewed when it expired. "By this time Kugler's patience was exhausted," McCrimmon and Kugler wrote in their joint memorandum recounting Koch's years at the U of I and the decision not to reappoint him. Kugler "had become convinced that though Koch was professionally competent as far as his knowledge of the subject was concerned he did not fit into a general education program but would be best employed in a course for botany majors. [Kugler] had also become increasingly dissatisfied with Koch's lack of cooperation in performing program chores outside of the classroom." Although the memorandum did not specify what those chores were, Koch reportedly did not contribute his expected share of questions to the examinations administered to beginning biology students, and he also did not contribute his expected share of laboratory specimens to the common stock used by biology instructors.[6]

Kugler and McCrimmon denied that Koch's writings had influenced their decision not to renew his contract, but by 1959 he had attracted attention for numerous outspoken letters to the *News-Gazette* and *Courier* newspapers in Champaign-Urbana as well as to the *Daily Illini* student paper. He accused President Dwight Eisenhower and Vice President Richard Nixon of "stupid political obfuscation" in continuing nuclear arms testing. He similarly blasted Democrats for tolerating "Southern reactionaries," whom he described as "depraved, criminally minded mobsters who practice just the opposite of every decent, virtuous or ethical principle." Koch's favorite target, however, was religion. In asking why a local television station did not air any programs on humanism, he charged that "our so-called freedom of religion has degenerated into Christianity, or else no freedom of expression." Observing that human senses of sight, sound, and smell were markedly inferior to those of many other creatures, Koch puckishly wrote, "Why the suprarational intelligence which 'designed' the universe should have been so niggardly with the human being, I cannot understand." More seriously, he lamented that "Buchenwald, and more so, Hiroshima and Nagasaki, not to mention the current mad race to stockpile bombs and destroy the human race, illustrates the complete inability of the medieval Christian system of ethics to solve the ethical problems of a scientific age."[7]

Koch also made news beyond his letters to the editor. He unsuccessfully ran for the Champaign school board in 1959, arguing for expanding science education across the curriculum now that science and technology "dominate our lives as surely and thoroughly as did theology in the middle ages." He delivered a speech at the University of Illinois advocating birth control, including for teenagers. And in December 1958, he told a campus forum on evolution that the "soul of man is nothing more than his personality plus a halo around his endocrine glands." Coverage of the forum in the *Daily Illini* caught the eye of U of I president David Henry, who asked the provost, Gordon Ray, what he knew about Koch ("I have noted his letters to the editor in the same vein," said Henry). The two men discussed the matter but took no action.

Koch's secular humanism carried over into his academic writings and his teaching, as he regularly paid homage to John Dewey and biologist Oscar Riddle. Writing in *Scientific Monthly* in 1957, Koch approvingly quoted from Riddle's book *The Unleashing of Evolutionary Thought*, in which Riddle had argued that "the worthy facts concerning man's origin and destiny come not from the religious traditions but from investigations made in biological and other sciences within the time of men now living."[8] Koch was faculty adviser to the campus Humanist Society (whose president remembered him as a "militant atheist"). He also frequently lectured on humanism to U of I professor Harry Tiebout's philosophy classes, sharing with Tiebout a "religious manifesto" that Koch wrote in February 1960: "Religionists Awake! You have nothing to lose but millstones of ignorance and lethargy.... Methinks Christians profess their God too loudly." After receiving word that his U of I contract would not be renewed, Koch wrote a letter to *Science* magazine that disparaged the likes of Otto Kugler and James McCrimmon. According to Koch, "the greatest impediment to the improvement of college courses in biology and botany seems to be a dogmatic and narrow-minded view of heads and chairmen of departments as to what such courses should include and how they should be taught." Such people, he said, were nothing but "academic dry-rot."[9]

It was in that frame of mind—eager to continue combat with pious religionists, no longer caring (if he ever did) about how university administrators viewed him—that Koch sat down in his campus office in March 1960 with a copy of the *Daily Illini*. A headline caught his eye: "Sex Ritualized."[10] The accompanying article and Koch's response to it would unexpectedly trigger a raging controversy over gender, sex, and academic freedom on college campuses. It also would end Koch's U of I career much sooner than he ever could have anticipated.

Gender and Sex on Campus in the Postwar Era

Women had been admitted to the U of I almost from the time of the university's founding in the 1860s, even though the U of I's first regent, John Milton Gregory, had thought coeducation to be an "innovation of doubtful wisdom." The U of I's early years had been heady times for women. When Isabel Bevier (a pioneer in home economics) arrived on campus in 1900, she found it brimming with "a spirit of adventure, open-mindedness and experimentation." The campus opened its Woman's Building in 1905. According to Paula A. Treichler, the building's name—"with *woman* in the singular—was intended to give every individual woman on campus a sense of proprietorship and belonging."[11]

Treichler also observes, however, that women during the subsequent decades were subject to "increased institutional hierarchy and control" at the U of I and other universities. The post–World War II climate in higher education would be significantly different from what it had been at the start of the century. "By 1950, a total picture of the American college woman to replace the older image of the bluestocking was clearly in sight," writes historian Paula S. Fass. "Eager for husband and children, disgusted with angry feminists, and knee deep in diapers and dirty dishes, American women seemed eager to trade their much vaunted academic heritage of the enlightened best in Western civilization for a mess of pottage." The average marriage age for women was barely twenty years old, as female undergraduates seemed to pick up cues from their educators that marriage and children should be what they wanted most out of life. So young women were caught in what Fass calls "the female paradox: the fact that women were receiving more education than they seemed to need." College-educated women did work outside the home; historian Barbara Miller Solomon notes that about three-fifths of women holding college degrees would join the workforce by the early 1960s. Yet married women commonly put off careers until their children reached a certain age, and Solomon says that female undergraduates of the day often were reluctant to appear too ambitious: "The idea of stating that one would become a writer, a doctor, or a professor would have sounded absurd."[12]

A host of ideologies shaped women's outlooks. According to Linda Eisenmann, they included a patriotic ideology saying that "women should defend the home front against threats of communism and domestic disruption," an economic ideology saying that women should leave more prestigious and higher-paying jobs to men, a cultural ideology saying that women's family ties were of paramount importance, and a psychological ideology saying that "women were best fulfilled through acceptance of their reproductive role." Those ideologies were not all-powerful. Eisenmann observes that they were challenged both by the labor market's increasing demands for women workers and by "a growing ease with sexual experimentation and publicity around healthy American sexuality."[13] Historian Jessica Weiss argues that stereotypes of postwar women as paragons or victims of cozy or stifling domesticity are oversimplified. In reality, those women helped to "create a more egalitarian marriage pattern, pioneering changes in men's and women's family roles" while setting the stage for the feminist resurgence of the years to come. Weiss also suggests that those changes placed stresses on both women and men. They "struggled to come to terms with the increasing instability of American marriage" (exacerbated by the fact that people were marrying at such a young age), as well as with the "heightening expectations of the sexual revolution and feminism."[14]

The conflicting pressures took their toll on female undergraduates of the day. Psychiatrist Carl Binger wrote in the *Atlantic* in 1961 that many women students showed symptoms of depression: "a loss of zest, a feeling of apathy or fatigue, and an apparent need for extra hours of sleep, a very much lowered self-esteem, with sensitivity to other people's opinions and reactions, and, above all, an inability to get work done." Some young women fell into binge eating, which Binger said could result from stress over academics or relationships; it even could turn into "a kind of chronic addiction."[15]

Part of college women's angst may have stemmed from their tacit understanding that marriage and childrearing alone might not be enough to fulfill them. A 1960 study found that female undergraduates tended to see a career outside the home as "an interlude, at best a part-time excursion away from full-time family life—the family life which the coeds yearn for, impatiently look forward to." At the same time, though, the young women feared that family life would be "largely monotonous, tedium, and routine." Then there was the treacherous path that had to be trod just to reach the point of marriage, a path that many women felt that they had to navigate on their own. "The contemporary sexual mores of young people are so different from those which governed their parents' or teachers' lives that a common meeting ground between them scarcely exists," Carl Binger observed.[16] The Kinsey reports on men's and women's sexual behavior (published in 1948 and 1953) already had exposed the hypocrisy underlying traditional mores; as one historian says of the reports' impact, "No longer could masturbation, premarital or extramarital intercourse, and homosexuality be viewed as occasional deviations." The reports highlighted that a wide range of women were indulging in a wide range of sexual activities. Another impetus to the liberalization of attitudes would come in 1960 when the oral contraceptive pill was introduced. "The belief that pleasure in sex was created only to insure the production of children seems to have disappeared with the idea that if God meant man to fly, He would have given him wings, and at about the same time," wrote Gloria Steinem in 1962.[17]

That did not mean that sex became an uncomplicated, guilt-free experience for young people; far from it. Instead, it devolved into what historian Beth Bailey describes as "a series of skirmishes that centered around lines and boundaries: kissing, necking, petting above the waist, petting below the waist, petting through clothes, petting under clothes, mild petting, heavy petting. The progression of intimacy had emerged as a highly ordered system." Sociologist Winston W. Ehrmann in the early 1960s described petting as a way of allowing a "couple to experience in varying degrees the emotional gamut of sex from sensory titillation to a deeply committed love relation without running the risk of an out-of-wedlock pregnancy and the extreme social stigma of promiscuity"—for premarital sexual intercourse still did bear a widespread stigma. That in turn placed certain expectations on young women. "I suppose the ideal girl is still technically a virgin but has done every possible kind of petting without actually having had intercourse," Nora Johnson commented ironically in 1959, adding: "This gives her savoir-faire, while still maintaining her maiden dignity."[18]

That petting-without-intercourse (also known as "everything but") could be great fun is suggested by the title that Roger Ebert gave to a blog post late in his life: "Making out is its own reward." While he was an undergraduate at the U of I in the early 1960s, Ebert worked at the *Daily Illini*. The secluded room where the newspaper's photograph negatives were stored turned out to be ideal for romantic assignations. Ebert also had a car (a magazine of the time noted that "the boudoirs of modern collegians" were "the motel and the automobile"), and he used his 1955 Ford to be transported in more ways than one. "I experienced delights made all the more exciting because they were restricted," he happily remembered. "We kissed. I fondled breasts. My hands strayed to her netherlands. My own movables were rummaged." Orgasms—which Ebert described as "Oops!" moments—sometimes occurred for one or both participants, but, as he noted, "Part of the game was to get . . . right . . . up . . . almost . . . to the Oops! Point," without necessarily passing it.[19]

Young men such as Ebert did not venture toward "Oops!" with just any young woman; "you had to know the girl pretty well," he recalled. Beth Bailey notes that "a whole new set of 'official' statuses emerged to designate the seriousness of relationships: going steady, lavaliered, pinned, engaged. Each of these was more serious than the last, and each step allowed greater sexual intimacy." Of course, not every young person followed this tidy progression when it came to sex. For his part, Ebert as an undergraduate never made it to the point of getting engaged; nor would he have intercourse with another student in Champaign-Urbana until a few years later while he was in graduate school. Having grown up in Urbana, Ebert lived at home during much of his time at college. He had a close but fraught relationship with his mother, who had wanted him to become a priest, and she would go so far as to check his jeans for signs of sexual activity, once telling him that he had "wasted a baby." So the fun of making out was accompanied by embarrassment, guilt, and frustration. Ebert was convinced that he was far "behind the curve" in his sexual experience (he knew of couples who lived together or who said that they "were 'going to Chicago for the weekend,' wherever Chicago might happen to be"), and he pitied himself as being "the most ill-served young man of my generation."[20]

Ebert was hardly alone in his self-perceptions, for the double standard of youthful sex—succinctly summarized by Beth Bailey as "'Nice girls' said no; boys kept pushing"—made young men feel that something was wrong with them if they did not want to keep pushing or did not have intercourse. A 1961 scholarly study found that "virgin men of college age, regardless of their desire or lack of desire to remain virgin, generally do not receive support and acceptance for their virginity from either their peer group or adults, including their parents." But the pressures on young men did not approach the pressures on young women: the "nice girls" who were supposed to know when to say no. "The boy is willing to go as far as you let him. So you have to fight him *and* your own inclinations," a woman student told journalist Gael Greene, while another young woman complained that a "girl has double the responsibility and gets twice the blame." Greene herself observed that the pressure to engage in "everything but" represented a "perversion of traditional concepts of female purity when it rests its claim on nothing more than a slender membrane preserved intact before the aggressions and blandishments of 10, 20, 50 young males."[21]

Popular culture dramatized young women's dilemmas. The year 1960 saw the release of the Shirelles' number-one hit song "Will You Love Me Tomorrow"—which implicitly addressed a girl's hopes and fears about letting a boy go all the way—and the movie *Where the Boys Are*. The film was based on a novel of the same name, in which a college student has sex with multiple young men during spring break and ends up pregnant: by whom, she does not know or care. In the movie version, a young woman asks a female professor whether a girl should "play house before marriage" (the aghast professor sends her to the dean's office); another young woman tells her friends that she plans to become

Poster promoting the 1960 movie *Where the Boys Are*. Although the poster promised lighthearted entertainment, the movie also dealt with premarital sex and sexual assault.

"a walking, talking baby factory—legal of course"; and a third young woman has sex with two different young men on separate occasions before being sexually assaulted by one of the men despite having repeatedly told him "no."²²

Whatever their limitations as art or social critique, such works as *Where the Boys Are* addressed real-life concerns. Feeling that they could not turn to their elders for advice about sex, young women turned to their peers. "A good many girls try to solve their bewilderment in college by constantly comparing notes with each other," wrote Nora Johnson in 1959, although that approach had its limitations. Johnson quoted one of her friends: "Freshman year, the problem is what to do when a boy tries to unbutton your blouse; sophomore year, when he reaches up your skirt; and after that, everybody shuts up." Gael Greene found astounding ignorance among college women about contraception and pregnancy. Many of the women were having intercourse despite the stigma against it, and many of those women who ended up pregnant resorted to illegal abortions. One undergraduate told Greene that women students "often act like we still think the stork brings babies and screwing has nothing to do with it."[23]

Then there were the young men who ignored the word "no." A mid-1950s survey of women undergraduates on one campus found that 55.7 percent of them had experienced one or more unwanted attempts at sexual contact during the past year, 20.9 percent had experienced "forceful attempts at intercourse," and 6.2 percent had experienced "aggressively forceful attempts at sex intercourse in the course of which menacing threats or coercive infliction of physical pain were employed." Many of the young women experienced "fear and guilt reactions"; virtually none of them reported the perpetrators to police or university authorities. In a study published a few years later, Phyllis and Eberhard Kronhausen quoted one college man who likely was representative of many offending males. He told the researchers that "I have never been deliberately cruel to a girl or have absolutely forced myself upon one." But he also recounted incidents in which he "couldn't—or wouldn't—stop," and in which he believed that "the muffled 'No, please don't' wasn't really a signal for me to stop."[24]

The U of I would experience two horrific cases in the early 1960s relating to unwanted pregnancy or violence against a woman student. In January 1962 a twenty-four-year-old U of I graduate student gave birth prematurely while alone in her dormitory room. (She later said that she had been impregnated by a professor at a different university.) Believing the baby to be stillborn, she attempted to flush the body down a toilet and then dropped it down an incinerator shaft, where a custodian found it. After it was determined that the baby actually had been born alive—although nonresponsive—the young woman faced murder charges. A subsequent investigation found that she had always been an excellent student and had never before been in trouble. Charges were reduced to "concealing the death of a bastard," a misdemeanor. The woman was placed on probation and was allowed to continue her studies elsewhere.[25]

A few weeks before that incident, a U of I female student was killed by a male student in a murder-suicide. "They were very close together; then they began to drift apart," an acquaintance of the couple told the *Daily Illini*. The truth was much uglier. Susan Stout, a twenty-five-year-old doctoral student in psychology, had been living with James Mautz, a forty-year-old undergraduate. Mautz had served as an Urbana police magistrate for several years before losing that position for misappropriating funds; after working at a number of other jobs, he had enrolled at the U of I. In September 1961, when Stout attempted to end her relationship with Mautz, he tried to strangle her and also threatened to harm her graduate adviser. Stout was checked into the university hospital as a protective measure. After she was released, Mautz began following her car and spying on her with binoculars while continuing to threaten her in writing and by telephone. Stout appealed for help from the local district attorney, only to be told that Mautz (a longtime friend of the district attorney and many police officers) would hurt no one. The psychology department set up its own ad hoc security system to try to protect her, but to no avail: on the evening of November 8, Mautz fatally shot Stout and then turned the gun on himself in a dormitory lounge near a large group of people who had been watching television.[26]

Stout's murder stirred anguish and anger, particularly within the psychology department; its faculty and students had greatly admired Stout and were appalled by the collective failure to keep her safe. A group of her fellow graduate students sent U of I president David Henry a four-page letter recounting the details of the case, saying that attempts to protect Stout had been afflicted by "debilitating informality" and "crippled by an inadequate set of tools and techniques." The letter outlined two possible courses of action: "The University should either relieve itself of responsibility for protection of the University community, or it should institute an organization adequate to the demands of general protection. It is our feeling that the latter alternative is the appropriate one." The gist of the university's official response came from liberal arts and sciences dean Jack Peltason. He wrote that if the university assumed "that it has anything approaching total responsibility for the well-being of the University members," it would produce "a paternalistic atmosphere in which the University might assert authority over the lives of its staff members beyond that which would be appropriate," for the U of I was "not a welfare or police agency." President Henry indicated that he "concur[red] heartily" with Peltason.[27]

Deans of Students and Parietals

The U of I's hands-off approach toward its staff and older students contrasted dramatically with its long-standing approach toward younger students, especially the female ones. The university had pioneered the dean of students position in 1901 in the person of Thomas Arkle Clark. According to one historian, Clark resembled "a sheriff in an old-time Western movie" who "walked the streets and ruled by various forms of intimidation, skill, and a bit of luck." Students wrote an ode to him: "Oh, the dean of men and women at dear old Illinois / Is a father to the girls, and a mother to the boys / He looks out for their morals, especially after dark / Our matriarchal, patriarchal, Thomas Arkle Clark." In actuality, Clark's formal title was dean of men; there was a separate dean of women at Illinois and at many other universities. Paula Treichler notes that "it was an office in which intelligent, well-qualified, well-educated women could exercise administrative skills and professional leadership and exert a unifying influence on behalf of women." It also was an office that could generate considerable frustration among the individuals who held it, as they struggled with both unsympathetic male administrators and resentful female undergraduates. A U of I dean of women named Ruby Mason responded to her forced departure in 1923 by destroying all the records in her office.[28]

Well into the 1960s, the deans' offices at Illinois and elsewhere helped enforce what were known as parietals, a key component of the principle of in loco parentis ("in the place of a parent"). As described by historian Kelly Morrow, "Parietals attempted to control female students' sexuality by limiting their mobility and opportunities to have sexual interactions with men." Roger Ebert recalled how parietals worked at the U of I: "The university took aggressive steps to prevent sex among undergraduates. They weren't allowed to live in their own apartments. In women's dormitories, a strict curfew was enforced, and too many 'late minutes' in a semester would get you hauled up before a disciplinary committee. Campus cops patrolled the parking lots of motels, looking for student stickers." Couples meeting in university housing lounges had to comply with the "three-foot rule" mandating that at least three of the couple's four feet had to stay on the floor at all times.[29]

The three-foot rule applied to male-female couples; same-sex couples usually had to remain closeted on college campuses. When the Leo Koch controversy erupted, a man who had been a U of I student back in the 1940s wrote President Henry's office to say that the university counseling center had subjected him to "psychotherapy, counseling, and hypnotism" to try to "cure" him of his gayness before finally booting him out of school altogether. Even in the 1960s, homosexuality among college students still was viewed as a problem in need of therapy, and it could make otherwise progressive young people feel exceedingly uncomfortable. When Roger Ebert saw two men kiss each other on the mouth in a bar near campus, he and his friends "all fell silent, our eyes evading one another's, and none of us bold bohemians could utter a single word." Likewise, in Gael Greene's interviews with college women about sex, she found that "homosexuality appears to be a subject the college girl of the sixties finds difficult or impossible to discuss"; information about sexual activity between women never rose above vague "hearsay and gossip."[30]

During the postwar era, Fred Turner held the title of dean of students at the U of I, with separate deans of men and women working below him. Turner was considered to be an able administrator, even if he did not match the swagger of his predecessor Thomas Arkle Clark. (Turner also was known for reputedly admonishing male students that a "stiff prick has no conscience," although it seemed that no one had ever actually heard him say it.)[31] The U of I's dean of women from 1947 to 1967 was Miriam Shelden. She and other women in her position had to confront stereotypes that one historian says included being seen as "either matronly, curmudgeonly chaperones dedicated to scrutinizing boyfriends and conducting bed checks or innocuous mother figures who offer[ed] advice on hem length and proper fork choice at formal dinners." A *Daily Illini* columnist would target Shelden by referring to her as "Dear Granny": "Just why should a coed have to be in her own little house by 10:30 on week nights? Is it the intention of Granny in the Dean of Women's office to make sure all her little girls are getting enough sleep? Or is she making sure that they're not out being seduced by some awful, lascivious man?"[32]

The truth was that Shelden was an impressive person in her own right; she had served as a reserve commander in the US Navy during World War II, received a doctorate from New York University, and earned a commercial pilot's license. She would staunchly support the 1960s civil-rights movement and also was a forceful advocate for young women, just as other deans of women were. Speaking to high school girls in Chicago in 1960, Shelden urged them to think beyond just marriage and children while telling them never to sell themselves short:

Miriam Shelden, University of Illinois dean of women from 1947 to 1967. Over time, Shelden became an increasingly assertive advocate for gender and racial equality. (Courtesy of the University of Illinois Archives, Miriam A. Shelden Papers, RS 41/3/21)

"There are many of you here today who have capabilities far beyond those of men who are securing higher education. If you complete your college training you must not be content to fill clerical jobs. Clerical jobs must be done, but women of high intelligence must do more." She recommended that the young women pursue additional education beyond their undergraduate degrees. And she added that women were "able to compete successfully on a level with men, although you will find that your boyfriend will argue this point. Unfortunately for him and fortunately for you, statistics are wholeheartedly in your favor."[33]

Shelden did not go so far as to tell the high schoolers that women could choose to stay single and childless, even though she herself would never marry. She said that a woman "must assume two jobs and do an outstanding piece of work on both of them. She must bring up her children and she must make her contributions to her community, to her state, and to her nation. A basic college education is the soundest dowry parents can give their daughters." Most likely, women would have to wait until their children were sufficiently grown before they could use their education to realize their fullest potential. Shelden was expressing a widely held perspective in higher education that historian Paula Fass says "splintered [a] woman's roles into worker, citizen, housewife, and mother and sliced up her life over time." That placed the onus on women to make constant adjustments to meet society's—and men's—expectations. "It's almost like the problem a girl has when she dances with a boy," Shelden told the high schoolers. "He may know only one step—in which case there is no difficulty.... But when you change partners, you may find that your new partner has a brand new step and you must be adept enough to adapt to his dancing. You must be prepared by the same token to assume whatever role presents itself to you within your lifetime in terms of educational training and life patterns."[34]

When it came to parietals, Shelden backed the principle of in loco parentis, saying that "students would be quite surprised to find out how many parents expect this function from the University." She supported more flexibility in women's curfew hours but rejected dropping them altogether. She also rejected any notion that students should be free to conduct their sex lives as they pleased, saying that there was no such thing as "freedom without restraint." In fact, she believed that the U of I had to teach and uphold restraint: "We have assumed ethical values as a part of education. The University has obligations in the field of ethical values and as such has the right to make certain demands of students." As for sex researchers such as Albert Kinsey, they were "pseudo-scientists."[35]

Shelden did realize that young people were changing along with the times, for better or worse. "The shift in student attitudes and conduct is noticeable," she wrote in her office's annual report in 1960. "It may be the beatnik influence, a return to individualism from conformity, or simply a breakdown in family and societal controls with a loss of concern for others." But Shelden also came to believe that behind their incipient rebellion, students were searching for belonging and a higher purpose in life, and adult society bore responsibility for not providing them with the "love, respect, and tenderness" that they needed. Other educators began to see that traditional methods of dealing with students might be losing their effectiveness. Arthur S. Adams, past president of the American Council on Education, said that some universities still believed that the main responsibility of deans of women was "to see that the girls don't get into trouble"; too many educators were "not yet aware of the societal changes which hold so much meaning for the woman of the future." Psychologist Kate Hevner Mueller wrote that one of the biggest changes was "a moving away from a prudential (fear and authority) ethic toward a social ethic (the greatest good of the greatest number)." She asked, "Will this social ethic alone serve to restrain the impetuosity and inexperience of youth?"[36]

Questions about sexual ethics assumed greater urgency. The 1953 Kinsey report on female sexuality had sharply criticized the strictures against premarital intercourse, saying that "the attempt to ignore and suppress the physiologic needs of the sexually most capable segment of the population has led to more complications than most persons are willing to recognize. . . . Many youths and older unmarried females and males are seriously disturbed because the only sources of sexual outlet available to them are either legally or socially disapproved." Earlier, Kinsey had blasted the "utter illogic" of petting-without-intercourse, as well as the educational system's failure to nurture the healthy attitudes toward sex that were necessary for producing happy marriages: "Our ignorance of copulatory techniques, which is the direct outcome of the impressions that are imprinted on the young, our ignorance of satisfactory contraceptive devices above all, produce attitudes which make our concepts of sex wrong."[37]

According to historian Regina Markell Morantz, the Kinsey reports "disturbed, shocked, and threatened not just ordinary men and women but professionals as well." Many news stories and commentaries about youthful sex reflected that anxiety. The headline to a 1958 *Ladies' Home Journal* article left no room for doubt about the article's viewpoint: "Why Premarital Sex Is Always Wrong." Anthropologist Margaret Mead argued that parents and educators tolerated premarital sex as long as it led to marriage, which Mead said did young people a disservice: "Instead of encouraging them to realize the opportunity to remain single and abstinent and responsible during their developing student years and giving them a rationale for doing so, they are only speeding their children into early, irresponsible marriage, triggered in an increasing number of cases by premarital pregnancy."[38]

But as the 1950s gave way to the 1960s, a growing number of educators and journalists would call for a more vigorous debate and dialog on sex and gender. "Snarled-up sex emotions are at the chaotic hub of contemporary problems in the individual, the family, and the broader society," wrote Robert and Frances Harper. "Until educators courageously face the full truths about sex, a most crucial social need will go unmet." Gloria Steinem implicitly pointed to the need to school young men: "The real danger of the contraceptive revolution may be the acceleration of woman's role-change without any corresponding change of man's attitude toward her role." For onetime dean of students John T. Rule, the problem was "the failure of the college to carry on a constant, intelligent, constructive debate with students" and "to listen with calmness rather than outrage" to young people who wanted to talk about sex. Milton I. Levine and Maya Pines argued that "suppression of information on this vital aspect of life" mocked "the 'freedom of ideas,' 'education of the whole man,' and other clichés of the academic world." According to Lester A. Kirkendall, it was "only through hammering out ideas and concepts in prolonged and vigorous discussion that misconceptions can be cleared away and convictions established." And Gael Greene called for "a new moral orientation" that would "provide both a convincing argument against exploitive, destructive sex and a respect for the immense potential of fulfillment possible in joyous and responsible sex that builds both a relationship and the self."[39]

That was the debate—still emerging as of March 1960—that Leo Koch was about to jump into with both feet as he sat down in his office to read the *Daily Illini*.

Advice on Sex

As depicted in the pages of its independent student newspaper, the U of I was a relatively tranquil place at the start of the sixties. The undergraduate student body was 70 percent male and 30 percent female, and the U of I proudly embraced its title as "Fraternity Capital of the World." Lists of pledges to fraternities and sororities regularly appeared in the *Daily Illini*, as did lists of students who had gotten pinned, engaged, or married. In January 1960 it was reported that the Delta Gamma sorority was having trouble participating in the campus's annual Sheequon festival because too many of its members had moved out of the sorority house to get married. The U of I hosted at least thirty queen contests each year, including Homecoming Queen, May Queen, Dolphin Queen,

Interfraternity Queen, Men's Residence Hall Queen, Sno-Ball Queen, St. Pat's Ball Queen, Skull and Crescent Ball Queen, Star and Scroll Ball Queen, Pin and Paddle Ball Queen, Plowboy Prom Queen, and Little International Horse Show Queen. Some members of the student senate felt that the sheer number of queen contests was diluting their value, but a proposal to eliminate most of them was rejected.[40]

For titillation, students could visit downtown Champaign's Illini Theater. It played such pictures as *The Mating Urge*, *The Respectful Tramp*, *Naked Amazon*, and *Call Girls*, the last of which was billed as "the sin-side story" of "the girls who can't stop—and the ones who won't!" Although the community tolerated those movies, a citizen's group met in January 1960 to discuss removing "obscene, immoral and indecent magazines" from local newsstands. (It was not reported whether the list of offensive periodicals included *Playboy*, which had been founded a few years previously by U of I graduate Hugh Hefner.) Champaign police also ordered the removal of a male nude painting from the Turk's Head coffeehouse near campus for purported obscenity. When students published a satirical newspaper called the *College Tumor* that featured sniggering sexual innuendo and pictures of scantily clad women, U of I administrators took exception, and the *Daily Illini* published a scolding editorial.[41] Student demonstrations were few and far between, but each spring saw an impromptu campus water fight that paralleled similar events with sexual undertones at other universities. Students would open fire hydrants and toss people—especially young women—into the torrents. In the 1958 water fight, at least four thousand students had rampaged through the U of I campus. They shouted "we want panties" at sorority houses and "we want tear gas" at the police. They also doused both police and U of I dean Fred Turner with water balloons. Nineteen students were subsequently expelled.[42]

Despite the frivolities, there were glimmers of a growing political and social consciousness among U of I students. In the fall of 1959, the campus NAACP chapter (with Harry Tiebout as its adviser) began its Fair Play campaign. It asked campus-area businesses to sign a nondiscrimination pledge and to display window decals that said "We hire and serve without regard to race, creed or nationality." The following February—in a signature moment of the civil-rights movement—African American students began sit-in protests against segregated lunch counters in the South, and the U of I student senate sent telegrams of support to the protesters. That same month, U of I students formed the Committee for Liberal Action to fight "general apathy on the part of University students and the administration on social action and other issues in general." The committee expanded the local antidiscrimination campaign to target segregation in fraternities and other student housing. The *Daily Illini* approved the committee's efforts, saying in an editorial that "the unceasing clinging to the status quo" in the university and the surrounding community "makes 'action' a most worthwhile purpose."[43]

There also were signs on campus of mounting frustration with parietals. Women in U of I residence halls grumbled that they sometimes were being disciplined on the basis of spurious complaints from unknown accusers. "A coed who was accused of being noisy and another who had been accused of 'unseemly' conduct and even of 'holding immoral conversations' feel that no effort at all was made in determining the correctness of the charge," the *Daily Illini* reported. Women also felt that punishments were applied inconsistently or were unnecessarily burdensome. Some students were "campused," requiring them not only to remain in their dormitories but also to sign in every half hour. "You can't study at all—the whole evening is constantly interrupted—and you keep looking at your watch the whole time," one young woman complained, while another one said, "if you have to do this for a whole weekend, it makes you just about go nuts."[44]

Meanwhile, an effort was underway on campus to try to jump-start a thoughtful conversation about love, marriage, and sex. The U of I's liberal-minded YMCA-YWCA announced that it would bring William and Doris Cole to campus for a series of talks in late March. William Cole was a university president who had written the books *Sex in Christianity and Psychoanalysis* and *Sex and Love in the Bible*. In announcing the Coles' visit, the Y said that it was "important to present the Judeo-Christian understanding of relationships and of sex so students can get some idea of ethical and religious guides which can really help them face specific situations." The Y gave the upcoming event a deliberately innocuous title: "Relations between Men and Women in the 20th Century."[45]

U of I students Dick Hutchison and Dan Bures both served on the university Y's cabinet. Wanting to bring attention to the Coles' visit and to the underlying issues that the Coles would address, the two young men decided to cowrite a column for the campus press. Bures later would say that they wanted "to cause a stir" and that the resulting column was "poorly written, not widely read, and much misunderstood."[46] But it succeeded in highlighting concerns that young people were grappling with on college campuses across the country. The column appeared in the *Daily Illini* on March 16, 1960, under the headline "Sex Ritualized."[47]

"Fraternities and sororities have ritualized sex in an organized fashion and independents have ritualized it in an unorganized fashion," the column began. It described how the ritual manifested itself in a sorority lounge on a Saturday night. The lounge was full of couples "sitting, smooching and now and then mumbling passionately." Even though it was only a little after midnight, the couples were obligated to continue making out until the one a.m. weekend curfew for women, irrespective of any boredom or fatigue. Ending the smooching before the curfew was a grievous faux pas liable to embarrass a young woman in front of her peers and to provoke wrath against any young man who wanted to go home early. In their column, Hutchison and Bures then turned to the campus ritual of searching for a Saturday night date. Men were not particular about whom they went out with, just as long as she was "female and good looking enough to have some prestige value."

"This, girls, is what most campus males think of you," Hutchison and Bures continued. "You are not people, you are not complex human beings, you are not the sum of eighteen or more years of various experiences and environments which have made you the person that you are—you are only female sex units." That many young women similarly viewed young men as male sex units served as further proof that the dating scene was rife with "reciprocal neglect" and that "male-female relations on campus, in general, [have] stultified into a predetermined ritual." In conclusion, the authors argued that "most students do not seem to recognize the obvious. They cannot recognize reality because they don't want to recognize reality. They fear it. People fear and seem incapable of opening their souls to one another—especially to one of the opposite sex!"

Despite the emphasis on sex in the column's headline, Hutchison and Bures actually had focused on male-female relations beyond sex. In doing so, and despite Bures's later disparagement of the column, the two young men were several years ahead of the curve. Historian Beth Bailey notes that during "the late 1960s and early 1970s many young people began to rethink the role of gender in relation to sex." They increasingly "explored the possibilities of friendship" between women and men, and they sought to redefine gender roles more than they tried to expand sexual freedom. That in effect is what Hutchison and Bures seemed to be striving for when they wrote in 1960 that "the first stage of dating—meeting each other—[should be] only the structure which makes possible further acquaintance, understanding, and appreciation of another person as an individual."[48] Such earnest sentiments were not nearly so racy as the physical aspects of sex, which might explain why the column escaped the notice of most readers.

It did not escape the notice of Leo Koch, who would remember that it was only by "some mysterious quirk of fate" that he happened to read the *Daily Illini* issue that contained Hutchison and Bures's column. The headline "Sex Ritualized" captured his attention, for, as he later said, "There is a long history of association of religious ritual with sexual activity among primitive societies and in some not so primitive. In our modern society, we still retain the vestiges of this association in the religious teachings which to a large degree govern our sexual mores. These ethical teachings form the core of our cultural inheritance from the ancient Jewish tradition in our presently Christian culture." As a dedicated humanist who was skeptical—to put it mildly—of religious influences on social ethics, Koch apparently expected to read an exposé of the crude and repressive impact of Judeo-Christian morality on youthful sexual behavior.[49]

Needless to say, that was not what Koch found in Hutchison and Bures's column. Although he would remember that he "sympathized deeply with the concern of these students for the superficial nature" of the campus dating culture, he found the column "quite stuffy" in its devotion "to certain rather unimportant details of student behavior. Nor did I find in this student article any mention of the most important problem of all, namely sexual intercourse." He also felt that the column ignored the broader social context affecting sexual mores. Koch reviewed the column as he would a student essay, "making mental notes of these points which I would have used if I were grading that essay. No doubt, egotistically, I found these so fascinating that I typed them in the form of a letter to the editor of the *Daily Illini*." It was perhaps more accurate to say that the letter represented the column that he felt Hutchison and Bures should have written. Composing the letter took Koch no more than twenty minutes.

The "Sex Ritualized" column had appeared alongside a *Daily Illini* editorial supporting the local Fair Play campaign and the sit-ins in the South ("no white person can know, and few can imagine, what it is like to be a Negro in most of the southern United States").[50] Koch began his letter by taking a light poke at the student paper's editorial bent: "You have made a great show of liberalism in racial problems whose center of physical and emotional disturbance is a safe, 1,000 miles away. I will be interested to see how your social conscience operates with a problem which strikes very close to home, here on campus." He then took a light poke at Hutchison and Bures's "narrow-minded, if not entirely ignorant perspective" on student sex. They had failed to acknowledge the social pressures that drove "healthy, sexually mature human animals into such addictions (of which masturbation is likely the least objectionable) to unhealthy and degenerative practices"—including what went on in sorority lounges.

Koch went on to write that it was impossible to talk frankly about sex. The main culprits in shutting down discussion were religious leaders who believed that "youngsters should remain ignorant about sex for fear that knowledge of it will lead to temptation and sin." That brought Koch to his main argument: "I submit that the events described by Hutchison and Bures are merely symptoms of a serious social malaise which is caused primarily by the hypocritical and downright inhumane standards engendered by a Christian code of ethics which was already decrepit in the days of Queen Victoria." The fact that students did nothing more than neck in sorority lounges pointed to "an extreme degree of brainwashing" that prevented young people "from satisfying their needs in more obvious and healthy ways."

Koch ended his letter with language that could have come straight from Kinsey:

> With modern contraceptives and medical advice readily available at the nearest drugstore, or at least a family physician, there is no valid reason why sexual intercourse should not be condoned among those sufficiently mature to engage in it without social consequences and without violating their own codes of morality and ethics.
>
> A mutually satisfactory sexual experience would eliminate the need for many hours of frustrating petting and lead to much happier and longer lasting marriages among our younger men and women.

The letter was signed "Leo F. Koch, Assistant Professor of Biology." Koch later said that he had added his academic title to his signature "to stress the fact that I was analyzing the subject from a particular perspective for which I felt myself qualified."[51]

Koch recalled that he personally delivered the letter to the *Daily Illini* offices, where editor-in-chief Rich Archbold read it. As an independent student newspaper, the *Daily Illini* was not subject to editorial control by the U of I; the paper could print what it wanted to print. Archbold consulted with other editors and staff members, most of whom laughed over Koch's letter and none of whom argued against its publication. The editor-in-chief wanted to print the letter, he later said, because it would tie in with the impending visit of William and Doris Cole to the U of I and serve "as a jumping off point for a serious discussion on the problems of sex on college campuses." Although Archbold did not personally agree with Koch's viewpoints, "the professor was only expressing an idea. He was not coercing anyone to practice his idea on his next date."[52]

First, though, Archbold needed to confirm that Koch actually wanted the letter published—it had been addressed to Archbold himself rather than to the newspaper. When the editor called the professor at home, Koch was emphatic: "If you have any guts, any gumption, you will print it." The professor already had shown the letter to his wife Shirley, who according to Koch, had been "deeply perturbed" by it; she never had been fully comfortable with her husband's frequent letters to the editor, and she noted that "gentlemanly hints at theological heresy did not pack the same kind of explosive qualities as did ungentlemanly suggestions of sexual enlightenment." Nonetheless, Koch said that he "belittled her fears."[53]

So it was that on the morning of March 18, 1960, Koch's letter appeared on the editorial page of the *Daily Illini* under the headline "Advice on Sex." Apart from a brief article reminding readers of the Coles' upcoming talks on campus, the only other remotely salacious item in that day's paper was an ad on the back page that featured a U of I woman student (described as a "pert, young freshman") in a one-piece bathing suit sold by a Champaign department store. By far the day's biggest story was the Illinois high school basketball tournament that was set to begin that day at the U of I; thousands of teenagers and their family members from across the state were visiting the campus. The timing was not advantageous for Leo Koch. As Rich Archbold recalled, "it was extremely difficult to find copies of the paper after noon. What papers could be found had Koch's 'Advice on Sex' ripped from the editorial page."[54] It was not certain who exactly was picking up the paper or doing the ripping, but clearly the letter had sparked an immediate sensation.

Koch himself began to grasp the impact of his letter that same day after a faculty friend "called me to ask if I preferred to hand in my resignation then or later." Once on campus, Koch found himself having to deny rumors that he already had been fired, although he could not fathom the possibility of such a thing actually happening. It was true that he already was on a terminal contract, but it was not set to expire until the end of August 1961. Koch's only sin had been to write a provocative letter to the student newspaper. He thought to himself, "After all, academic freedom and all that."[55]

Yet within days, anticommunist activist Ira Latimer would seize on Koch's letter as proof of all the immorality and subversion that he believed were consuming the U of I. Even more ominous for Koch was the reaction of members of the U of I Board of Trustees. They too had read Koch's letter, and they soon would make it known that they were not at all pleased.

CHAPTER 3

Seriously Prejudicial

For the first couple of weeks after the March 18 publication of Leo Koch's letter, the public debate over what Koch had written seemed to be confined mostly to the pages of the *Daily Illini*. The student newspaper published several letters in response to Koch, both pro and con. One correspondent praised him for his "intelligent, perceptive, and objective commentary" and argued that "smut and the need for censorship would decrease if our society would stop regarding sex as evil and see it in its proper relationship to a happy society." Another writer (a member of the campus Humanist Society) observed that "Koch is not asking us to roam the streets as animals in search of sensual pleasure, but rather to put our beliefs and actions to constant re-examination and possible amendment under the assumption that the greatest good is not obedience but development."[1]

Less sympathetic was a letter from a University of Illinois freshman who rejected Koch's arguments about Christianity: "I have on several occasions talked with my pastor about sex, and each time the advice I received was sound, completely moral, and not in the least Victorian." Reverend James Hine of the campus McKinley Foundation accused Koch of "the grossest oversimplification of facts and inadequate treatment of a complex and important aspect of human experience I have had the agony to read." Hine argued that "the sex relation happens to be part of a greater relationship known as 'love,' which incidentally Mr. Koch doesn't mention, and which cannot be expressed or enjoyed in its entirety apart from the privacy, security and sanction of the institution we know as marriage."[2]

William and Doris Cole arrived on campus on March 21 to begin their series of talks on sex. William Cole said that he shared "many of Koch's criticisms of the controls invoked by society, but I don't agree that all control should be abandoned. We don't need to frighten individuals to death about the nasty, dark, frightening thing sex is. Rather we should make them socially responsible." The Coles' subsequent talks attracted packed houses all week long, and the *Daily Illini* praised the events as a "well-executed attempt to clear the air that surrounds a most complicated subject." Overall, it seemed that Koch's letter and the Coles' visit had accomplished what Koch later would say had been his intent all along: to inject "ideas into the campus intellectual brew" on a topic that badly needed serious discussion.[3]

Then, on April 2, the *Daily Illini* reported on its front page that the recently formed Committee for Liberal Action was investigating the "pending dismissal" of Koch. The members of that student group were confused over Koch's status because he had told them about his terminal contract that he believed had been issued to him in retaliation for his humanist activities.[4] But, in fact, a process was nearing completion to accelerate Koch's departure from the U of I. Just five days later, on April 7, the university announced that he had been relieved of all duties and that his appointment would be terminated at the end of the current academic year instead of the following year as originally planned.

How and why would Leo Koch be fired? Speculation began almost immediately that the university had caved in to external pressure from a letter campaign by anticommunist activist Ira Latimer. The real impetus to the firing, though, would come from within the university's own hierarchy.

Removing Leo Koch

Ira Latimer already had been gathering material on Koch as part of his dossier documenting alleged subversion at the U of I. One of his file cards on suspicious organizations focused on the Humanist Society. The card quoted from Koch's talk on evolution in 1958 in which he had said that the "soul of man is nothing more than his personality plus a halo around his endocrine glands." The dossier also contained handwritten notes on Koch's attendance at campus appearances by US Senator Paul Douglas of Illinois and socialist Norman Thomas, both in November 1959; the handwriting in the notes resembled that of Grace Oliver, whom Latimer had recruited to help his antisubversion campaign. According to the notes, Koch hectored Douglas with questions about why the senator would not admit Red China into the United Nations, and Koch introduced Thomas's talk by declaring that America's "only chance for survival as a nation is to embrace the principles of Marxism."[5]

After the *Daily Illini* published Koch's letter on sex, Latimer responded with a lengthy screed attacking both Koch and the U of I. It was dated March 25, one week after Koch's letter. Latimer charged that Koch's missive had been deliberately timed to appear when vast numbers of high schoolers were on campus. It was clearly part of a strategy to "demoralize a nation as a necessarily preliminary to taking it over," consistent with the communist blueprint. "Animal Koch would reduce us to a sub-animal level," Latimer opined. "Come the Revolution, there will be free sexual intercourse for everyone." In making "glib double-talk in violation of common sense pass as 'intellectual' and 'progressive,'" Koch sought to "destroy the capacity for criticism which enables men to detect and denounce the fallacies and semantic perversions of Communist propaganda."[6]

Latimer proceeded to blast the U of I Board of Trustees for having registered its objection to a so-called oath of disbelief that was required nationwide of students applying for federal loans (by law, the students had to swear that they had never been affiliated with a subversive group before they could receive the loans). He also excoriated the U of I for having given a fellowship to Edward Yellin, the ex-communist graduate student who had just been on trial for refusing to name his past associates. And Latimer denounced the university for "using the taxpayers' money" to finance the bond-issue campaign, although in actuality no tax money was being used for that purpose. He signed the letter "Reverend Ira H. Latimer" and added that he was a member of the U of I Dads Association.[7]

Latimer addressed his letter to the *Daily Illini*, which did not print it. It was then sent to the parents of a reported twenty-five hundred women students at the U of I along with a reprint of what Koch had written. At least some of the mailings were organized by Eloise Mount of Tuscola, Illinois, a town not far from the university. Mount had been state president of the American Legion Auxiliary and had participated in campaigns to investigate sex education in local schools; now she represented an organization calling itself the League for Moral Responsibility. Mount forwarded Latimer's letter to parents with an accompanying letter of her own dated April 2. It encouraged the recipients to "write your Senator at The State House, Springfield, Illinois, and demand an investigation of the University. Ask the editor of your local newspaper, the manager of your local radio station, and your friends, to help you."[8]

One of Mount's letters was sent to U of I trustee Wayne Johnston. It included a typewritten addendum at the bottom: "WHAT ABOUT YELLIN AND THE

OTHER COMMUNIST'S / WE HAVE THE NAMES AND THE TRUE FACTS / YOU ARE PROTECTING THE COMMUNIST'S BY YOUR SILENCE." A bewildered Johnston wrote to U of I president David Henry on April 5 to inform him about the letter, and Henry wrote back on April 7, the same day that Koch was relieved of his duties: "Since the letter is an unreasoned attack on the Board of Trustees and transmits a vicious smear on the University and the faculty composed by Mr. Ira H. Latimer, I doubt if the communication should have any answer.... Such irresponsible communications serve only to create misconceptions and misunderstanding in the minds of the readers. Perhaps that is what was intended." The university later gave all the trustees a copy of a form letter that was being sent to people who wrote to the U of I in response to Latimer's attack; the form letter repeated the essence of what Henry had written to Johnston. The university also sent trustees information about Latimer's checkered past, including a detailed account of his failed attempt to be admitted to the Illinois bar.[9]

The communications suggest that Latimer's attack on Koch had little direct bearing on the decision to remove the professor, although the university had in fact heard from many parents by the time that Koch was removed from his teaching position. On April 5, the *Chicago Daily News* (in a story creatively headlined "U. of I. Moss Expert Gathers Verbal Stones for Love Views") reported that a "storm of letters" protesting Koch had reached President Henry's office; later news stories estimated their number as somewhere between two hundred fifty and five hundred.[10] It appears that the brunt of those letters did not arrive until just before Koch was removed, by which point his fate had been all but sealed. The process to rid the university of Koch actually had begun much earlier—right after his letter to the editor had been published—and it had started with formal expressions of concern from two of the trustees themselves.

Frances Best Watkins was the only woman trustee. She wrote to President Henry on Sunday, March 20, two days after Koch's letter appeared. Noting that she had seen Koch's provocative letters to the editor in the past, she now felt that he had gone too far: "I am concerned about the high school pupils who may have taken Friday's issue of The Daily Illini home with them, and also the result of the press's use of such material if it came to their attention. It seems to me that many parents would hesitate about sending their sons and daughters to a school where a member of the faculty advocated such conduct.... I think he should be removed from the faculty and hence from his position of influence on students." The president's office followed up with a call to Watkins.[11]

Two days later, Watkins sent fellow trustee Johnston a copy of Koch's letter to the editor, and the day after that—on March 23—Johnston wrote his own letter to President Henry: "To have what I presume to be a prominent professor at the University of Illinois openly advocate sexual relations—and, I would presume from the article, by the youth of the campus—prior to having been lawfully and legally made man and wife seems to me to be advocating a principle which is not only out of place but both socially and ethically wrong. It seems to me that if I have properly interpreted the context of this letter it ought to be dealt with in a very definite way, even though the damage has already been done."[12]

The U of I president answered directly to the Board of Trustees, which effectively had the power to hire and fire the president. Both Watkins and Johnston had served on the board when it voted no confidence in George Stoddard back in 1953, leading to his immediate resignation (Watkins had voted against Stoddard; Johnston had voted to support him). The two trustees also had been on the board when Henry was hired as the permanent replacement to Stoddard. What is more, as of 1960, the trustees themselves were voted in and out of office by the people of Illinois. That said, there was nothing in Watkins's or Johnston's letters that could be interpreted as a threat to Henry, who had cultivated a much better relationship with the board than had existed between the trustees and Stoddard. In their letters, Watkins and Johnston both apologized to Henry for adding to the burdens that the president already was bearing. Neither trustee wrote anything implying a fear of being ousted by voters if no action were taken on Koch. Instead, they seemed genuinely offended by what Koch had written and concerned about his impact on young people.

Henry also was offended. After all, he had been raised with a fundamentalist upbringing, which he later would say "perhaps made me more understanding than I might have been otherwise of the conventional attitude toward social mores and the religious experience." His education and administrative experience had broadened his outlook considerably, and as to Ira Latimer, Henry was not likely to be moved by red-baiting since he had been red-baited himself when his name was first floated for the U of I presidency. Nevertheless, the president believed that Koch had "flouted the moral code" and could not possibly claim the protection of academic freedom. Henry would compare Koch's actions to a doctor who condoned abortion when it was still illegal: "A hospital not only would not violate the first amendment if it discharged such a man, but would itself be guilty of irresponsibility if it did not do so."[13]

Koch might have maintained a faint hope of keeping his job if he had had the vigorous support of his home unit on campus, but of course that was not the case; the Division of General Studies already had given him a terminal contract. One week after Koch's letter appeared, he was called in to meet with DGS chair James McCrimmon and DGS biology head Otto Kugler, the two men who had decided the previous year that Koch's contract would not be renewed. McCrimmon summarized the meeting in a memo to the dean of the College of Liberal Arts and Sciences, of which DGS was a part. McCrimmon criticized Koch for identifying himself as a U of I biology professor when he signed his letter to the *Daily Illini*: "Any biologist who discussed sex conduct as he had discussed it, especially any biologist who advised undergraduate men and women that drug store contraceptives were dependable, raised a question about his competence as a biologist and thus tended to bring discredit on himself and on the department of which he was a member." In addition, in that at a university "sex was a touchier subject than religion," Koch "was under a professional obligation to handle the subject with restraint and good taste," which he had abjectly failed to do. It lent credence to rumors that the professor had acted in bad taste in the classroom. (Two of Koch's former graduate assistants later reported that he once had "displayed a carrot with what might be described as phallic gestures" in class; on another occasion, he had told students that if they thought an examination was rough, "they might do as in rape—relax and enjoy it." Neither incident came to light until after Koch was relieved of his duties.)[14]

McCrimmon followed up the meeting with Koch with a memo to the biology professor telling him that other DGS faculty had called to express concern about his letter to the editor. The DGS head concluded the memo with a swipe at Koch: "I know that your image of yourself is that of a fighting liberal battling courageously against the ignorant forces of society. May I tell you frankly that I am not easily persuaded to confuse arrogance with courage nor intolerance of opposing beliefs with a search for truth."[15]

McCrimmon's memorandum to Koch amounted only to a reprimand, but the executive committee of the College of Liberal Arts and Sciences (LAS) also was considering the case. Committee members later would say that they were not exposed to the letters that the public was sending to the president's office about Koch. After a preliminary meeting in late March, the committee met again on April 6, and LAS dean Lyle Lanier reported its verdict in a memorandum to President Henry: it had voted five to one that Koch's letter "constituted a breach of professional responsibility so serious as to justify a recommendation that he be relieved of his university duties." Dean Lanier expounded on that breach of responsibility by writing to Koch that his letter to the editor had been "excessively intemperate" and "needlessly derogatory." Lanier added that the LAS executive committee "in no sense would deny the right of a faculty member to criticize the American sexual mores, provided that the subject were treated in a spirit of serious, reasoned inquiry commensurate with its importance as a social problem. Unfortunately, the Committee could not feel that your letter measured up even to minimal standards in these respects."[16]

Koch's academic freedom protections were circumscribed by U of I statutes, the most recent version of which had gone into effect in 1957. Although the statutes did assert the "full freedom, within the law, of inquiry, discourse, teaching, research, and publication," they also said that a faculty member could be discharged for "conduct seriously prejudicial to the University through deliberate infraction of law or commonly accepted standards of morality": in brief, conduct that threatened the "best interests of the University." The statutes also admonished faculty to be mindful of "accuracy, forthrightness, and dignity" in their public speech.[17]

The American Association of University Professors (AAUP) and the Association of American Colleges had issued a "Statement of Principles on Academic Freedom and Tenure" in 1940 that also left the likes of Leo Koch vulnerable. It declared that faculty members' "special position in the community imposes special obligations. As scholars and educational officers, they should remember that the public may judge their profession and their institution by their utterances. Hence they should at all times be accurate, should exercise appropriate restraint, should show respect for the opinions of others, and should make every effort to indicate that they are not speaking for the institution." Back in 1940, during discussions over what the "Statement of Principles" should include and not include, a line had been deleted that had said that the "judgment of what constitutes fulfillment of these obligations should rest with the individual." Such language would have given faculty much more protection from universities seeking to discipline a professor over extramural speech; it would have indicated that the professor's individual conscience took precedence over any other consideration.[18]

As it was, Koch could claim no such protection. His unit heads, along with the dean and the executive committee of his college, all had made it abundantly clear that they believed that Koch's letter to the editor had met the criteria of being prejudicial and of not demonstrating restraint or respect. In addition, they all believed that, through his signature to his letter, Koch had inappropriately made it seem as though he were speaking for his profession and his university. Those viewpoints on Koch's conduct were fully in accord with those of the trustees, who already had communicated their displeasure to President Henry, and with those of President Henry himself. Henry noted as much in his April 7 letter to LAS dean Lyle Lanier, using language carefully crafted to adhere to the university statutes: "With you, I consider Professor Koch's letter a grave breach of academic responsibility. The views expressed are offensive and repugnant, contrary to commonly accepted standards of morality, and their public espousal may be interpreted as encouragement of immoral behavior. It is clear that Mr. Koch's conduct has been prejudicial to the best interests of the University." Consequently, Henry directed Lanier to "relieve Professor Koch of his duties immediately. His appointment will be terminated at the University at the end of the current academic year."[19]

That same day—April 7—the U of I issued a news release announcing that President Henry had approved Koch's removal from his duties. In the eyes of the president and other U of I administrators, the proper channels and procedures had been followed and the university's best interests had been served. But the timing of the announcement immediately raised suspicions, for it came just after Ira Latimer's attack on Koch had been circulated across the state. Even if Latimer had played no actual role in Koch's removal, it *appeared* as though he had, suggesting that public attacks on faculty could help get them fired. Latimer's reference to the bond issue, whose passage the U of I had made a top priority, only deepened the suspicions. In addition, the U of I's news release implied that Henry had personally ordered Koch's dismissal, which the president did not have the authority to do; that authority rested with the Board of Trustees. Overarching everything else were questions that would command the U of I's attention for years to come: How did one define "academic responsibility," and just how "responsible" did a faculty member have to be? What was more "seriously prejudicial" to a university's best interests—keeping faculty members who were deemed troublesome, or jettisoning them?

"Not Free Love but Free Speech"

Leo Koch immediately made it clear that he would not depart silently. The same day that the university announced his removal from the classroom, the professor issued a public statement of his own: "Unfortunately, the University of Illinois has chosen to violate the traditions of free speech which most academic institutions the world over are striving to strengthen. If there is academic responsibility, it surely is to maintain the academic freedom of expression and exploration of ideas." The biology professor charged that "in the face of the upcoming bond issue, President David D. Henry has exercised poor judgment in the execution of his duties." The whole affair reeked of McCarthyism, according to Koch: "If the citizens of this country do not have the intellectual vitality to come to their own conclusions after weighing the evidence pro and con, without persecuting those who believe differently than they do, then this country is no longer a democracy." A *Daily Illini* photographer snapped a picture of Koch reading

Oscar Riddle's *The Unleashing of Evolutionary Thought*, a book extolling the power of science over superstition.[20]

Early the next morning on the U of I campus, normally placid save for the odd water fight, students hanged President Henry in effigy from a tree in front of the university YMCA-YWCA. According to the *Champaign-Urbana Courier*, the effigy was "a well-dressed mannequin complete with spectacles and mustache," and attached to it was a sign: "Hanged for Killing Academic Freedom." That night, the campus Committee for Liberal Action held an emergency meeting to discuss Koch; instead of the usual crowd of twenty or so students and faculty, more than two hundred people (including Koch himself) showed up to the meeting. The attendees approved a resolution to "censure the actions and words of President Henry and demand a public apology to Koch and the students of the University." They also discussed Ira Latimer's written attack on Koch, which they knew had been sent to the parents of women students. And they scheduled a campus rally for the next afternoon on the same day as the annual Sheequon parade celebrating the coming of spring.[21]

That rally would produce what the *Courier* described as "an astonishing demonstration" of support for Leo Koch. Undeterred by early-spring snow flurries,

Demonstrators for and against Leo Koch in front of the University YMCA-YWCA on April 9, 1960. This picture appeared in the 1961 *Illio* campus yearbook.

a crowd of more than a thousand protesters and spectators gathered in front of the U of I administration building. (President Henry was not present, it being a Saturday.) The protesters carried a small coffin said to bear the corpse of academic freedom. They also waved signs reading "Not Free Love but Free Speech," and "World's Great Purgers: Stalin in the '30s, Henry in the '60s." There was a song to the tune of "Battle Hymn of the Republic": "Leo Koch has seen the end of all his academic rights / Henry crumpled up his contract with conservative delights / And the reason was that student sex was brought into the light / As Sheequon marches on." A speaker at the rally hammered home the conviction that Henry had "pandered to the popular pressure exerted to remove Dr. Koch so that the passage of the bond issue might more easily be secured." Although onlookers cheered the speeches and laughed at the parodies, there were a few taunts ("go home, beatniks!"), and one naysayer shouted that "I'd rather have the 195 million dollars [from the bond issue] than Dr. Koch." Koch stayed away from the rally, but afterward the *Champaign-Urbana Courier* quoted him as being gratified: "This might be a good university after all."[22]

The following week, the U of I student senate condemned Ira Latimer's letter as "a serious threat to the civil rights and liberties of the American people." The *Daily Illini*—which had editorialized that "Koch's only crime seems to be that of crying 'Sex' in a crowded campus"—received sixty-six letters opposing Koch's firing and only twenty-three supporting it. United Press International polled more than three hundred U of I students; they too opposed the firing by a nearly three-to-one margin, although most of them indicated that they did not agree with Koch's views on sex. In an open letter, a group of U of I graduate students asserted that they could "find no statutory justification for the dismissal of Professor Koch" and that his dismissal "would be prejudicial to the best interests of this University and the people of Illinois."[23]

If Koch had the support of many students, the same was not true of the four Chicago newspapers. *Chicago's American* blared the news of his dismissal with a front-page headline: "Fired Prof Tells His Code of Love." The *American* editorialized that Koch's advocacy of "free love" eminently justified his firing, and the newspaper ominously added, "There should be, perhaps, more firing." The *Chicago Tribune* also trumpeted the Koch story across its front page ("OUST PROF FOR SEX VIEWS"), and although it did not publish its own editorial on the case, it reprinted one from the *Cincinnati Enquirer*: "If [Koch] cares for our advice it is this: Go quietly!" The *Chicago Daily News* mocked Koch's claims that his academic freedom had been violated: "Is a man, once he gets on a college faculty, forever thereafter immune to the consequences of whatever viciousness or folly he may adopt as personal doctrine? Such an idea is patently absurd." And the *Chicago Sun-Times*, although acknowledging that Koch had his rights, also said that he had "transgressed on the right of every student at the University of Illinois—the right to instruction by and association with responsible, mature professors with ideals higher than those of dogs in the alley.... Dr. Henry did right in booting him out."[24]

President Henry's office, which only days earlier had been receiving angry letters demanding Koch's ouster, now was flooded with messages of praise for Henry from across Illinois. They came from the Hauge Lutheran Church in Chicago, the Board of Education in Harrisburg, the Flower Club in Eldorado, the Knights of Columbus in Quincy, the Laesch Dairy Company in Bloomington, and the Americans for Moral Decency in Chicago. That last group did not seem to be affiliated with Eloise Mount's League for Moral Responsibility, which had helped circulate Ira Latimer's attack on Koch. Even so, another Latimer ally, Howard Barham of Champaign, sent Henry his own laudatory note: "I want to thank you and your wife for a job well done. Koch is a disgrace." The president also was praised by several U of I faculty. An English professor wrote that he could "only applaud those men who, knowing what they had to face, came to the stern position that this wretched man must go. I can only apologize for a faculty that has allowed him to go as far as he has gone unchecked." The U of I Dads Association (of which Ira Latimer had identified himself as a member) backed Koch's firing, as did the U of I Moms Association—and both groups also endorsed the bond issue.[25]

Yet as the Koch story gained national attention from *Time*, *Newsweek*, and other media, the U of I president also heard from critics across the country. "Surely after the many published studies of sexual behavior and the prurience of much of our entertainment, no institution dealing with young people can hope to maintain a Victorian hypocrisy and suppression of the subject," wrote a woman in New York. A California man observed that "Dr. Koch's ideas are not new or unusual and many experts in medicine, psychology and hygiene have published identical suggestions." From Alabama came a letter saying that a university was "a small society where freedom is practiced, displayed, and in fact created. You will cut off your knowledge of freedom at its source if you discourage your teachers from speaking their minds and if you show your students, America's future citizens, that speech-freedom is neither good nor practical nor safe." There was criticism from overseas as well, with a group of forty-two Norwegian academics protesting the U of I's apparent abandonment of "the search for and the spreading of scientific truth." Much closer to home, a U of I physics graduate student pithily chided Henry: "The voters can give you the bond issue but they cannot give you a University!"[26]

Other campuses took up Koch's cause. Four hundred sixty-two University of Iowa students and faculty signed a letter protesting the firing, and the student government of the University of Michigan issued a pro-Koch statement. The *Harvard Crimson* wrote of the U of I that "more inquisitive and adventurous minds are advised to seek employment at a less stagnant institution."[27] At the University of California in Berkeley, the student government adopted a resolution that supported Koch, declaring that "the University as an institution should, by its very nature, encourage freedom of thought and expression." When the Berkeley chancellor voided that resolution on top of existing restrictions on campus political activity, the *Daily Californian* student newspaper editorialized, "Student government should not be the puppet of the administration." The Koch case proved to be an early impetus toward the Free Speech Movement that would blossom in Berkeley four years later.[28]

U of I philosophy professor Harry Tiebout was especially distressed over Koch's dismissal; he had regularly invited Koch to his classes to lecture on humanism. In a letter to LAS dean Lyle Lanier, Tiebout wrote that "a great university would have been able to shrug off the whole Koch incident as of no importance. The drastic reaction by University officials seems to me to be symptomatic of a deep sickness, and I think reinstating Dr. Koch would be the first big step on the road toward health." Tiebout observed that Koch's teaching method deliberately provoked "consternation, shock, dismay, and indignation" among students, and that was all for the good: "I would say that Dr. Koch does a singularly poor job of convincing students of the truth of the particular religious and social beliefs which he espouses, but does an outstanding job in getting students to think, and think hard, about serious issues. . . . In short, I think Dr. Koch is an admirable gadfly and that a great university needs more gadflies, not fewer."[29]

For his part, Koch publicly tried to distance himself from the "free love" label, equating it to casual sex between strangers as opposed to "well-planned" premarital intercourse between couples intending to marry. (In private, Koch was more caustic. He said that if the only acceptable means for young people to address their sexual impulses was through so-called petting, then "we must also agree that the correct procedure for a starving person with food is to caress it gently until the need for it disappears.") When reporters asked Koch about his teenage daughter, he responded that she saw sex as being "of no special significance. The subject is discussed frankly at home but without any particular emphasis, just like many other topics." Koch also would note that no one ever asked him about his two sons, highlighting the double standard for young people and sex. In the meantime, the professor had begun the process of appealing his dismissal. The day after he was relieved of his duties, he asked to have his case reviewed by the Committee on Academic Freedom of the U of I faculty senate; a few days later, he requested and was granted a formal hearing before the U of I Board of Trustees.[30]

The academic freedom committee was the first to consider Koch's appeal. One of its members was Victor Stone, the U of I law professor who recently had tangled publicly with Ira Latimer over Latimer's failed bar application (see chapter 1). Stone would recall that three of the committee members were negatively predisposed toward Koch, including chair Glenn Salisbury. Despite his anti-Koch position, according to Stone, Salisbury would come to believe that his committee's handling of the Koch case later cost him the chance to become U of I agriculture dean. That was because the committee's report on the case was in many ways sharply critical of the university and President Henry.[31]

The report wrestled with the seemingly irresoluble conflict between academic freedom and academic responsibility. On the one hand, the committee began by declaring that it was "only through the freedom to pursue truth without fear of reprisal or censure and through the unfettered competition of ideas that the democratic society can progress to higher intellectual and moral levels. This freedom cannot be reserved only for those who agree with majority beliefs and those who have the wisdom to be right. To so restrict academic freedom would render it meaningless." On the other hand, the committee also declared that a "faculty member does not have the right to urge students, or anyone else, to engage in illegal or immoral behavior," and it went on to echo language from the 1940 Statement of Principles on Academic Freedom and Tenure: "In publicly expressing his views, particularly on controversial matters, the faculty member, in keeping with his University association and his position as a man of learning, has the obligation to be accurate, to exercise appropriate restraints, and to show respect for the opinion of others."

The committee then applied the competing principles of freedom and responsibility to the Koch case. Sexual behavior was in fact a proper subject "for public discussion by a faculty member as a citizen, even though this member may have no special professional competence on this subject"; merely discussing sex was "not in itself an infraction of commonly accepted standards of morality." But Koch still had been academically irresponsible, "not because he publicly expressed controversial views on sexual mores, but because of the way in which he expressed them." His letter to the editor was "not in keeping with those standards of temperateness, dignity, and respect for the opinions of others which should characterize public expression by members of the academic community." He also had displayed poor judgment in sharing his views about sex in a student newspaper. For that reason, the letter had been "prejudicial to the best interest of the University, in that it may have damaged the standing of the University in the eyes of many people in the State of Illinois; the administration therefore had a legitimate concern with this damage and valid reason for action to minimize it."

And yet, by summarily announcing that Koch's contract would be terminated at the end of the current academic year, by widely publicizing the actions against Koch, and by failing to provide Koch with a proper hearing, the university and President Henry had overstepped their bounds and had not followed correct procedure. Thus their actions also had been "prejudicial to the standing of the University in the academic community in this country and abroad; and may have an unfavorable effect on the status of academic freedom within the University." As the committee put it, "freedom cannot be real unless its bearers have no doubts about their rights to exercise it and do not feel compelled to assume the attitude, 'I had better be careful.'" In conclusion, the committee unanimously recommended that Koch be reprimanded but not dismissed, that university statutes be revised to ensure a fair hearing for faculty facing discharge, and that administrative action be taken to clarify that controversial opinions were not in and of themselves violations of academic responsibility.[32]

President Henry did not take kindly to the academic freedom committee's report. He refused a request from the U of I chapter of the AAUP to make the report public prior to the Board of Trustees' hearing on Koch. Henry also prepared a detailed rejoinder to the report. He had not been guilty of overstepping his authority just because some people had misinterpreted his letter saying that Koch would be dismissed (again, only the trustees had the power to discharge a faculty member). The university had to publicize Koch's removal from duties because of the widespread attention that already was being paid to the professor's letter to the editor. There had been no need for a hearing prior to Koch's removal from duties; everyone involved in the case, including Koch, agreed on the facts of what had happened. "College and universities will have academic freedom as long as the profession holds the respect of the public in the responsible application of the precepts of the tradition," Henry wrote. "Should the University of Illinois appear to condone, by its silence or by Mr. Koch's continued employment, the infraction of the moral code inherent in his behavior, academic freedom at this institution would be injured beyond repair." Henry sent the Board of Trustees the academic freedom committee's report and his response to it for the trustees to consider during their hearing on Koch.[33]

That hearing took place in the faculty lounge of the Illini Union on June 14, 1960, with spectators lining up outside the building to get one of the small

Seriously Prejudicial • 77

Leo Koch (center) on June 14, 1960, the day of his hearing before the University of Illinois Board of Trustees. Koch is flanked by his wife Shirley and his attorney Donald Moore. (Courtesy of the Champaign County Historical Archives, Urbana Free Library, Urbana, Illinois)

number of seats inside. Thirty journalists also attended, as did Koch and his wife along with President Henry and other U of I officials. The university was represented during the hearing by its legal counsel Ralph Lesemann. Koch had two representatives: Donald Moore, the former staff director of the ACLU in Chicago; and David Danelski, a lawyer and U of I political science professor. Danelski had first taken on Koch's case after the biology professor could find no other counsel. To help cover Koch's legal costs, anonymous people had slipped envelopes with cash in them under Danelski's door. Later, Moore and the ACLU also gave Koch their backing.[34]

During the hearing, Lesemann quoted liberally from Koch's letter to the editor, provoking muffled snickers from a handful of students in attendance. Lesemann noted that Koch had sent his letter in response to the *Daily Illini*'s "Sex Ritualized" column, which the lawyer insisted had been "written in a humorous vein" with no pretense of being factual (an assertion the column's authors likely would rebut). Regardless, "Sex Ritualized" had discussed only "smooching"; Koch had discussed intercourse, and he had dismissed opponents of premarital sex as being "prudes and puritanical old maids." To Lesemann, that defamed "the good sound citizenry and residents of this state who are against the use of obscene language, of obscene literature, of obscene letters." By taunting young people who did no more than smooch, Koch was inciting immoral behavior by effectively daring them to have sex: "Now, when you accuse a red-blooded young American attending this University or any other of having been brainwashed so that he will limit his activities in a certain way and is inhibited from doing something else, what is his reaction to that? Stop and consider it!" To bolster the U of I's case, Lesemann cited 1940's *Kay v. Board of Higher Education*, in which the New York Supreme Court had denied Bertrand Russell a faculty appointment at the City College of New York because of his controversial writings on sex and religion.

Moore and Danelski took turns defending Koch (who, on the advice of his lawyers, did not speak during the hearing). "It looks to me like the big charge against Leo Koch here is—they call it 'incitement,'" Moore told the trustees. "Of course it's incitement. He's inciting thought. If we're going to fire every professor who says something that incites discussion, debate, and controversy . . . we're not going to have any professors who are going to be willing to open their mouths." Danelski argued that faculty were morally compelled to express their beliefs: "Take for example in the thirties in Germany. If a professor thought it was wrong to kill Jews and make slaves out of them, do you not think he had an obligation . . . that he go forward and talk about this? And today in the South, if a professor believes that the Supreme Court is right in its [decision against school segregation], do you not think he has a moral obligation to go forward and say that?" Danelski also blasted the U of I counsel's reference to the Bertrand Russell case, which Danelski called "one of the blackest pages in American jurisprudence" in that it had wrongfully denied faculty employment to "one of the greatest minds of our time." In conclusion, Danelski urged the trustees "to decide for freedom and not to give in to the whims and passions of a few irate letter writers. There are more important principles involved here. It is the principle of whether or not a man, because he is in the minority, is free to express a view that hurts nobody."

Danelski and Moore's defense was for naught. The trustees voted unanimously to confirm Koch's termination, saying that they regretted having to take "such drastic, but proper and essential, action against him."[35]

Censure and Change

U of I president David Henry had reason to feel vindicated by the trustees' vote. To the end of his days, he would argue that "no issue of academic freedom was really at stake" in the Koch case, and he would look back on it as "a rude interruption to the rapid progress of the early years" of his presidency. The university's progress received a giant boost five months after Koch's dismissal when Illinois voters approved the higher education bond issue. "In retrospect, had the bond issue not succeeded, the Chicago development [of that city's new U of I campus] would not have been possible in the time frame that later occurred," Henry would recall. "The Urbana campus could not have accepted the large enrollments that the new buildings made possible.... To maintain a distinguished University without adequate facilities for its people is not possible."[36] If Koch had not been fired, and if angry voters had somehow rejected the bond issue as a result, certainly the university's best interests would have been harmed.

Of course, there is no way to know what would have happened had Koch been retained for one more year until his contract expired. What is known is that at least in the short term, Koch's firing hurt the university's academic standing, to the consternation of many of its faculty. Coleman Griffith had been removed as U of I provost by the trustees in 1953 at the same time that they ousted George Stoddard as president. Although Griffith (who remained on the U of I faculty) wrote Henry a supportive note at the time of the Koch case, he gloomily told a fellow faculty member that the "damage is done. Koch is the unhappy victim. We must now live with an unfortunate mistake.... Intense pressure was exerted on the President and he pushed the 'panic button.'" Eight distinguished U of I professors, including Nobel laureate John Bardeen, wrote a statement on academic freedom that was endorsed by the faculty senate and timed to coincide with the trustees' vote on Koch. "The ultimate test of any new opinion is its soundness, not the immediate reaction of public opinion to it," the professors wrote. "Because the University is charged with advancing the process of scientific and scholarly inquiry, it must be careful not to inhibit the responsible expression of views, even though they are unpopular and even though in the end they may prove untenable." A more explicit rebuke to President Henry and the trustees came from two hundred twenty-nine U of I faculty members, who signed an open letter condemning Koch's firing: "We believe the president and the Board of Trustees have done this University a disservice. Precedents have been established which are likely to diminish the effectiveness of the faculty.... It will be more difficult to retain our best scientists and scholars and to attract men of high quality to this campus."[37]

Worse was yet to come. In the spring of 1961, the national office of the AAUP informed the university that it would conduct an investigation of Koch's dismissal. That investigation came only after considerable prodding from the U of I's AAUP chapter and from Koch himself. (Academic freedom historian John K. Wilson notes that "Koch was not an ideal victim" in the eyes of the national AAUP; he was an obscure assistant professor who had written a snarky letter about student sex as opposed to taking up a more righteous cause of the day such as racial discrimination in the South.) The AAUP's report was not completed until the fall of 1962 and was not made public until the following March. It would lead to a formal AAUP censure of the U of I.[38]

The Leo Koch case made news for years at the University of Illinois. This headline and picture appeared in the *Spectator*, a campus newspaper cofounded by Roger Ebert in 1961. (Courtesy of the University of Illinois Archives, *Spectator* File, RS 41/8/803)

The report was in three parts, with the first section relating the findings of the AAUP's ad hoc investigating committee chaired by Yale law professor Thomas I. Emerson. The committee found that the U of I's president and trustees had violated Koch's due process and had not sufficiently involved the faculty in the decision to fire him; moreover, some lower-ranking U of I faculty seemed reluctant "to espouse unorthodox or deviant views in controversial areas." The committee declared that for the U of I to achieve its full potential, "its top administration and its Board of Trustees must be ready to recognize its maturity, its ability to absorb a few gadflies, and its need for uninhibited freedom of discussion."[39]

In the second part of the report, the ad hoc committee grappled with the broader questions raised by the Koch case. The committee argued that "a faculty member should have the same right of expression as any other citizen and that university discipline should not be invoked under any standard of 'academic responsibility.' Such sanctions as are appropriate in this situation are the unofficial judgment and pressures derived from the basic standards of the academic profession and the intellectual community." In other words, faculty should be judged by fellow faculty and not by administrators or members of the public who might find unorthodox expression irresponsible. "The concept of 'irresponsibility' is exceedingly vague," the committee went on to say. "Any serious application of the standard would tend to eliminate or discourage any colorful or forceful utterance." It was true that the 1940 Statement of Principles on Academic Freedom and Tenure had said that faculty should demonstrate respect and restraint, but those were merely admonitions, not mandates. Nor should the alleged incitement of immorality or unconventional behavior be automatically disciplined: "As Justice [Oliver Wendell] Holmes has said, 'Every idea is an incitement.'" A great university was not a shepherd to a flock of sheep conforming to commonly accepted ideas; it instead should be "an enlightened and lively center of investigation and controversy. If it falls too short of this ideal, the very concept of academic freedom in such an institution becomes degraded into meaninglessness."[40]

The third and final part of the report contained comments by members of the AAUP's "Committee A," which was charged with matters of academic freedom and tenure. Committee A provided small comfort to the U of I, saying that its dismissal of Leo Koch had been "outrageously severe and completely unwarranted." However, the committee also asserted that the U of I "did not err in proceeding on the assumption that a violation of academic responsibility on the part of a faculty member fell within the disciplinary powers of the institution," for "we can hardly expect academic freedom to endure unless it is matched by academic responsibility." To that argument, Committee A member Warren Taylor of Oberlin College wrote a passionate dissent. Institutional discipline should be imposed only for "dereliction of duty and professional incompetence," Taylor said. To invoke violations of academic responsibility as a basis for discipline was "to open a Pandora's box of all the coercive and compulsive crusades of sectarian, political, and economic pressure groups together with consequent attempts at dismissal by administrators who are unable to resist the public pressure engendered by such groups whose causes often contain more heat than light."[41]

Whatever its internal differences as regards academic responsibility, the AAUP was united in its stance that the U of I had erred badly in the Koch case, and it voted to censure the university in April 1963. President Henry was no happier with that development than he had been with his own campus's academic freedom committee when it had recommended against Koch's dismissal or with the scores of U of I faculty members who had signed the open letter rebuking Henry's administration. In his official response to the censure, Henry doubled down on his contention that the university had not violated Koch's due process or academic freedom; he also made his unhappiness clear to members of the U of I's AAUP chapter, which had urged the national AAUP to investigate Koch's dismissal. At the same time, Henry fully realized that, for the university, the "censure was, of course, some embarrassment. It is supposed to have that effect." He quickly expressed his willingness to help make changes that would remove the sanction, particularly by revising the university statutes, much as the U of I's academic freedom committee had recommended when the Koch case first erupted.[42]

The long, tedious process of statute revision had begun shortly after Koch's dismissal, meaning that it had already been going on for three years by the time of the AAUP censure; it then would grind on for three years more. The process required ongoing negotiations among the president's office, the faculty senates of each U of I campus, and the Board of Trustees, with input from both the U of I AAUP and the national AAUP. When the revised statutes finally took effect in 1966, the code that covered faculty dismissals had been dramatically altered. Gone was the old language that had doomed Leo Koch: that a faculty member could be discharged for "conduct seriously prejudicial to the University" through violations of "commonly accepted standards of morality." Now the code stipulated that due cause for dismissal existed only when faculty had been "grossly neglectful of or grossly inefficient in" their university duties or when their conduct outside the university "clearly and convincingly" demonstrated that they no longer could perform their university duties "consonant with professional standards of competence and responsibility." Again, it was the standards of professional academics that counted, not the standards of public opinion or morality. The new statutes also meticulously outlined a multistep procedure that the university had to follow whenever it sought to dismiss a faculty member.[43]

In the end, according to U of I law professor Victor Stone, the U of I emerged with "the best statutes on academic freedom and tenure in the country." The new statutes also succeeded in persuading the AAUP to remove its censure of the university in February 1967. In an odd and accidental way, the Koch case turned into one of the "succession of partial victories" that David Henry had said that he wanted to bring about as U of I president: the faculty ended up better protected than they had been before the whole affair began.[44]

The Koch case also prompted a reexamination of academic freedom protections nationwide. Historian Joan Wallach Scott observes that "academic responsibility" often had been used as a pretext to fire faculty during the McCarthy years: "Sometimes the need to protect the university from legislative intervention was the reason, sometimes the refusal of the professor to come clean with his colleagues inside the university was the issue, sometimes it was that communism was by definition antithetical to free thought.... This logic substituted for any need to provide concrete evidence of scholarly or pedagogic unfitness." The disputes within the AAUP over academic responsibility's applicability to Leo Koch's dismissal pointed up the pressing need to clarify the concept, especially as it applied to "extramural" speech in which a faculty member spoke as a citizen.[45]

As a result, the AAUP's Committee A in 1964 issued a "Statement on Extramural Utterances" relating to cases such as Koch's. According to the new statement, "The controlling principle is that a faculty member's expression of opinion as a citizen cannot constitute grounds for dismissal unless it clearly demonstrates the faculty member's unfitness to serve. Extramural utterances rarely bear upon the faculty member's fitness for continuing service." That language also was codified in 1970 in the "Interpretive Comments" that were appended to the 1940 Statement of Principles on Academic Freedom and Tenure. For John K. Wilson, the new language represented a decisive shift away from a "gentleman scientist model" of academic freedom that stressed "propriety and obligations" and a shift toward a "liberty model" that stressed the rights of faculty to speak their minds. In contrast, Hans-Joerg Tiede argues that "the AAUP's understanding of extramural speech has changed very little throughout its history," and the Koch case simply prompted the organization to clarify the intent of the original 1940 statement.[46]

None of those statute revisions or philosophical debates over extramural speech did Leo Koch much good. His firing left him and his family in substantial debt, as he detailed in an appeal for money: he owed $550 to a Champaign-Urbana grocery, $350 to other local stores, $200 to gas stations, $850 to a credit union, and more. In the spring of 1961, a few U of I faculty members opened the Leo F. Koch Fund at a local bank to help him pay his bills; the AAUP chipped in with additional funds. At about the same time, an international group of academics formed the Committee for Leo Koch to raise money and awareness about academic freedom. The committee sent out more than twenty-eight thousand brochures about the Koch case, and although it succeeded in bringing in a few hundred dollars for Koch himself, it also went into debt while doing so.[47]

What Koch wanted most of all was to force the U of I to pay him the full year's salary that he was supposed to have received during the final year of his contract (since the university had terminated him one year early). That was something that the U of I steadfastly refused to do, even when the national AAUP indicated that such a gesture could help remove the censure against the university. When the AAUP finally lifted the censure anyway, Koch was bitterly disappointed. "My dismissal resulted in severe financial and total professional damages that far exceeded the $5,900 that the University owed me under that contract," he wrote to the AAUP. Members of the U of I's AAUP chapter also protested the decision not to insist on compensation for Koch. In response, a national AAUP representative wrote that the organization had decided that any such attempts would be futile: "We reached the point where it seemed virtually certain that if redress to Professor Koch was to remain an issue, then the University of Illinois would remain on the list of Censured Administrations essentially forever. It is a real question whether one or more fossilizations of that type, however faithfully they might preserve the history of a crime, would permit the censure list to be used flexibly as a dynamic instrumentality." Eventually, the national AAUP itself paid Koch the year's salary that he had lost.[48]

While Koch was seeking to address his money woes, he also was seeking a legal judgment against the U of I with help from the ACLU. He first filed suit in the Superior Court of Cook County, Illinois, asking for damages for breach of contract, but the court ruled against him. Koch then turned to the Illinois Appellate Court, which also ruled against him: "When the plaintiff entered into his employment contract with the University of Illinois, he voluntarily agreed to the University's rules and procedures for determining the causes of discharge, the quasi-judicial framework for determining the existence of those causes and the procedure whereby he might be discharged as a result of those causes. What his present complaint amounts to is an assertion that he should not be bound by the agreement to which he voluntarily assented." A subsequent appeal to the Illinois Supreme Court ended again in failure, and in January 1964 the US Supreme Court declined to review the case.[49]

By then, Leo Koch was long gone from Champaign-Urbana. After paying off some of his debts, he moved his family to California in the summer of 1961 to take a position at a research company. That job lasted only a year, and then he taught grade school in San Francisco for a time. When he decided to experiment with LSD in 1963, he observed rather wanly that "I suppose I am still 'ambitious,' but see no constructive or plausible avenue of attaining these 'ambitions' at the present time."[50]

In fact, Koch still had plenty of adventures ahead of him. In the summer of 1963, he traveled to North Carolina to work at a libertarian free school called Camp Summerlane; the job ended after just one week when a mob set the school ablaze over rumors of racial integration and other social taboos.[51] After the US Supreme Court refused to hear Koch's case against the U of I, he joined Jefferson Poland in founding the Sexual Freedom League in New York City. Koch remained as outspoken as ever not just about sex, but also about religion and academic freedom. In notes that he prepared for a media interview, he asserted that organized religion remained the "last stronghold of antiscientific orthodoxy." Should society embrace nudism, "obscenity, pornography, [and] voyeurism would be immediately ameliorated." According to Koch, birth control should be subsidized, prostitution and abortion should be legalized, and educators "ought to be bold thinkers, not conformists."[52]

The irony was that the writing for which Koch would forever be known had not been especially bold or original in its thinking, not even for 1960. In his letter to the *Daily Illini*, he had said only that sex should be tolerated "among those sufficiently mature enough to engage in it" and among those who felt ethically comfortable with it. Kinsey had argued much the same thing several years previously. However, Koch would say that if David Henry "or any member of the Board of Trustees of the University of Illinois understood the content of the Kinsey Reports, then it is obvious that none of them have the courage to admit so in public." In firing Koch, the U of I president and trustees had acted according to their own moral convictions and had done the politically prudent thing. Yet they also had forsaken a chance to demonstrate courage and faith in their own university. In a sermon delivered soon after Koch had been dismissed, Reverend David Harris Cole of the Universalist-Unitarian Church of Urbana argued that the United States "never has fully accepted the concept of intellectual freedom" and that it "has always had a strain of demagogy and intolerance." The Koch case represented a failed "opportunity to show the public that one can allow for dissent, that we can allow the examination of ideas, even controversial ones, which are dogmatically held, in the confidence that the truth will win."[53]

For Koch, the most dangerous dogma was the "mass hypocrisy implied by the prevalence of sexual behavior which is publicly condemned but privately condoned." He said that the primary victims of that hypocrisy were young people, who by 1960 were beginning to question received wisdom about sex (a topic of keen interest and importance to them) and a host of other concerns. At the very least, they wanted to be able to hear and participate in discussions about those issues without being told that it was immoral or irresponsible. So it is not surprising that many U of I students—even ones who disagreed with Koch's views on sex—protested his firing. Just after the U of I dismissed him, Koch wrote that the "enthusiasm, vigor, and discipline" of those students had convinced him that "they are capable of meeting any responsibilities which they might accrue as well as, if not better than, their preceding student generations. I am convinced that their difficulties are greater only because of the shortcomings of their parents and teachers."[54]

Students would have plenty more opportunities to display their enthusiasm and to aim ire at their elders in the years ahead. Great changes were in store for the U of I and the rest of the world.

CHAPTER 4

Storm Coming

One of the many groups of people whom Leo Koch had managed to anger with his letter about premarital sex was the Iowa Regular Baptists, who in April 1960 adopted a resolution "deploring the great indifference and blindness of those who would condone such practices under the guise of liberty of conscience, freedom of speech and academic freedom." The group also approved a separate resolution opposing the election of a Roman Catholic as US president. The unnamed target clearly was John F. Kennedy, who had emerged as a leading Democratic presidential candidate.[1]

Despite such anti-Catholic sentiment, Kennedy proceeded to win the Democratic nomination; and by October he was in a tight race with the Republican presidential nominee, Richard M. Nixon. Illinois being one of several states that could tilt either way, Kennedy visited the University of Illinois on October 24 as part of a whirlwind tour of five cities in the state. He took advantage of recent changes to the long-standing rule that had banned U of I buildings and grounds from being used for political purposes (supposedly to keep the university above partisan politics). The rule changes made exceptions for most candidates for office; Nixon's running mate Henry Cabot Lodge Jr. already had campaigned on campus the previous month.[2]

Kennedy's brief speech on the quadrangle in front of the university auditorium drew some ten thousand spectators, some of whom climbed trees, craned out of windows, or perched on roofs to get a better view. When he began to speak, the crowd surged forward, breaking through rope barriers and nearly trampling people closer to the candidate. The *Daily Illini* amusedly reported that young women seemed to be especially taken with Kennedy. (The paper's "Campus Scout" columnist quoted one such woman: "He's so handsome; it's a shame to waste such a hunk of man on a job that will age him.")[3]

Kennedy told the U of I crowd that the 1960 presidential election was "a contest between the contented and the concerned, between those who wish to stand still and those who wish to move ahead." Naturally, he identified himself with the concerned movers camp determined to reestablish the global image

John F. Kennedy speaking in the front of the auditorium on the University of Illinois main quadrangle, October 24, 1960. (Courtesy of the University of Illinois Alumni Archives)

Kennedy's speech drew some ten thousand spectators. A local newspaper later said that no other visitor to campus ever "created the excitement and almost near riot" that Kennedy did. (Courtesy of the University of Illinois Alumni Archives)

of the United States as "a new, strong, vital, revolutionary society." Kennedy finished by invoking Illinois's most famous resident, Abraham Lincoln:

> One hundred years ago in the campaign of 1860, Lincoln wrote to a friend: "I know there is a God, and I know He hates injustice. I see the storm coming and His hand is in it. But if He has a place and a part for me, I believe that I am ready." Now, one hundred years later, we know there is a God, and we know He hates injustice, and we see the storm coming. We see His hand in it. But if He has a place and a part for us, I believe we are ready.[4]

Two weeks later, Kennedy was elected president, narrowly carrying Illinois. The three years that would follow would indeed be tempestuous and would end in tragedy. They also would be a time of social and intellectual awakening for young people across the political spectrum as they engaged with the great issues of the day—particularly civil rights and the Cold War.

Confronting Racism and the Arms Race

The U of I never had been very hospitable toward African Americans. In a history of U of I Black students, Deirdre Lynn Cobb notes that they "rarely had the privilege of being treated fairly or as first class citizens"; the students "had to bear the shame and humiliation of attending an institution that promoted education and equality, but they were overlooked daily." Until the Illini Union opened in 1941, African American students could not buy a hot meal on or near campus and sometimes had to resort to using an empty classroom as a place to eat a sack lunch. Even after World War II, they found it difficult to find an adequate place to live or to get a haircut.[5]

At the start of the 1960s, African Americans still constituted a tiny minority at the U of I: only an estimated two hundred or so students out of more than twenty thousand total on campus. (The numbers did increase slightly by the middle of the decade, but not until 1968 was there a concerted effort to attract more Black students to Illinois.) The students endured slights. Carol Easton remembered that when she arrived at her residence hall on her first day at the university, "I had been assigned a roommate who was a young White girl. And she came into the room and she saw me, and then she turned around and she left. And I never saw her again." So Easton spent her first semester living in a dormitory room by herself. As an English major at the U of I, Easton (who later would hold an endowed professorship at Northwestern University) never read a work by an African American writer, nor was she ever taught by an African American professor. In fact, there was not a single tenured Black faculty member at the university.[6]

For all that, Easton felt that she "had reached heaven" when she transferred to the U of I from a private university; her previous school had had only ten African American students. She formed close ties at the U of I with her sorority sisters and other Black students. "Even though we were in a sea of White faces, we found our own social world," Beverly Effort would recall. Connie Rolison remembered that "we had to do well because we were representative of our race, and we were careful not to bring discredit in any way, shape, or form. Because we were essentially surrounded. But it also encouraged activism, because back then was the beginning of the whole civil rights thing." Some African American students joined the U of I chapter of the NAACP, and they participated in the Fair Play campaign that began in 1959 and asked campus-area businesses to sign a nondiscrimination pledge. When some student groups resisted the campaign, a person (who chose to be identified only as "An American Negro") wrote to the *Daily Illini* to say that people should not be afraid of insulting local businesses: "I believe that it is time we insulted men who constantly violate the Constitution by their practices of discrimination since they are little better than the bigots we fought in World War II."[7]

In 1961 students renewed an effort originally launched during the previous decade to fight discrimination among campus-area barbers; they also boycotted the local Coca-Cola bottling company for its hiring practices. Most prominent was a campaign targeting the new J. C. Penney's store in downtown Champaign. When the store opened in April 1961 with two hundred employees that included no African Americans except for custodians and stock personnel, Reverend J. E. Graves and other Black community leaders organized picket lines that included Black students from the U of I. White students and faculty eventually joined the picketing. After three weeks, the store as well as others in Champaign-Urbana agreed to hire more African American staff. The local Council for Community Integration, which had helped lead the picketing, boasted that the "campaign originated with and was conducted by Negroes, speaking clearly and forcefully in their own behalf on an issue of moral as well as practical, bread-and-butter importance." U of I philosophy professor Harry Tiebout, adviser of the campus NAACP chapter, pronounced the campaign a "social revolution."[8]

Tiebout was as formidable a gadfly as his friend Leo Koch. Student Lew Collens (later president of the Illinois Institute of Technology) recalled that Tiebout used to taunt members of one fraternity by demonstrating their secret handshake in front of everyone in his classes. The professor helped lead efforts to fight discrimination in U of I fraternities and sororities as well as in off-campus housing. To people who said that Greek houses should be free to pledge whomever they wanted, Tiebout argued that the U of I should approve only those organizations that operated according to the university's core values. By that criterion, Phi Beta Kappa—which promoted scholarly excellence—had a right to be exclusive, but an Illini Young Nazi Club had no business being on campus: "Promotion of antisemitism is not consonant with the ideals and purposes of the University. . . . Only when the principle of selectivity is cruel, stupid, and immoral does the question of discrimination arise." In October 1961, the campus Committee on Student Affairs (CSA) passed a bill calling on the university to withdraw recognition of any fraternity or sorority that practiced discrimination; the bill also asked the university to stop approving discriminatory off-campus housing. The following February, the U of I Board of Trustees endorsed the CSA bill; but it would not go into effect until 1965, and it would not apply to Greek houses. (The Interfraternity Council did approve its own antidiscrimination pledge, but that too would not take effect until 1965.)[9]

92 • CHAPTER 4

A picketer in front of the new J. C. Penney's store in Champaign, Illinois, in April 1961. The picketers were protesting the store's hiring policies toward African Americans. (Courtesy of the Champaign County Historical Archives, Urbana Free Library, Urbana, Illinois)

While the university was proceeding with all deliberate speed on discrimination, it also was grappling with concerns about militarism and nuclear proliferation. The U of I had long required all freshmen and sophomore men to participate in the Reserve Officers' Training Corps (ROTC), consistent with Illinois state law. Many students believed that compulsory military training was a waste of time. The student senate polled the campus in December 1960, with twenty-five hundred students opposing the compulsory program and only a thousand students supporting it. The following March, some students tried to picket the annual campus military ball, but they were blocked by the City of Champaign. Martin Cobin—a U of I speech professor, Quaker, and World War II veteran—argued in the *Daily Illini* that "military training is necessarily and quite properly in conflict with training in democratic citizenship"; it also was contrary to the university's mission to promote "free inquiry, independent thought, [and] respect for learning." Yet it was not until June 1963 that U of I president David Henry urged the state legislature to end compulsory ROTC, and then it was on the grounds of the university running low on money and space to handle the burgeoning number of students who would be required to participate. ROTC became a purely voluntary program as of the fall of 1964.[10]

During the ROTC fight, U of I students enlisted in efforts to bolster world peace. After President Kennedy in 1961 announced the formation of the Peace Corps, interest in the program surged among students at Illinois and at other campuses nationwide.[11] That same year, Illinois students formed a Student Peace Union. They picketed a meeting that was discussing the effectiveness of campus fallout shelters, and they also protested nuclear arms testing by carrying signs reading "Neither Red nor Dead" and "No Contamination without Representation." Peace union member Joe Tuchinsky wrote in the *Daily Illini* that the world faced the threat of "the greatest catastrophe ever inflicted on the human race." (He soon would leave graduate school at the U of I to devote himself fully to the causes of peace and nonviolence.) Even students who were otherwise apolitical commented ironically on the arms race. *Daily Illini* writer Stu Cohn noted that the winning entry in the 1961 campus Stunt Show competition started with "a radio flash telling all people to proceed to their civil defense shelters, and ended with the death of the last five people on earth." Cohn wrote that it was "a sad situation when college students, the cream of the intellectual crop, come face to face with our country's greatest menace only through stunt shows and parodies," and he objected to the notion that universities were ivory towers isolated from the rest of the world: "Should education, understanding, and research stop at the boundary of a course number?"[12]

Some U of I faculty connected their academic work to pacifism. Communications professor Dallas Smythe denounced the Cold War as a "spiral of terror" and called for the creation of a U of I peace research center with a budget of a million dollars. (According to his graduate student James Carey, Smythe also asked students to lie across the railroad tracks near campus to protest US foreign policy, creating consternation among Carey and his classmates: "We all thought: That goddamn engineer may not see us!")[13] Psychology professor Charles Osgood formulated a strategy dubbed GRIT (Graduated and Reciprocated Initiatives in Tension reduction); in return for such efforts, he was accused of appeasing communism.[14] Eugene Rabinowitch (editor of the *Bulletin of Atomic Scientists*) pleaded for "cooperation among the Western nations and the Communist nations in order to promote world peace," and Oscar Lewis (internationally known for his studies of the culture of poverty) scoffed at suggestions that civilization could survive a nuclear war. One hundred eighty-three U of I faculty members signed an open letter to President Kennedy questioning the building of fallout shelters; a like number of faculty and community members signed another open letter criticizing the government after the failed Bay of Pigs invasion of Cuba: "Our government's complicity in the Cuban invasion, coupled with the continuing support of corrupt, undemocratic regimes in Latin America, Laos, South Vietnam and other parts of the globe, strike at the system we are pledged to defend."[15]

The October 1962 Cuban missile crisis struck fear into many students and faculty members at the U of I just as it did elsewhere across the nation. "It is hard to write these words, not really knowing if they will ever be set into type and read," wrote Roger Ebert in the *Daily Illini*. Alluding to Fidel Castro, whom many Americans had first viewed as a romantic or humorous figure, Ebert noted that the Cuba situation "began with a comic book hero and a thousand wisecracks and may end with the end of it all." People interviewed on the street about President Kennedy's quarantine of Cuba expressed worry and dread: "I'm terrified, but I'm proud of Kennedy." "We're going to have war plenty soon." "We're the aggressors, and I don't like it." Champaign County Civil Defense conducted a practice alert of an impending nuclear strike by directing twenty police cars to drive around the community with all their sirens blaring at once. Charles Osgood said that he was "terribly disturbed" by the crisis, which he feared was "opening a Pandora box of trouble." Dallas Smythe told young people that he felt "guilty of forcing you to grow up so that every day of your lives you have lived with the threat of nuclear war hanging over you."[16]

When the quarantine appeared to have the desired effect and tensions eased, students whom the *Daily Illini* interviewed backed Kennedy, as did the student newspaper's editorial page: "Although we were probably as frightened during the past 48 hours as most people throughout the country, we certainly give our wholehearted support to President Kennedy's action in the Cuban crisis." *Daily Illini* columnist Don Henry belittled individuals who had criticized the quarantine as being too bellicose: "Before we came to college we would have called such people cowards, but we can't do that now. We are sophisticated; we must refer to them as 'concerned people searching for peaceful alternatives.'"[17]

It soon became clear, though, that life would not simply revert to what it had been before the crisis. Dallas Smythe—one of those "concerned people searching for peaceful alternatives"—decided at the end of the academic year to abandon the United States altogether and move his family to his native Canada: "If we and our two children were to die in a nuclear war, we didn't want to do it as Americans." And only days after it had backed Kennedy's Cuba policy, the *Daily Illini* questioned the broader US stance toward the world and lamented the country's failure "to successfully identify itself with social and economic reform and revolution. . . . Will we someday shelve our nuclear playthings and attempt to conduct foreign policy on the only realistic battlefield—the negotiating table, the United Nations, and the minds of men?"[18]

Student Fads and Factions

Of course, students did not spend all their days fretting about the perilous state of the planet. The twist dance craze hit the U of I in late 1961, and the *Daily Illini* featured several pictures of the fad, including students dancing to the "Jingle Bell Twist" next to a Christmas tree. Women residents of Busey Hall invented the "snoot boot," a small, knitted nose covering that was advertised as stopping "beak leak." The women sold the snoot boots for charity while making gifts of them to U of I president David Henry and Chicago radio personality Dick Biondi (who joked that it would "keep the pizza outta my nostrils"). Other students in U of I residence halls staged "talkathons"; they set a record by talking for 609 straight hours on the telephone, or a little more than twenty-five consecutive days without a break. One campus tradition—the annual water fight—ended ignominiously after a local radio journalist was blinded in one eye while covering the event.[19]

Another campus fad dovetailed with heightened social consciousness. Music aficionados founded the U of I Folksong Club in the spring of 1961 and created a newsletter called *Autoharp*. Some of the most renowned folksingers in the country played on campus, among them Josh White (who sang "Free and Equal Blues" at the U of I); Rambling Jack Elliott; Odetta; Peter, Paul, and Mary (who told the campus audience, "We have a message, and we're not at all bashful in singing about it"); and Joan Baez, who was just twenty-one years old when she appeared at the U of I in November 1962. "I don't like cute songs, snappy songs, little ditties," Baez said before her concert in the university auditorium. "I like beautiful songs, mostly sad songs, and that's what I sing." She added that she hoped her music was "getting through to mostly people my age" and that she felt "a very close kinship with the sort of lost generation today that feels the bomb hanging overhead."[20]

If folksingers and their fans tended toward pronounced liberal sympathies, young people whose politics were of the opposite bent also were asserting themselves. Journalist Robert Novak—who had attended the U of I from 1948 to 1952—wrote in the *Wall Street Journal* in 1961 that although students on both the left and the right were increasingly active on college campuses, the "most obvious evidence of reawakened political interest is the highly articulate, efficiently organized and usually well-financed campus conservative movement centering on Sen. Barry Goldwater as a leader." *Time* magazine commented that same year that the "new trend is youth's natural rebellion against conformity, and to many the liberalism of their New Deal-bred elders is the most ironbound conformity." The magazine quoted the president of the University of Wisconsin's Conservative Club: "You walk around with your Goldwater button, and you feel the thrill of treason."[21]

The conservative movement also was "percolating" at the U of I, according to Jim Nowlan, a U of I undergraduate who later would serve as an Illinois state legislator. Although he would recall that he was only a "fringe activist," Nowlan participated in campus Republican groups as well as the Conservative Coordinating Council, which published its own newsletter, *New Voice*. "In the past Liberalism looked on the campus as its empire," wrote U of I students David Young and Robert (Bob) Auler in *National Review*. "The winds of change continue to blow, as evidenced by the hurricane damage suffered by the Liberal installations at the University of Illinois." One of the young conservatives' heroes was Indianapolis newspaper editor M. Stanton Evans. In his 1961 book *Revolt on the Campus*, Evans argued that two evils afflicted contemporary American culture, the first being permissiveness: "We no longer believe in the absolute standards of behavior handed down by our tradition.... We are no longer concerned with doing what is 'right' but with 'getting along,' adjusting." The second evil was statism: "We have tended to yield the governance of our lives to the group, or to the state. We no longer believe in individual self-reliance, but prefer to huddle in the shadow of the mass." Evans also praised the Young Americans for Freedom, a conservative group founded in 1960 at the Sharon, Connecticut, family home of William F. Buckley Jr. The Young Americans for Freedom issued its Sharon Statement of principles promoting free markets and anticommunism.[22]

The U of I Conservative Coordinating Council joined the YMCA-YWCA and other campus organizations in creating the Great Debates series, which pitted conservative speakers against liberal speakers. According to a university Y spokesperson, the series was "carefully planned to meet a need seriously lacking on this campus—a program frankly presenting the political problems facing the United States today." In May 1962 William F. Buckley debated Oberlin political science professor Carey McWilliams Jr. before more than thirty-five hundred spectators in Huff Gymnasium. Buckley criticized the "thinking elite" whose "moralistic rhetoric" was hampering US policy toward the Soviet Union, while McWilliams said that the US preoccupation with material wealth made the nation appear to the rest of the world as a land of "plenty—not freedom." Liberals and conservatives also faced off on the U of I campus in a more lighthearted way: a student basketball game. The conservatives won 56–28 with the help of a six-foot-six ringer specially recruited for the occasion. "The liberals were aided by three cheerleaders," the conservative *New Voice* reported gleefully, "but the Conservatives needed none."[23]

The captain of the liberal team was Rennie Davis, and one of the cheerleaders was Liz Krohne, Davis's girlfriend at the time. Davis—who later would become one of the "Chicago Seven" accused of inciting riots during the 1968 Democratic national convention—spent the 1962–63 school year as a U of I graduate student in labor and industrial relations. "While students in other parts of the world are trying desperately to alter events, we choose good times with happy sorority sisters, two dates a week, an early marriage with all the Things," Davis argued in the *Daily Illini*. "Can we afford to take as narrow a social, vocational or financial view of our university 'experience' as we are doing?" In March 1963, after the censure of the U of I over the Leo Koch firing, Liz Krohne presented a letter from students to the Board of Trustees asking for the Koch case to be reopened. Later that spring, after firehoses were turned against civil rights protesters in Birmingham, Alabama, Krohne introduced a measure in the student senate that would have called on President Kennedy to intervene in the crisis. When the senate defeated the measure, Krohne immediately resigned her senate post. "Until Student Senate involves itself responsibly but aggressively in major issues, local or otherwise, it cannot hope to command the respect, let alone the attention, of the general student body," she said afterward. Krohne and Rennie Davis presided over a regular lunchtime klatch of left-leaning students in the Kaeser "K" Room café in the university Y basement. Roger Ebert would remember Krohne "vividly for her radicalism explained with a confiding smile."[24]

Just as students on the right had the Young Americans for Freedom, students on the left had the Students for a Democratic Society (SDS), which formed a U of I chapter in May 1963. The SDS issued its own declaration of principles—the Port Huron Statement—which advocated replacing "power rooted in possession, privilege, or circumstance by power and uniqueness rooted in love, reflectiveness, reason, and creativity." Young liberals also had their own heroes, including Paul Goodman, author of *Growing Up Absurd* and other works of social critique. Goodman argued that higher education should dispense with the "*external control, administration, bureaucratic machinery and other excrescences that have swamped our communities of scholars*" in favor of reclaiming "the ancient function of the universities as the loyal opposition and watchdog of society." The lunchtime group in the university Y's K Room sometimes read Goodman's writings aloud to one another.[25]

Roger Ebert and Student Discontent

Ebert was a K Room regular, but he later acknowledged that his political commitment never matched that of the more radical students who gathered there. He ironically commented that he "used journalism to stay at one remove from my convictions: I wouldn't risk arrest but would bravely report about those who did." Still, by the time of his undergraduate days at the U of I, Ebert already had come a long way from the eight-year-old altar boy he had once been who had solemnly expressed his ambition "to be a policeman, do my duty, and respect the laws of the community."[26]

Ebert grew up in Urbana as the son of a U of I electrician. Raised Roman Catholic, he lost his faith by his teen years, although he retained the liberal social values that his Dominican nun teachers had helped instill in him in parochial school. Ebert published his own neighborhood newspaper while he was still a child; after he enrolled in Urbana's public high school, he worked at the school paper while holding down a part-time sportswriting job for the Champaign-Urbana *News-Gazette*. On top of that, he also swam on the school team, acted in plays, won a statewide speech contest, and served as senior class president, among other activities. "We knew nothing of violence and drugs," he recalled of his high school cohort. "We looked forward to the future. We were taught well. We had no idea how lucky we were." By his senior year, Ebert did seem to have a healthy idea of how bright and talented he was as well as a predilection to let others know about it. The staff of his high school yearbook inserted a mischievous inscription below his senior portrait: "Here's a self-made man who adores his creator."[27] As Ebert prepared to graduate in 1960, he had ambitions of attending Harvard, just like his literary idol Thomas Wolfe and also like John F. Kennedy, who was running for president that same year. After he learned that his father had fallen terminally ill with lung cancer, Ebert remained in Urbana to attend the U of I.

He had been brought up by his father to hold a certain awe for the U of I, believing that the "university had the first, the biggest, or the best of everything." Ebert pledged a fraternity and was duly hazed (he claimed to have eaten twenty-six raw eggs); it planted the seeds of disenchantment with the Greek system. Soon he latched on to a mentor, U of I English professor Daniel Curley,

ROGER EBERT
Editor, *Daily Illini*

Roger Ebert in the 1964 *Illio* campus yearbook. Ebert would say late in his life that editing the *Daily Illini* was the best job he ever had. (Courtesy of the University of Illinois Archives, *Illio* File, RS 41/8/805)

who would teach Ebert in multiple classes and become a father figure to him after his own father died. In time, Ebert became editor-in-chief of the *Daily Illini*, which he would say was "the best job I ever had." He would form similarly warm memories of the U of I as a whole: "I loved the university. It took me from childhood to my life." But Ebert expressed those sentiments late in his life. As a student journalist, he often was more acerbic toward the university and its denizens, seemingly assuming for himself Paul Goodman's "loyal opposition and watchdog" role. (Indeed, Ebert often carried a copy of *Growing Up Absurd* in his coat while walking on campus.)[28]

As a U of I freshman, Ebert went as far as to view the *Daily Illini* as "shamefully right-wing," thanks to the influence of a fellow student named Si Sheridan. Ebert and Sheridan created a rival paper of their own called the *Spectator*, and they published it weekly from the basement of Ebert's family home in Urbana. Ebert declared that the new paper's goal was "to accomplish what the Daily Illini cannot because of University control." The *Spectator* published lengthy essays by U of I professor Harry Tiebout on the civil-rights picketing campaign against the local J. C. Penney's; it also published essays by Ebert himself. He took aim at what would become familiar targets for him: the aimlessness of his student peers and the shortcomings of the educational system that purported to serve them. "To this generation, a dry boredom [along] with a rejection of life has become an unavoidable cultural diet," Ebert wrote. "Members of our generation have been surrounded with it almost from the time of their first maturity, and they often see it reflected in the attitudes of their teachers and contemporaries. What course of action is left to them, beyond a mindless obeisance to the mass will?"[29]

Ebert quickly sold the *Spectator* and joined the *Daily Illini*, setting aside whatever political reservations he may have had originally. He would cover the William F. Buckley–Carey McWilliams Great Debate and many of the folk music acts that appeared on campus. In the summer of 1961, he launched his own regular column called "Ars Gratia. . . ." (The column title, with the ellipsis attached, seemed intended to raise the question of what or whom art was really for.) Portentously enough, Ebert's debut column was a pan of the Disney film *The Parent Trap*. He soon branched out to take on censorship and cultural squeamishness. When multiple US states in 1961 tried to stop sales of Henry Miller's novel *Tropic of Cancer*, which up until then had been banned in the United States, Ebert protested: "Miller's message may not be a very clear one, a very careful one, or, in the end, a very valid one. But it is unique, and it is sincere. We should think carefully before silencing him." After some communities tried to eliminate religious-themed Christmas displays, Ebert wrote that the "real danger is that all religious customs, all folk customs, all genuine traditions of the many peoples which make up our nation, will be sifted out one by one, leaving only the homogenized, sterile stew of conformity. This nation was once a melting pot. It is fast becoming an automatic blender."[30]

Ebert also addressed national politics. He questioned the "clever public relations" behind President Kennedy's image: "I have not seen a John F. Kennedy bubble-gum card. Perhaps there are none. But I wonder if the President's popularity rests on any more stable foundation?" If there were any doubts about where Ebert's true loyalties lay, though, they were erased when he became embroiled in a public spat in the fall of 1962 with conservative standard-bearer Barry Goldwater. It began when the Arizona senator sharply criticized the University of Colorado after its student newspaper published an anti-Goldwater editorial. Ebert responded by blasting Goldwater for his "baldly political jingoism" and for opposing freedom of expression. In return, Goldwater—who somehow had read Ebert's column—sent an angry letter to the *Daily Illini*: "I would suggest that Mr. Ebert, if he has serious intentions of becoming a reporter, a writer, or an editor get it through his head that he won't go far stating untruths or half-truths." Ebert promptly wrote two more columns attacking Goldwater, calling him a thin-skinned "bully-boy." The modern conservative, charged Ebert, was "not prepared to stand up, to speak out, to move bravely into the world with ideas as his weapons. He seeks to cower behind a protective shield of war machines and committees designed to 'investigate' other Americans."[31]

When he was not sparring with US senators, Ebert often turned his disapprobation back toward higher education. He said that university faculty should be free "to stand up, shout out, advise and persuade a society which in its faceless confusion sometimes seems willing to sacrifice everything to the pursuit of creature comfort"—and yet Ebert argued that the faculty had sold out to the point of shunning all conviction or controversy. The average college student was little better, avoiding the passionate commitments that had begun to form on both ends of the political continuum: "He is willing to applaud those speakers who echo bland, inspired mediocrities. But today's student is not part of a revolt to the right or left. He is a stand-patter from the word 'stop.'"[32]

Ebert was hardly alone in his criticism of his fellow students, which echoed the "Silent Generation" critiques that already had been circulating for years. *America* magazine published a satirical essay by a University of Pennsylvania graduate student saying that most contemporary young people were "apathetic clods" who ought to form an organization called "Young Americans for Nothing." *Mademoiselle* wrote that college students were afflicted by a host of anxieties and ills that included vocational confusion, religious doubts, homesickness, irrational panic, cosmic despair, interpersonal difficulties, and communication failure, as well as a general malaise dubbed "The Flops." The *Saturday Evening Post* quoted a young woman at the U of I: "You exist from one assignment to the next, one weekend to the next, living for the time the exam is over—only to start right in on the next one. The pace doesn't let you stop and take a look at *what* you're doing or *why*. That's how I've managed to make the honors list—big deal! I don't even know why I care—or *if* I care."[33]

However, just like Ebert, many young people were in fact starting to question what they were doing and why, and they were discovering that they cared very much indeed: not just the activists who joined the likes of Students for a Democratic Society or Young Americans for Freedom, but also the ones occupying the vast gulf in the middle. Historian John R. Thelin notes that, by the early 1960s, students were growing irritated by the bureaucratization of higher education; they also felt frustrated by administrative constraints on what they could say or do. "There was little tolerance for dissent about substantive issues of campus life," Thelin writes. "In short, deans and presidents did not want problems": particularly not while their attention was increasingly being consumed by fund-raising and public relations.[34] But the problems posed by their students would steadily mount as the decade progressed.

At the U of I, dissent was muted at first, especially in comparison with the vocal demonstration after Leo Koch's firing. But when the university imposed restrictions on campus picketing in 1961, some students objected. The restrictions had come after picketers targeted the annual military ball to protest compulsory ROTC. "In an academic community, picketing is not consonant with the spirit of intellectual analysis and rational discussion which should characterize the consideration of controversial issues," U of I president David Henry declared, stressing propriety and restraint just as he had done during the Koch case. In response, a student who had participated in anti-ROTC protests said that most restrictions on picketing were unwarranted: "These regulations do not belong on the American scene and are a restriction to the freedom of speech." The university ended up allowing picketing on campus provided that foot and vehicle traffic was not impeded and advance notice was given; student picketing also took place off campus, as with the J. C. Penney's protest. But tensions remained, and when students carried signs and distributed handbills alerting visiting high schoolers to racial discrimination within U of I fraternities, dean of administration Royden Dangerfield was heard to exclaim, "Get those damn picketers out of here."[35]

Another source of contention was the issue of visiting speakers at the U of I. Although political candidates now were permitted on campus, the Clabaugh

Act—which the Illinois legislature had enacted back in 1947 and which forbade "subversive, seditious and un-American" speakers and organizations—was still on the books. Speakers also were subject to prior approval by a university committee. In March 1962 *Daily Illini* editor-in-chief Wade Freeman helped launch a campaign to liberalize the rules, saying that it would help tear down the "fabric of fear for both the controversial and what 'could damage us when the next budget comes up.'" Although Freeman acknowledged that the university already allowed most speakers to appear, as witnessed by the Great Debates series, he also said that "the mere existence of controls on campus speakers is contradictory to the principle of academic freedom." The U of I student senate studied the visiting-speakers issue, but the issue would remain unresolved for years; the Clabaugh Act remained in force and became the focus of protests during the Vietnam era.[36]

The biggest controversy during the early 1960s over a visiting speaker in Champaign-Urbana presaged similar controversies that would erupt decades later on college campuses. The Channing Murray Foundation, which was affiliated with the Unitarian-Universalist church in Urbana, sponsored the Forum for Dissent. Because the foundation was technically off campus (even though it was located just off the main U of I quadrangle), it was not subject to university regulations on speakers. In October 1962 the Forum for Dissent announced plans to host American Nazi leader George Lincoln Rockwell, who advocated sending Black Americans to Africa and who insisted that the Holocaust never had happened. When Urbana police said that they could not guarantee Rockwell's safety, the visit was canceled. Rockwell blamed the cancelation on a "liberal conspiracy" that was "in control of American campuses" and that feared that "students will be won over by our ideas, which of course they would be." U of I graduate student Ron Szoke, who chaired the Forum for Dissent, defended letting Rockwell speak. The *Daily Illini* quoted him as saying that "communism, fascism, and other repellent doctrines are better resisted by letting their advocates discredit themselves publicly than by suppressing or ignoring them." Several people took exception. A letter writer to the *Daily Illini* said that there was no legitimate controversy that Rockwell could address—deporting Black people and denying the Holocaust were not ideas that should be open for debate.[37]

Students might disagree over who should be brought to town to speak, but if there was one issue that united them irrespective of their politics, it was discipline and the student code. There were two main sources of friction. The first was double jeopardy: students protested being punished twice for the same offense (they could face penalties from both the criminal justice system and the university's subcommittee on undergraduate student discipline). The second source of friction was the vagueness of the code itself. Reminiscent of the clause in the U of I statutes that had helped get Leo Koch fired, the undergraduate code said that students could face discipline for "conduct [that] is deemed undesirable or prejudicial to the University community's best interest." The discipline subcommittee frequently announced that someone had been punished for "conduct unbecoming a student," which, as the *Daily Illini* said, conceivably could cover "everything from spitting on the sidewalk to murdering your Rhet[oric] 101 teacher." Students complained that discipline was applied unevenly (with star athletes getting away with things that other students could not); they also increasingly resented the university's in loco parentis intrusion into their drinking habits and sex lives. "Under this system, the quickest road to maturity and complete adulthood is to flunk out, so to avoid several more years of child-like relationship with our University parents," argued student senator Cliff Steward. Although the student senate undertook a massive review of the discipline system and proposed an overhaul, the issue continued to fester.[38]

Discontent extended to the U of I's best and brightest. During the 1962–63 school year, Philip Martin was named the university's first Rhodes Scholar in thirteen years. He was executive vice president of the student senate, he had spent time with his brother Eden at Harvard, and he had attended (at the U of I's expense) a prestigious annual conference on world affairs at West Point. As Martin later recalled, those experiences had "contributed to an acute awareness of unrealized possibilities at Illinois centering loosely on the question of the somnolent state of student life." Early in 1963, he "had a kind of 'last straw' moment" when he witnessed a reporter corral a random student to be photographed next to a university official, which seemed to Martin to symbolize undergraduates serving as mere props for administrators. At about the same time, U of I president David Henry issued his annual "State of the University" report outlining what Henry saw as the university's top priority for 1963: to "more directly and more effectively translate the research and professional resources of the University into the practices of industry and business for the strengthening of our economy." It was a frank acknowledgment of the many constituencies that the U of I now was expected to serve, as well as a logical extension of the public outreach that Henry always had prioritized as president. It also corresponded with the ascendancy of what University of California president Clark Kerr labeled the "multiversity." According to Kerr, the typical large university had evolved into a complex "mechanism—a series of processes producing a series of results—held together by administrative rules and powered by money." That impersonal, mechanistic conception of higher education would not sit well with many students, including Philip Martin.[39]

Martin decided to write his own State of the University report from a student perspective, and the *Daily Illini* published it in February 1963. Martin began by acknowledging that running the U of I was a complicated enterprise, and so it was not surprising if university administrators saw "the process of higher education as a problem in factor analysis, with the entering freshmen constituting a set of inputs" and "the graduating class composing the output." But undergraduates wanted more out of college than simply to be molded into productive cogs in the economy. They resisted "being portrayed as a piece of raw material, like a carload of wheat," and they feared that they were "coming to occupy a status of increasingly low priority as the University sinks more and more of its money, attention, and creativity into a bottomless pit of highly specialized research and training programs for industry and government." Charging that the U of I discouraged "student inquiry and participation because things are quieter when they are muzzled," Martin called for "a more complete philosophy of undergraduate education which stresses people and not grades as the mainspring."[40]

The *Daily Illini* attempted to get reactions to Martin's essay from President Henry and other administrators. "Top University officials had nothing to say to undergraduates on the subject," the newspaper pointedly reported, quoting one such official as responding "Even if I had read the article I would have no comment." Martin recalled feeling disquieted by his "sense that I had offended people in the administration, who could with some plausibility view me as biting the hand that fed me. I could not help feeling that I had naively bitten off more than I could chew." Yet he did succeed in provoking discussion. The head of the U of I French department, Charles A. Knudson, wrote a lengthy retort to Martin that said that there were no "solid grounds for the charge that undergraduate instruction is suffering from neglect"; Knudson also dismissed the *Daily Illini* as "chiefly a chronicle of undergraduate frivolities." University trustee Irving Dilliard, the former editorial page editor of the *St. Louis Post-Dispatch*, was more conciliatory. "If the undergraduates are getting less than their due in the totality of interests that make up the University, or if thoughtful students think that this is so, then I, for one, want to know about it," Dilliard wrote in the *Daily Illini*. He also praised the student paper itself: "I hope you Illini editors will continue to publish a provocative, challenging, constructively critical paper. The extent to which you do so is a measure of the educational stimulation you are receiving, by whatever means and influences, at the University of Illinois."[41]

The Storm Breaks

The editor-in-chief of the *Daily Illini* when it published the Martin essay was U of I senior Karen Lucas. Her interest in newspapers had been sparked at an early age by the Brenda Starr comic strip, and she would go on to have a long career in journalism. Lucas would remember the *Daily Illini* as fun and full of camaraderie. It also was comparatively "forward-thinking" in terms of gender relations, so that "if you had talent and ability, it was welcomed." Working on the paper offered a side benefit as well: she had permission to stay out past the campus curfew for women. While Lucas was editor-in-chief, the student paper issued a twelve-point editorial platform that called for in loco parentis to be "reduced in keeping with the modern education trend toward student self-responsibility." The platform also asserted that the university should not restrain or discourage "the right of members of the University community to hear, discuss or express opinion," nor should it punish such expression. Among the staff whom Lucas helped bring to the paper was Bill Nack, later a star writer for *Sports Illustrated*.[42]

As for Roger Ebert, Lucas recalled that he was "quite a challenge, but a lot of fun." Ebert would be less charitable toward himself. By his own memory, he was "a cocksure asshole," and after taking over from Lucas as *Daily Illini* editor-in-chief, he was "tactless, egotistical, merciless, and a showboat." He did say that one of his strengths was being a good talent scout. Ebert recruited Liz Krohne as a columnist; her radical perspective would appear on the editorial page alongside right-leaning ones from such writers as Bob Auler, who would remain friends with Ebert for the rest of both men's lives despite their political differences. (Said Ebert of Auler, "He calls me the Mad Bomber and I call him a Fascist Baby Eater.") Another Ebert recruit to the paper was Ron Szoke. He chaired the Forum for Dissent at the Channing Murray Foundation, and for a time he also had worked on the ORDVAC computer for the US Army, an experience that he said had impressed on him "the enormous wastefulness of the military." Not seeing himself as one of the "firebrand radicals," Szoke served as the *Daily Illini*'s film critic, and Ebert later would say that he "learned as much from him as from anyone since."[43]

Ebert's ascension as the newspaper's editor-in-chief in 1963 corresponded with momentous happenings in the world as issues that had been mounting on campus—civil rights, peace activism, and free speech—all came to a head. August saw the March on Washington where Martin Luther King Jr. delivered his "I Have a Dream" speech. U of I dean of women Miriam Shelden was there to hear King's address. She said that "for a moment, I thought he said, 'I *had* a dream.' But when he repeated, 'I *have* a dream,' I knew white America still had time to take massive steps toward achieving our true democracy of *all* the people." Shelden became a strong supporter of African American women students at the U of I. One of them, Eleanor Saunders, would remember Shelden as a "woman before her time" who "possibly without direction from the university or necessarily even support" had taken a "personal interest in us in the early sixties, for which I remain very grateful."[44]

Only one month after the March on Washington, Ku Klux Klan members bombed the Sixteenth Street Baptist Church in Birmingham, Alabama, during Sunday services, killing four Black girls. The day after the bombing, some three hundred fifty U of I students and faculty gathered for a silent vigil in front of the university auditorium. The vigils continued throughout the week and spread to other campuses across the country. U of I NAACP member Rudy Frank wrote a scalding letter to the *Daily Illini* heaping scorn on White people who were donating money to rebuild the church but doing nothing to stop racism: "I understand there is even going to be formed a 'Bomb-of-the-Month Club' for all those kind-hearted white Americans who wish to express their compassion for the plight of the Negro on a sustaining basis." In October, U of I student Earl Wordlaw wrote a firsthand account for the *Daily Illini* of what it felt like to walk on campus as an African American: "A terrifying despair possessed me, a despair that came because I felt outside of the activities, outside of the concern and feelings of my fellow students, outside of the University itself ... a despair from which I could never expect surcease because this is how America is." Wordlaw followed up with a series of essays that appeared under the heading "The Revolution of 1963" in the *Daily Illini*; the essays discussed the merits of integration versus Black separatism and of nonviolence versus armed struggle.[45]

There was one welcome piece of news during that fall of 1963, especially for students who had lobbied for arms control: by a lopsided margin, the US Senate ratified a treaty halting atmospheric testing of nuclear weapons. At the same time, though, the *Daily Illini* observed that the "Vietnamese situation has moved from bad to critical." After the Ngo Dinh Diem regime in South Vietnam was toppled in a bloody coup at the start of November, the student paper's lead editorial noted that "there is every reason to believe that the US Central Intelligence Agency was behind the overthrow of the Diems." The editorial concluded, "If the United States means what it says about self-determination, rule by democracy, and foreign policy based on fair play and mutual respect, it would be well advised to abandon its behind-the-scenes manipulations, decide once and for all whether 'friendly' military dictatorships are better than 'awkward' democratic rulers, and behave on the international scene as a great power with vision should."⁴⁶

A few days later, on November 9, US senator Strom Thurmond addressed a capacity crowd of seven hundred people in the Illini Union. He said that he was "proud to be a right-winger" and warned that communists had "penetrated colleges, churches, almost all organizations in one way or another." Twenty-five picketers protested Thurmond's appearance and his opposition to civil rights (one of their signs read "Justice Now or Blood Later"); handbills also were distributed encouraging people to laugh at the senator. Some people did laugh and hiss when he claimed that "in Russia the children are taken from parents at three of age." When one spectator chortled at Thurmond's reference to God, the senator shot back, "Do you believe in God? Aren't you proud of America? If not, why don't you move to a country which you will be proud of?" Singing picketers followed Thurmond to his car after his speech; according to some witnesses, the picketers also jostled him. ("I have never seen a member of the United States Senate in a cold sweat, but I saw one last Friday night," a student would say.) The picketers denied having made physical contact with the senator, but the student senate still issued an apology to Thurmond for his having feared "personal injury."⁴⁷

Thurmond's appearance at the U of I touched off a slew of letters and commentaries in the *Daily Illini*. In an editorial, the paper criticized the people who had picketed and heckled the senator, but it also questioned why the student senate had felt compelled to apologize to him. Graduate student Richard Schwarzlose (later a longtime Northwestern University journalism professor) also condemned the hecklers: "Freedom of speech is not a contest of who can shout (or laugh) the loudest or the longest. It is a privilege under which all, in their turn, may shout (or properly, speak) while the rest listen." But one letter writer compared Thurmond to Adolf Hitler in that the senator was a "super-racist [who] believes in large military armies." And *Daily Illini* news analyst Gary Porter challenged what he called "the new ravenous appetite for political freaks" on college campuses, which he said came at the expense of promoting true freedom of speech that served the "ongoing search for truth by confrontation of idea with idea."⁴⁸

The Thurmond kerfuffle quickly was followed by another free speech controversy at the U of I. A young man named Richard McMullin was arrested for trespassing after he set up a table in front of the campus library and handed out Christian literature to passersby. (He was not then enrolled as a student, and he had not received university approval to distribute the literature.) By all accounts, McMullin was a gentle soul who made a meager living by setting type in the

Daily Illini pressroom—where he also sometimes slept—and by selling copies of the paper. Roger Ebert and other students were outraged by what they saw as the university's abridgment of McMullin's freedom of expression. "God knows, there should be a thousand more like [McMullin] in this formal, official, correct, conforming desert of organization men," fumed Ebert in the student paper. In his memoirs, Ebert said that he freelanced a story on the case for the *Chicago Sun-Times*; it was his first-ever piece for the newspaper where he would spend his entire professional career as a film critic. (He also recalled that he received a byline, but no such byline appeared with the piece, likely because Ebert had quoted himself in it.) The *Sun-Times* published the McMullin story on the morning of November 22, 1963, and an elated Ebert was reading and rereading it in the Illini Union when suddenly he heard a radio bulletin: President Kennedy had been shot in Dallas.[49]

Ebert rushed to the *Daily Illini* newsroom in the basement of Illini Hall, where more than thirty staff members would crowd around the wire service teletypes transmitting the latest news about the assassination. "I swept everything off the top of my desk into a large wastebasket and made [the desk] a command post," Ebert recalled. He dispatched reporters to get reactions on campus, just as other local newspapers were doing. "Classes were dismissed. Businesses closed. The halls emptied," the *Daily Illini* would say. "An unnatural hush settled over the campus. The rain added to the gloominess of the atmosphere." The *Champaign-Urbana Courier* reported that through the window of a campus office, "one could see several typists just sitting at their desks doing nothing. One was looking out the window at the rain, chewing her fingernails. The red rings around her eyes told the story of her grief." The *News-Gazette* recalled Kennedy's campaign stop in 1960, saying that "no other individual who has visited the University of Illinois campus ever created the excitement and almost near riot as the late John F. Kennedy."[50]

The *Daily Illini* went to press at five the next morning after the assassination. Just as the presses began to roll, someone spotted a breezy Thanksgiving-themed ad for the *Illio*, the campus yearbook: "The 'Great Turkey' says—Help stamp out mental illness—Buy your Illio now (or we'll kill you)." The presses were stopped, the ad was pulled, and the paper was printed. The following Monday, more than eleven thousand people (including six thousand ROTC cadets) attended a memorial service in Assembly Hall, which had opened only a few months previously. According to the *Courier*, "the crowd stood for a minute of silence—a minute during which the slightest sound could have been heard, but wasn't." In his *Daily Illini* column, Ebert righteously denounced "this disgrace of a nation" that had given rise to Lee Harvey Oswald and Jack Ruby. A letter writer to the paper said that students "have not only lost a President; we have lost a friend. A friend, who, like us, was youthful and vigorous. He, probably more than any other president, associated himself with the young, the new generation."[51]

The grieving campus emptied for Thanksgiving break. Then the students returned, and attention shifted to happier matters. The Illinois football team, led by Dick Butkus, was headed to the Rose Bowl for the first time in twelve years. Ebert assigned himself to help cover the New Year's Day game for the *Daily Illini* and blissfully embarked for California, where he would visit Hollywood for the first time. The student paper's first issue of 1964 was dominated by coverage of Illinois's 17–7 victory. The U of I faithful had celebrated by tearing down both wooden goalposts, and one spectator proudly displayed "a blood spattered piece of crossbar in a gashed hand" while others "combed the ground for splinters and chips." Hundreds of fans turned out for a pep rally to welcome the football team back to Champaign-Urbana.[52]

One person shunned all the merriment. Revilo Oliver did not distract himself with such frivolities as football. Nor was the U of I professor the least bit impressed by civil rights, pickets, pacifism, or young people challenging the old, traditional ways. For him, all those atrocities pieced together into a single treasonous pattern—the same pattern that his friend Ira Latimer had tried to warn people about four years earlier—and John F. Kennedy, Lee Harvey Oswald, and Jack Ruby (or *Jakob Rubenstein*, as Oliver called him) fit the same pattern as well. Ebert had telephoned Oliver on the day of Kennedy's assassination to try to get the professor's reaction for the student paper, but no one answered the call.[53] That did not mean that Oliver had no comment: far from it. He would spend the holidays amassing his thoughts into a lengthy thesis. It would become his most remembered and reviled piece of writing, culminating an unlikely trajectory for a man once known only for his abiding devotion to ancient Athens and Rome.

CHAPTER 5

International Vermin

Revilo Oliver was a man of imposing physical size and formidable intellect who would spend nearly fifty years at the University of Illinois as a student and classics professor. His worldview was as odd and backward as his name, and over time he would descend ever deeper into a netherworld rife with hate.

To try to understand how the man ended up the way he did, it helps to know something of his family background. "My first name, an obvious palindrome, has been the burden of the eldest or only son for six generations," Oliver would write. That certainly was true of his own father—who also was named Revilo— but available records do not turn up additional palindromes in the family tree (in fact, one account holds that the U of I professor's father was the first to hold that moniker).[1] In the end, it does not matter how many Revilos there were. What is significant is that generations of Olivers bore a multitude of burdens, most of them self-inflicted or inflicted on them by fellow members of the clan.

The family patriarch, Franklin Oliver, arrived in central Illinois in 1833 to seek his fortune, and he was said to have been "the first white settler in what is now Chatsworth" in Livingston County. He came to own a vast tract of highly valuable land in the area; he also married three times and fathered nine children. When Franklin died in 1881 at the age of ninety-four, the Chatsworth newspaper commented that for some time he had been "very eccentric in many respects." That description did not do the man's eccentricities justice. According to another newspaper story (headlined "Old But Frisky"), he had fallen prey to "erotomania," becoming besotted with a succession of women who were not his wife. To underwrite his ardor, Franklin had been selling off his land, which he had jealously protected until then. His third and final wife divorced him not long before he died, and family members began suing one another over what remained of the Oliver estate. "A bitter animosity existed between [Franklin] and his wife and her two sons, Revi[l]o and John," said the *Bloomington Daily Leader*. "The record in the case shows that there was extreme cruelty and hatred on both sides." Animosity and cruelty within the Oliver family would persist for decades to come.[2]

After Franklin's death, his son Revilo (father-to-be of the U of I professor) served as Chatsworth mayor for a time. In a 1900 family history that sounds suspiciously as though it may have been written by Revilo senior himself, Revilo was said to be a "famous song composer" responsible for many "beautiful songs and poems"; he also was "both an author and inventor, a characteristic seldom found in one person." In addition, Revilo was said to be blessed with "a genial, kind-hearted and sympathetic nature"—and yet "when thoroughly aroused by injustice," he was "unyielding and of a warlike disposition." Not everyone agreed about the merits of Revilo's literary efforts. "This poetry of Revilo's is of the variety which makes its readers wish they had never been born," a local newspaper chortled. "After reading a stanza or two it is considered best to eat Limburger cheese to sweeten the breath and remove the yellow taste." But there was no disagreement over Revilo's belligerent demeanor: particularly not after he became afflicted with his own bout of erotomania, which triggered a whole new batch of lawsuits.[3]

Although Franklin had sold off the family estate, Revilo and his mother were able to acquire a sizable chunk of Illinois land of their own. When Revilo grew enamored with a woman of "quite notorious" reputation named Maude Barlow, he granted Barlow half of that land in return for her marrying him. After the wedding, he "was happy just one day," the press breathlessly reported. "His bride went to Bloomington, consorted with her old associates, and as he alleges, committed the unpardonable sin, most unbecoming to the bride of a day." Revilo was found "crying and wringing his hands" on a street corner, while telling a police officer, "They are after me." Hysteria and paranoia soon gave way to rage. Revilo was said to have been determined to "have everyone implicated in the row hanged by the thumbs before he will allow them to carry off their swag." Thus followed the latest round of litigation. Although a judge eventually ruled in Revilo's favor about the land that he had given to Barlow, she still came out of her exceedingly brief marriage several thousand dollars richer. Revilo and his mother then decamped for Texas, seeking a fresh start. While there, Revilo took out a want ad searching for a woman who could set his poetry to music. The woman who answered the ad, Flora Lang, consented to become his new wife, despite being more than twenty years his junior. In 1908 or 1909 (sources differ), Flora gave birth to a baby boy.[4]

Nobody lived happily ever after. The elder Revilo's sister seized the family land in Illinois, alleging that Flora Lang "was another adventuress of the type of Maude Barlow, and that she was another member of the old gang that had defrauded them before." The elder Revilo's mother died a pauper, and Revilo himself returned to Illinois with his wife and infant son, determined to win back his land. Still another lengthy string of lawsuits ensued. "Some member[s] of the Oliver family have been in litigation almost continuously since 1870," a newspaper observed in 1919, adding that "some evil genius has been following the footsteps of this ill-fated family." For a time, it appeared as though Revilo would succeed in reclaiming his property, but a central Illinois jury decided that a will that supposedly had bequeathed him the land was a forgery. He grew increasingly despondent, and in 1929 he hanged himself in the basement of his Springfield, Illinois, home, leaving behind a note saying that his troubles were finally over. His widow Flora, who seems never to have been an "adventuress," was left bankrupt.[5]

The Junior Revilo Oliver

Despite this bizarre and tragic family history, Revilo and Flora's son—who also was named Revilo—would in time make himself a respected professor of the classics. The young man showed early in his life that he had unusual talents. After attending Springfield public schools, Oliver left for southern California while he was still an adolescent, ostensibly to remove himself from Illinois winters (although one wonders whether the ongoing turmoil at home also might have been a factor). He took classes at Compton High School in the Los Angeles area. "The 'educators' there had already made great progress in sabotaging education," Oliver would recall contemptuously, "so, just to have something to occupy my mind, I began the study of Sanskrit." To that end, he obtained a Hindu tutor who he believed "had come to the United States to ease the financial burdens of dowagers who had more money than they could otherwise spend." Oliver soon became proficient in multiple languages, including Latin and Greek, and for recreation he journeyed "to watch the holy men and holier females [including Aimee Semple McPherson] pitch the woo at the simple-minded." He spent a brief stint at Pomona College in California, and by 1927 he had returned home to live with his parents. Oliver subsequently enrolled at the U of I.[6]

"He was unlike any student we had ever known," remembered a U of I undergraduate who lived in the same dormitory as Oliver. "He was like a character out of a Charles Dickens novel": tall, sallow, always dressed in the same brown suit whose sleeves and legs were much too short for him, and prone to charge straight ahead across campus, with nary a glance to the left or right. The young man seemed utterly credulous and hence was easy prey for practical jokes, such as repeatedly being told that a nonexistent telegram was waiting for him at a distant office. Then there were the notebooks that Oliver amassed on ancient tongues. "They were filled with immaculate typing done on a typewriter which had a keyboard with special Greek and Sanskrit alphabets," his dormitory mate recalled. "He was one of the most brilliant students to pass through the university." He was also obviously different from everyone else, having not been raised as his classmates had been "with fishing and swimming and lusty games and fistfights." And although in those days Oliver held an unswerving devotion to Abraham Lincoln—even letting his long dark hair fall across his forehead, as his idol had done—he seemed the type of person whose passions could escalate "into a strong prejudice or fanaticism."[7]

In 1930, one year after his father's suicide, Oliver married Grace Needham in Urbana; she was several years older than he and had two daughters from a previous marriage. Grace would become her new husband's fiercest champion. She was active in local theater, and in May 1935 the Illini Theater Guild mounted a production of the ancient play *The Little Clay Cart* in a new translation by Oliver from the original Sanskrit. The production was targeted at a Mother's Day audience on the U of I campus, but according to the *Daily Illini*, "it was a sad disappointment for a great many students and mothers who were much more interested in an evening of light entertainment than sitting through four solid hours of Hindu stage craft."[8] The University of Illinois Press later published Oliver's translation of the play along with copious annotations by Oliver; it would be his first book.

By that time—1938—Oliver already had completed his bachelor's and master's degrees at the U of I and had joined the Illinois classics faculty. He also was well on the way to finishing his doctorate under the supervision of William Abbott Oldfather, the head of the classics department. Oldfather would be remembered as "a brilliant scholar who basically invented the department as a player on the national scene." According to a biographical essay by Michael Armstrong, Oldfather had been trained in Germany, and his loyal students at the U of I "met each week with 'Der Herr' to drink beer and sing German folksongs." Armstrong also noted that "oral tradition at Urbana insists on whispering, with considerable glee, that Oldfather was a Nazi," although there seemed to be no documentary evidence supporting that allegation.[9]

In early 1938 Oliver wrote Oldfather a long letter outlining his emerging political philosophy, which he described as fundamentally "pessimistic." Clearly referring to his late father, Oliver said that he could "scarcely feel sympathy for the modern doctrine of *chrêmata anêr*" (an ancient Greek phrase meaning "money is the man") that had "destroyed an honourable and chivalrous gentleman whom I must ever regard with filial affection." Oliver also lamented the historical tendency in societies toward producing "two extreme factions, both actuated by motives equally ignoble or passions equally ruthless, [that] crush between themselves all advocates of moderation and deliberation and thus extirpate the political wisdom of their state even before they begin the task of destroying each other." He noted that some of his acquaintances assumed that he was a fascist merely because he was not a communist; there seemed to be no middle ground.

If Oliver held one overriding commitment, it was to preserving cultural tradition: "I suppose that this devotion may well approach fanaticism, for I am afraid that the answer would be shocking indeed if I were forced to set a human price on the poems of Homer or the dialogues of Plato." Despite his stated apprehension toward political extremism, he also was deeply skeptical of democracy and egalitarianism. According to Oliver, "some inexorable natural law seems to have given intelligence to only a minority of mankind and, if that be not a sufficiently pessimistic observation, the same natural law seems to have dealt out even more sparingly probity and unselfishness." The "road to freedom" inevitably seemed to lead "to Hitler, or to our own hypothetical Roosevel[t] III."[10]

Oliver completed his doctorate at the U of I in 1940 and moved to Washington, DC, two years later to oversee a department doing classified work during World War II. (According to one source, he helped break codes for the Army Security Agency.)[11] Oliver corresponded with Oldfather about resuming his academic career, but Oldfather told him that he probably would be drafted if he came back to Illinois. In May 1945 Oldfather drowned in a canoeing accident; and soon afterward, with the war now over, Oliver returned to the U of I to help run the classics department while it searched for a new head. Oliver offered the administration several names as possibilities, and his own name also seems to have been floated for the position. A professor absent from Oliver's list of potential candidates, John L. Heller of the University of Minnesota, was named the new U of I classics head in 1949. In time, Revilo Oliver would become a chronic headache for John Heller.[12]

For a few years, though, all seemed peaceful. Oliver rose through the academic ranks to become a full professor with tenure in 1954. He had earned a

Revilo Oliver with his wife Grace and their dog Boondoggle in 1946. Oliver recently had returned from doing classified work for the War Department in Washington, DC. (Courtesy of the Champaign County Historical Archives, Urbana Free Library, Urbana, Illinois)

Guggenheim Fellowship and was named a Fulbright scholar; those honors allowed him to visit Italy accompanied by his wife Grace. When his name appeared in the newspapers, it was only in connection with his Italian adventures. (A horse drawing a carriage in which Oliver was riding stepped on a broken wine flask and galloped off in pain and panic; Oliver's attempts to stop the carriage left him badly bruised. Afterward he blithely told the *Champaign-Urbana Courier* that he had taken "passive part in a rather curious concatenation of incidents.") Then, in 1956, Oliver joined the staff of the new conservative weekly *National Review*. His life and career would never again be the same.[13]

Oliver and the Postwar Right

It is not completely clear what would keep driving Oliver further to the political right and away from the moderatism that he had expressed to Oldfather before the war. Late in his life, after he had fully embraced neo-Nazism, Oliver claimed to have become disillusioned on multiple fronts. He said that he had learned while working for the military during the war that "the unspeakable monster in the White House [had] successfully tricked the Japanese into destroying the American fleet at Pearl Harbor" and that the "monster" (Franklin D. Roosevelt) had acted "to please his Jewish owners and gratify his own nihilistic lusts." Oliver said that he had been appalled by the Nuremberg war crimes trials after Nazi Germany's "valiant and heroic defense against the forces of virtually the whole world that the Jews had mobilized against her"; the sham trials had been staged to "confirm the foul Jewish hoax, the Big Lie that the Germans had 'exterminated' six million enemy aliens." He also said that he had been shaken in 1954 by the fall of Senator Joseph McCarthy—"abandoned by those whom he sought to save, and traduced by the great lie-machines and propaganda mills"—which had forced Oliver to dissuade himself of his naive conviction "that when the facts of the Crusade to Save the Soviet [i.e., World War II] and other operations became known, as they inevitably must, the indignation of the American people would produce a reaction of such vehemence and violence that it could never be forgotten in history!"[14]

If Oliver really was harboring such malignant thoughts in the years just after the war, he did not share them publicly. The explicit, virulent anti-Semitism would not manifest itself for some time to come. Yet whether it was by nature or nurture or both, Oliver had inherited the disputatiousness that seemed to be a defining family trait, and breaking codes during the war may have fueled his conviction that the world was full of dark secrets that needed uncovering and deciphering. Oliver's letter to Oldfather before the war had expressed deep-seated pessimism, partly shaped by his father's sad fate; he had held little hope for democracy's ultimate success. He also had asserted that genuine intelligence was possessed by only a comparative few, presumably including himself (surely he recognized that he was quite unlike most other people). Finally, he had acknowledged his near-fanatical devotion to the classics. According to classicist Donna Zuckerberg, there has been a "millennia-long use of classical antiquity to promote reactionary ideologies" that have viewed "the dead white men of the ancient world as the sources of ultimate wisdom." So it was with Revilo Oliver. Signs of reactionaryism—that is, reaction against perceived threats to the study and veneration of White male heroes and ancient occidental cultures—began appearing in Oliver's writings in the late 1940s and grew increasingly venomous.[15]

In 1949, for example, Oliver reviewed a book on Latin pronunciation. Toward the end of his review, he excoriated the decline of Greek and Latin instruction in American schools, which he blamed on "the happy hooligans who have for some time acted as the advance agents of totalitarian despotism." According to

Oliver, they had mounted a "concerted effort to stultify and brutalize the adolescent mind by concentrating its attention on the 'problems' of human existence on the animal level." Two years later, Oliver asserted in another review essay that all other humanistic scholarship was subservient to the study of the classics (he would approvingly quote a fellow classicist who defined humanism as the "scholarly and initially reactive enthusiasm for classic culture"). Should the classics be undermined, other disciplines were doomed either to "disappear or [be] made 'socially relevant' by conversion into agencies for the propagation of lies." One could only hope, wrote Oliver, "that the return of the Neanderthal is not yet a decisive victory, and that Occidental civilization in Europe and America will somehow survive the attacks of both its foreign and domestic enemies."[16]

Oliver's allusions to a siege against Western civilization by enemies at home and abroad resonated with the anticommunist fears of the late 1940s and early 1950s as epitomized by Joseph McCarthy. In Oliver's own state of Illinois, the legislature had enacted the 1947 Clabaugh Act that prohibited subversive speakers and organizations at the U of I with an eye toward thwarting those individuals who "sought to instill in the hearts of American youth contempt and hatred for ideals to which the people of this great nation have been dedicated." In addition, the Illinois legislature's Broyles commission undertook a lengthy investigation of subversion in the state (although a 1952 study would assert that the commission "failed to uncover any hitherto unknown activity of Illinois Communists" or "discover a single teacher in Illinois who was a communist or advocated communism in his teaching").[17]

Oliver's writings not only appealed to anticommunists but also resonated with conservative intellectuals, most notably William F. Buckley Jr., who burst into prominence in 1951 with his book *God and Man at Yale*. An impassioned critique of the university from which Buckley had just graduated, *God and Man* argued that the rhetoric surrounding faculty academic freedom was "liberal propaganda." According to Buckley, "academic freedom must mean the freedom of men and women to supervise the educational activities and aims of the schools they oversee and support." Trustees and alumni should have the power to compel the faculty to emphasize "democracy, individualism, and religion" in the curriculum. If a class covered "Marx or Hitler, Laski or the Webbs, Huxley or Dewey," it was the teacher's express responsibility "to 'deflate' the arguments advanced." Political scientist Nicholas Buccola observes that Buckley's list of targets is telling: "There is John Dewey, a democratic theorist and defender of a 'new individualism,' cheek by jowl with Adolf Hitler, one of the greatest mass murderers of the twentieth century." Oliver similarly viewed Dewey as one of the "happy hooligans" out to destroy all that he held dear. When Buckley's former professor Willmoore Kendall invited Oliver to write for Buckley's new magazine *National Review*, Oliver accepted. At least for a time, Oliver and Buckley were close friends, and Buckley even said that Oliver was "without any exception the single most erudite man I have ever known."[18]

National Review would firmly establish Buckley as a leader of the postwar conservative movement. In Nicholas Buccola's words, Buckley believed "that American society was basically good, and that it was the sacred duty of conservatives to defend it from any ideas, personalities, or movements that were deemed threats to it." *National Review* embodied that belief beginning with its 1955 inaugural issue in which it declared that it would "stand athwart history, yelling Stop, when no one is inclined to do so." Oliver seemed an ideal fit with the new magazine's editorial philosophy. He wrote book reviews that included a sharp critique of liberal Christianity, whose hopes for world peace and harmony were viewed by Oliver as "hallucinations that precede disaster." (Such a stance made Oliver "rather unremarkable for his time," according to religious studies scholar Damon T. Berry.) Oliver took aim at similar targets in a review of Jean Dutourd's novel *The Taxis of the Marne*, using language suggesting that his worldview was growing more apocalyptic: "Dutourd knows, as all men who are not cowards know, that in the last analysis, nations live and die by blood and steel alone. . . . This is a book that will dismay the epicene little intellectuals who twitter in our State Department, and blanch the cheeks of the sleek eunuchs who fawn upon female voters about the impossibility of war."[19]

Many years later, Oliver would observe that his mid-1950s decision to start writing about politics "was certainly a grave mistake from the standpoint of my career." Once he had made that choice, however, Oliver committed fully to it. He would become far better known as a right-wing polemicist and activist than he ever had been known as a classicist, and those extramural activities would consume more and more of his time. Addressing a Champaign meeting of the Daughters of the American Revolution (DAR) in 1957, Oliver charged that communists were indistinguishable "from the many persons who, either from sentimentality or to advance their own careers, agitate for schemes of 'social welfare' and 'world brotherhood.'"[20] Oliver also enthusiastically backed the movement against fluoridating municipal drinking water. That movement dovetailed with antivaccine movements in arguing that fluoridation was the tool of a "conspiracy of experts" that endangered public health. In the 1950s, it also was seen as the tool of communists. Oliver said that fluoridation represented a "campaign of fraud, concocted by trained professional liars—public relations men—who work in lie factories." He claimed that fluoride was mostly used "to poison rats and cockroaches," and putting it in drinking water could result in the births of "mongoloid idiot[s]."[21]

In 1958, Oliver accepted Robert Welch's invitation to help found the John Birch Society (JBS), although Oliver's association with the organization would not become public for some time. Welch had been a candy maker and vice president of the National Association of Manufacturers. His new organization sought to tip "the political scales in this country just as fast and far" as was humanly possible to "reverse by political action the gradual surrender of the United States to Communism." Welch—who believed that democracy was "a deceptive phrase, a weapon of demagoguery, and a perennial fraud"—ran the JBS as an autocracy. It published its own *American Opinion* magazine, set up its own reading rooms, and organized vigorous letter-writing campaigns to further its cause; one of its most visible crusades targeted Chief Justice Earl Warren for impeachment. Two years after the JBS's creation, it was reported that Welch had called President Dwight Eisenhower a "dedicated, conscious agent of the Communist conspiracy," stirring bipartisan outrage. (Asked one Republican in Congress: "Good God, should the American people permit this kind of spleen to be poured on a man who has dedicated his whole life to freedom?") Subsequently, according to historian Colin E. Reynolds, "the John Birch Society was beset by charges of extremism, charges that convinced many Americans that the politics the organization represented might lead to the kind of violence and social disorder that it was theoretically working to prevent."[22] Even before then, Revilo Oliver had himself begun drawing charges of extremism. In turn, he was rapidly becoming a problem for U of I administrators.

"Acute Embarrassment through Violent Expression"

Oliver continued publishing in respectable conservative journals, including Russell Kirk's *Modern Age*. In what had become a familiar argument for him, Oliver wrote that liberal education ought "to produce cultivated gentlemen and intelligent citizens." The proper means of doing so was by studying the classics, for "the history of the ancient world, particularly of the Athenian democracy and the Roman republic, including their final failures, are the world's most impressive lessons in the problems of society and hence most likely to impart to young men, so far as that can be done by education at all, a certain wisdom and maturity." Moreover, "classical literature, free from both the grotesque eccentricities of the Baroque (e.g. Rabelais, Cervantes, Shakespeare) and the wild irrationality of Romanticism, combines a restrained beauty with sober consideration of all the fundamental ethical problems of mankind." Alas, John Dewey–inspired pragmatism had converted the schools "into machines for destroying mind and character." Having summarily dispatched a giant swath of the humanities and social sciences, Oliver turned in a separate essay to contemporary conservatism. He wrote of a rising mass of Americans who were "bamboozled by do-gooders, hectored by sob-sisters and shysters, insulted by snobbish vulgarians, bled by tax-sucking parasites, and betrayed by traitors." Those Americans were put off by the "racial bigotry of 'Liberal intellectuals,' the racial agitation organized by the Communists, and the open pandering of political parties to racial blocs." The "inchoate and unvoiced" resentment of that mass of people was "potentially a force of great—and in some circumstances, explosive—power."[23]

Oliver stoked that simmering resentment in his public speeches. In March 1959 he warned the Illinois convention of the DAR about the dangers of domestic communism: "Remember that the tentacles of the conspiracy reach into your home town, where its puppets are promoting fluoridation, 'mental health,' and innumerable other plans to accustom us to gradually increasing slavery and intimidation." The following month, he told a group backing Howard Barham's (ultimately unsuccessful) candidacy for the Champaign city council that there were three communist cells at the U of I, implying that those cells were threatening to take over municipal government. The month after that, Oliver addressed the Knox County Taxpayers Association in Galesburg, Illinois. He asserted that the communist conspiracy controlled regional planning, school consolidation, the press, and the federal Department of Health, Education, and Welfare. Oliver urged his audience to resist all bond issues and tax hikes by branding their proponents as communists ("we can no longer afford to split hairs," he said). He also claimed that communists were driven by "overwhelming lust" and were involved in dope peddling and bank robberies. Even though he said that he had "irrefutable evidence" supporting all his allegations, he did not share any of that evidence with his audience. Oliver's speech provoked an editorial response from the *Galesburg Register-Mail*, which expressed amazement that he was a U of I professor: "If tuition-paying students in Mr. Oliver's classics classes in the university are subjected to his mouthings on the communist menace, they should be entitled to a refund. So should the taxpayers."[24]

In case Oliver's mouthings had escaped the notice of U of I administrators, *Register-Mail* editor Charles Morrow forwarded his newspaper's coverage of the speech to President David Henry's office. Morrow attached a letter: "I believe irresponsible talks such as these do great harm to the University, particularly among persons who do not understand that he is speaking as an individual and not as a professor of a great University." A Galesburg-area school superintendent also sent a letter, saying that Oliver "commands respect only because he is a professor at the U of I and is *always presented* as such.... My personal opinion is that someone is seriously negligent in his responsibility to the public if a person such as Dr. Oliver is allowed to remain on the staff." And a Galesburg insurance agent mailed the president's office a one-line note suggesting that Oliver be sent to a city notorious for its resistance to school desegregation: "Can't you get this crack-pot a job in Little Rock?"[25]

After conversations with U of I provost Gordon Ray, liberal arts and sciences (LAS) dean Lyle Lanier asked the LAS executive committee to investigate whether Oliver was injecting his political views into his teaching and whether he was making it clear in his public speeches that he was speaking only for himself and not the university. The committee consulted with John Heller, Oliver's department head. Heller met with Oliver to remind him of the U of I statutory admonishment that faculty comport themselves with "accuracy, forthrightness, and dignity." Heller said that Oliver's espousal of "conspiracy, fear," and "name-calling" in his scholarly reviews was "not dignified, and is properly the concern of the [classics] department." Heller also asked Oliver about his allegation of communist cells at the university. Oliver replied that the allegation originally had been made about a decade earlier at an Illinois legislative hearing and never had been refuted; therefore, it must be true. Despite Oliver's twisted logic, Heller found no evidence that he was using his classes as a political pulpit, nor that he was consciously making it sound as though he were speaking for the university in his speeches. In June 1959 Dean Lanier told Provost Ray that he felt that that no further action should be taken; Ray concurred and informed President Henry to that effect.[26]

The contrast is striking between what was not done to Revilo Oliver and what would be done to Leo Koch only a few months later. The LAS executive committee and Dean Lanier came to dramatically different conclusions in the two cases. As to Oliver, Lanier wrote that the executive committee "definitely felt that any official investigation of Professor Oliver's speeches would be far better conducted by a [separate] faculty committee, or perhaps by a committee of the A.A.U.P. [American Association of University Professors]." That same courtesy would not be extended to Koch prior to his removal from his duties. Of course, Koch was an untenured professor on a terminal contract, whereas Oliver was a full professor with tenure. Oliver also had yet to create anything like the commotion that Koch would stir with his letter on sex; in Oliver's case, the reaction so far had consisted mostly of a few unhappy letters and a critical newspaper editorial. Nonetheless, Lanier said that Oliver had been informed "that his speeches had caused embarrassment to the President," and the LAS dean left the door open for future action against Oliver should there be "any indication that his speeches or other activities transgress the bounds of propriety for a faculty member."[27]

If Oliver already had seemed paranoid about communism, that paranoia now extended to the U of I administration. He and his wife Grace had become friends with Ira Latimer, whose fear of an all-encompassing communist conspiracy matched that of Oliver. Grace Oliver would help funnel information to Latimer about purported subversives among U of I administrators and faculty, culminating in Latimer's attack on Leo Koch. In a January 1960 letter to Latimer, Grace Oliver bemoaned the university's "smear campaign" against her husband, saying that he was being called "horrible, trash, scum, fascist. . . . The U of Ill is out to get him." Latimer also was given copies of two form letters that the university was sending to people who wrote to criticize Oliver (those letters had been shared with Oliver himself). One letter came from John Heller, saying of Oliver that "few of his colleagues in the University share his extreme opinions"; the other came from President Henry, who said that "it is always embarrassing when anyone speaks in public beyond the limits of his professional competence." Both men stressed in their letters that Oliver still had a right to speak his mind, but that did not matter to the professor's supporters. "Goons are always at their work," Grace Oliver wrote to Latimer. "Let us hope they don't get R. before his work is finished."[28]

Oliver's allies stepped up their campaign in 1960. In addition to Latimer's broadside against Leo Koch and the university bond issue, the Anti-Communist League attacked the bond issue in mimeographed sheets sent to U of I fraternities. According to *Daily Illini* columnist Dick Icen, the sheets charged that the university had "helped to nurture the seeds of a Bolshevi[k] revolution because of its placidness in allowing teachers and speakers of leftist sympathies to appear in Urbana." Howard Barham led the Anti-Communist League, and he sent his own letters to U of I trustees: "Please clean up this rotten red subversion on the campus of the University of Illinois." Eloise Mount sent similar communications; she previously had helped circulate Latimer's attack on Koch across the state. After U of I professor W. Ellison Chalmers signed the faculty open letter criticizing Koch's firing—and after he also had written a letter to the editor criticizing Howard Barham for "distortion, innuendo and personal attack"—an anonymous note sent to U of I trustees claimed that Chalmers was a communist supporter of racial integration. "WHAT ARE YOU GOING TO DO ABOUT THE TREASON AND COMMUNIST BRAINWASHING ON THE CAMPUS OF THIS UNIVERSITY," the note demanded to know. Students were not immune from attack; when Lew Collens publicly criticized the House

Committee on Un-American Activities, he found himself listed among the "ten leading communists" in Champaign-Urbana.[29]

Oliver himself remained as outspoken as ever. In late 1959 the Democratic National Committee made the mistake of asking him for a donation. Oliver responded that he was "not a member of the Communist-front" created by Franklin Roosevelt, whom Oliver called a "foul mass of syphilitic venom." That response was forwarded to the office of Paul Douglas, a Democratic US senator from Illinois. When Douglas's executive secretary contacted the university, Provost Gordon Ray reasserted "the right of a faculty member to express himself freely as a citizen." But Ray also apologized: "This is by no means the first time that Professor Oliver has caused this University acute embarrassment through the violent expression of his extreme political views, nor presumably will it be the last." Indeed it was not. In February 1960 Oliver addressed the annual meeting of the Illinois Classical Conference. Before an audience of high school students and Latin teachers, Oliver abruptly digressed from the subject of his talk ("Arcadius Avellanus—the American Erasmus") to decry progressive education's corrosion of youthful morals. He cited the example of a pregnant fifteen-year-old girl infected with both gonorrhea and syphilis. In a note to a colleague at another university, the U of I's John Heller said that he had found Oliver's speech to be "inexcusable on such an occasion, especially as just a few weeks ago I had been reminding him of the wording of the University's statute on academic freedom" (specifically the language regarding "accuracy, forthrightness, and dignity," which Heller would keep repeating to Oliver to no apparent effect).[30]

Oliver also had begun writing for *American Opinion*, the John Birch Society magazine. His article in the summer 1960 issue extolled White colonialism while calling Black Africans "unsanitary" and "savages." It was not until the spring of 1961, though, that Oliver's association with the JBS became widely known. He acknowledged to the *Champaign-Urbana Courier* that he had helped found the society, and when the newspaper asked him whether he still believed that communists abounded at the U of I, he replied, "Sure." The JBS was facing a new round of condemnation for Robert Welch's remarks about Dwight Eisenhower being a communist; even the stalwartly conservative *Los Angeles Times* warned against "smearing as enemies and traitors those with whom we sometimes disagree." Oliver said that the criticisms of the JBS were the direct result of a Communist Party directive: "You can always get people to do your work for a few bucks." A few days after speaking to the *Courier*, Oliver was quoted in the *Chicago Tribune* as saying that the new John F. Kennedy administration was full of "weak-in-the-head" appointees who threatened national security. Oliver also said that he had "no means of knowing whether President Kennedy is a Communist or not."[31]

Oliver's remarks were republished in newspapers across the country. The *Springfield Leader and Press* in Missouri editorialized that the "tragic thing about such movements [as the JBS] is that educational and cultural background are no safeguards against their appeal," as Oliver clearly demonstrated. Back at the U of I, the *Daily Illini* spoke out in favor of the "fundamental right of each individual to express his or her opinions on a subject without fear of reprisal," but it added that the "local professor has put himself so far out on the limb with his unqualified backing of [Robert] Welch that, if the ship must go down, Oliver too must follow." When the *Daily Illini* contacted U of I president Henry, he averred that Oliver was "using his right to speak as a free citizen" and that he had not said "anything that would occasion University interference." John Heller was more pointed in a letter to the student paper: "I feel it necessary to say in public that Professor Oliver's views are not shared by all members of the [classics] department, that nothing in the study of the Classics leads necessarily to the formation of such views, that in fact most scholars of the Classics hold quite different views of contemporary issues, and that, to the best of my knowledge, no member of the department allows his views, whether of the right, left, or center, to obtrude themselves in the classroom."[32]

Heller met with Oliver before sending his letter to the newspaper. According to his notes, Heller thought that his colleague looked "disheveled" and sleep-deprived. The two men clashed over the JBS, with Heller saying that "its primary aim was not anti-Communism, but anti- any sort of social betterment" that might get in the way of accumulating wealth. Oliver retorted that property was the underpinning of civilization, and then he launched into a "long discourse" about communist methods. "He feels himself as [a] crusader in [a] cause for which he will be vilified," Heller wrote of Oliver, adding that he "soberly defended his statement that his appointment to [the] Council of the John Birch Society was [the] highest honor that had ever been given him." When Heller asked him if that included all the honors that he had received for his classics scholarship, Oliver replied yes.[33]

By the end of 1961, "virtually the entire religious, civic, and political Establishment of the nation rose to denounce the John Birch Society by name," according to Alan F. Westin, a Columbia University legal scholar. He and other postwar professors tried to explain the essence of what they called the "radical right." Westin wrote that such organizations as the JBS assumed that "there are always solutions capable of producing international victories and of resolving our social problems; when such solutions are not found, they attribute the failure to conspiracies led by evil men and their dupes." Harvard sociologist Daniel Bell similarly pointed to the conspiracy-mindedness of people on the far right, adding that they also believed that "old-fashioned patriotism has been subverted by the cosmopolitan intellectual." For Bell, the right's real target was "essentially 'modernity'—that complex of attitudes that might be defined most simply as the belief in rational assessment, rather than established custom, for the evaluation of social change—and what it seeks to defend is its fading dominance, exercised once through the institutions of small-town America, over the control of social change." Columbia University historian Richard Hofstadter wrote of what he called a "pseudo-conservative revolt" that expressed "a profound if largely unconscious hatred of our society and its ways."[34]

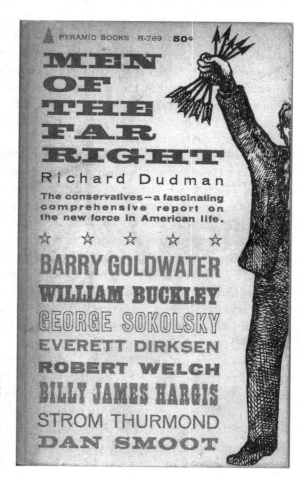

Cover of a 1962 book on the burgeoning right-wing movement in the United States. One of the subjects was Robert Welch, who had founded the John Birch Society four years earlier.

Such critiques from cosmopolitan Ivy League intellectuals irritated many conservatives, particularly the notion that (as historian David L. Chappell has described it) "you had to be uneducated, backward, provincial, xenophobic, to oppose liberalism." William F. Buckley Jr.—a cosmopolitan Ivy League intellectual himself—particularly resented the a priori assumption that "anyone who is opposed to the welfare state is likely to be 'unenlightened' in his attitudes toward science and religion; that such persons tend to accept the authority of an organic moral order, to hate Jews and Negroes, to entertain an unconscious desire to grind their heels in the faces of the weak." Yet Buckley was keenly aware of the potential damage that such assumptions could inflict on the conservative movement and its ambitions for Barry Goldwater and like-minded politicians. Buckley also was aware that there indeed were self-described conservatives who did not like Jews, African Americans, or other people who were deemed to be weak or inferior. Thus, in 1960, Buckley expelled Revilo Oliver from *National Review*; and, in February 1962, he publicly renounced Robert Welch in a *National Review* editorial: "Mr. Welch, for all his good intentions, threatens to divert militant conservative reaction to irrelevance and ineffectuality.... [He] has revived in many men the spirit of patriotism, and that same spirit calls now for rejecting, out of a love of truth and country, his false counsels."[35]

Even though Buckley knew full well of Oliver's increasingly overt racism and anti-Semitism, he still strove to maintain his friendship with the U of I professor. Buckley visited the university in the spring of 1962 to participate in the campus's Great Debates series. Oliver had issued the *National Review* editor a long-standing invitation to stay at his house in Urbana, and now Buckley took him up on it ("probably to his embarrassment," Buckley recalled, but "he had only the alternative of explicitly rejecting me"). While the two men talked in Oliver's home after the debate, Buckley heard an odd, garbled voice coming from the kitchen. Oliver was making high-speed copies of a taped speech of Edwin Walker, a former general who recently had resigned from the US Army in a controversy over his far-right ties. Buckley asked Oliver why he thought *National Review* had broken with Robert Welch and the JBS. Oliver offered three possible explanations: that Buckley caved in to pressure from his fellow editors, that Buckley feared that Welch might supplant him at the head of the conservative movement, or that Buckley was a communist agent. "Which of the three explanations do you lean to?" Buckley asked Oliver. The professor was charitable: "I lean toward the first two."[36]

Oliver had continued to make news in ways that disturbed his home university. In a 1959 speech that did not become widely public until a couple of years later, he had said that the right-wing Batista regime in Cuba had been "as good a government as one could reasonably expect to find in an island largely populated by mongrels." In that same speech, Oliver had targeted Felix Frankfurter, the only Jewish justice on the US Supreme Court. The professor called Frankfurter (who had been born in Austria) "the most brilliant and dangerous immigrant ever imported into this country. . . . Frankfurter is recognized as the dominant mind in the Supreme Court that has consistently and with ever-increasing effrontery advanced the Communist cause and subverted the American Constitution." Then, in early 1962, Oliver addressed a meeting of the Christian Crusade organized by right-wing minister Billy James Hargis. Oliver complained of "supine leaders" who were determined "to win the favor of every mangy cannibal in Africa." He also said that the European Common Market was part of the communist conspiracy's plot "to destroy those remote islands of white civilization such as Australia, New Zealand and the Republic of South Africa."[37]

In March 1962, John Heller met yet again with Oliver to admonish him yet again about accuracy, forthrightness, and dignity. Heller "begged him as [a] friend" to think carefully about what he was doing and then quoted some of Oliver's more outrageous accusations back at him, telling him "that he was only damaging his own reputation by such statements." According to Heller's notes from the meeting, Oliver replied that "he considered it his duty as a citizen to speak out and 'tell the truth' about this fearful conspiracy, etc. etc. I said that I honored him for his interest in public affairs, but that this did not justify him in using such language or conducting himself in this way. I pointed out that there would inevitably be a conflict between what he felt to be his duty (if he continued to speak in this manner) and his duty to the profession, to the cause of the Classics, and to the University." But, yet again, it "made no impression; he was off on a long speech when I said I had heard enough and hoped he would remember what I had said." Heller met afterward with LAS dean Jack Peltason. It now had been two years since the Leo Koch case, and Peltason said that although the university was "anxious *not* to take any action" about Oliver, he feared that it might "be forced into it." (To a person who had written the university to express outrage over Oliver, Peltason responded through gritted teeth that "a professor has a right to espouse any political views he wishes, even those which I consider false, dangerous, extreme, irresponsible, and embarrassing to the University.")[38]

Marxmanship in Dallas

Although Oliver was not formally disciplined, he received no salary increase for the 1962–63 school year. That year passed comparatively peacefully in the classics department, with Heller reporting to Peltason that Oliver had "cooperated very well in his teaching and all departmental functions." Heller thus recommended that Oliver's salary for the 1963–64 school year be increased to twelve thousand dollars, which, according to Heller, was still substantially less than what other full professors in the department were making. Oliver's raise did not stop him from writing inflammatory articles for *American Opinion*—including a piece advocating that the state act "to induce or compel the superior to have children and to prevent the inferior from proliferating"—and he was citing such avowedly racist and anti-Semitic figures as Francis Parker Yockey, whose book *Imperium* would become a lodestone for Oliver. The professor also continued his speaking engagements across the country while being prominently identified as a U of I faculty member, even if he avoided making it sound as though he were expressing an official university viewpoint. Prior to a talk to South Carolina members of the JBS in early November 1963, Oliver even was called "one of the top three philologists in the world," an assertion that his fellow classicists might have disputed. But his scholarly affiliation and reputation were important badges of credibility, particularly for someone spouting the views of the JBS. As William F. Buckley noted, Oliver was the JBS's "single literary light."[39]

The political left and center had many such lights, one of the most prominent being Richard Hofstadter, who already had written of a "pseudo-conservative revolt." At about the same time that Oliver was speaking to South Carolina JBS members, Hofstadter was delivering a lecture at Oxford University in England. It was later published as "The Paranoid Style in American Politics," and it became his most enduring essay.

"American politics has often been an arena for angry minds," Hofstadter began, arguing that the JBS was only the latest historical example. After drawing some parallels between contemporary right-wing politics and earlier political movements, Hofstadter then outlined three pillars of JBS-flavored thought: first, that there was a communist-inspired conspiracy to undermine capitalism and free enterprise; second, that communists had infiltrated the highest echelons of government ever since the time leading up to Pearl Harbor; and third, that communists also had infiltrated the schools, churches, and media to prevent effective resistance. "The paranoid spokesman sees the fate of conspiracy in apocalyptic terms—he traffics in the birth and death of whole worlds, whole political orders, whole systems of human values," said Hofstadter. "Like religious millennialists he expresses the anxiety of those who are living through the last days and he is sometimes disposed to set a date for the apocalypse." For the paranoid person, only total victory against the conspiracy would suffice: "Even partial success leaves him with the same feeling of powerlessness with which he began, and this in turn only strengthens his awareness of the vast and terrifying quality of the enemy he opposes."

That enemy was viewed as "a kind of amoral superman—sinister, ubiquitous, powerful, cruel, sensual, luxury-loving." The "superman" was especially associated with sexual libertinism (perhaps one reason why the likes of Leo Koch provoked such a violent reaction from the likes of Ira Latimer). Still, the respectable paranoid took pains not to seem too wild-eyed. "Paranoid writing begins with certain broad defensible judgments," observed Hofstadter, and it also was fastidious in its attention to detail: "The enemy may be the cosmopolitan intellectual, but the paranoid will outdo him in the apparatus of scholarship, even of pedantry.... One of the impressive things about paranoid literature is the contrast between its fantasied conclusions and the almost touching concern with factuality it inevitably shows. It produces heroic strivings for evidence to prove that the unbelievable is the only thing that can be believed." Hofstadter concluded by saying that paranoids never developed the awareness that history regularly happens without it resulting from an evil, all-encompassing conspiracy: "We are all sufferers from history, but the paranoid is a double sufferer, since he is afflicted not only by the real world, with the rest of us, but by his fantasies as well."[40]

On November 22, 1963, just after Hofstadter delivered his Oxford lecture, President Kennedy flew to Dallas. The city was a hub for the JBS, which had circulated letters claiming that the communist conspiracy was aiming "to (A): create tension between Negroes and Whites; (B): to transform the South into a BLACK SOVIET REPUBLIC; (C): to legalize and encourage intermarriage between Negroes and Whites *and thus mongrelize the American White Race!*" When United Nations ambassador Adlai Stevenson had spoken in Dallas in October, an anti-UN protester had hit in him in the head with a placard while other protesters spat at him. The protests had been organized by supporters of Edwin Walker, the right-wing ex-general from Dallas whose taped speech Revilo Oliver had been copying. Just before Kennedy flew to the city, Walker's backers circulated handbills with mug-style photos of the president and an accompanying headline: "WANTED FOR TREASON." On the morning of Kennedy's visit, the *Dallas Morning News* ran a full-page, black-bordered ad that had been written and paid for by JBS supporters; among other things, the ad accused the president of having ignored the Constitution and having "scrapped the Monroe Doctrine in favor of the 'Spirit of Moscow.'"[41]

Later that day, as Kennedy's motorcade drove past cheering crowds in downtown Dallas, the president was shot and killed. Lee Harvey Oswald was quickly arrested as the suspected assassin. It soon was reported that he was a Marxist

The "Wanted" handbill circulated in Dallas prior to John F. Kennedy's fatal visit to the city on November 22, 1963. The John Birch Society and backers of Edwin Walker vociferously opposed Kennedy.

who had defected to the Soviet Union before deciding to return to the United States. Two days after Kennedy's assassination, Jack Ruby shot Oswald dead; the day after that, Kennedy's funeral took place, and he was buried at Arlington National Cemetery.

Revilo Oliver quickly went to work. He had said that he considered it his solemn duty to tell the truth about the conspiracy that already had begun taking over America. Now he would uphold that perceived duty by sharing what he believed to be the truth about John F. Kennedy and the forces that had eliminated the president.

When Oliver's article "Marxmanship in Dallas" appeared in the Birch Society magazine, it was preceded by a note establishing the professor's bona fides: "Revilo P. Oliver is Professor of Classics in the University of Illinois.... [He] is an academician of international reputation who has published scholarly articles in four languages within the pages of twelve learned periodicals in the United States and Europe." What followed was Oliver's argument that a conspiracy underlay President Kennedy's murder and that the commission that had been appointed to investigate the killing would likely whitewash the details. That was not an outlandish notion in and of itself; on the contrary, as Richard Hofstadter had suggested, it could be considered a "broad defensible judgment" of the assassination and the Warren Commission, a judgment that many other people have shared in the years since. At the very least, no one could take exception with what Oliver said at the beginning of his article—that it was "imperative that we understand" what had happened in Dallas.[42]

Oliver cited widely agreed-upon facts: Lee Harvey Oswald was a former US marine; he had lived in Minsk in the Soviet Union and had married a Russian woman; while being interrogated after his arrest, he had "asked for a noted Communist attorney" (John Abt, chief counsel for the Communist Party USA). Oliver also contended that Oswald previously had tried to assassinate Edwin Walker in Dallas, an assertion that the Warren Commission later would endorse. Oliver even added a footnote citing the *Congressional Record* as evidence supporting his argument.

But the particulars of that argument were—to put it mildly—questionable. Oliver charged that Oswald had been "trained in sabotage, terrorism, and guerilla warfare (including accurate shooting from ambush) in the well-known school for international criminals near Minsk, and while there he married the daughter of a colonel in the Soviet military espionage system (and possibly also in the Secret Police)." After Oswald's training was complete, he and his wife "were brought to the United States, in open violation of American law, by our Communist-dominated State Department." It was in connection with those assertions that Oliver cited the *Congressional Record*. (In actuality, a conservative Ohio Republican, John M. Ashbrook, had merely raised questions about why Oswald had been in Minsk and what he had been doing there, as well as about Oswald's wife's family background.)[43]

Oliver rejected out of hand any notion that Oswald had acted alone; it was as ludicrous as the idea that Kennedy had not been killed but instead was "now a guest aboard a 'flying saucer' on which he is heroically negotiating with Martians or Saturnians to Save the World." Oliver offered three possible explanations for the assassination (much as he previously had offered three possible explanations for *National Review*'s renouncement of the John Birch Society). The first explanation was that "Kennedy was executed by the Communist Conspiracy because he was planning to turn American," a premise that Oliver found difficult to support because it gave the late president too much credit. The second explanation was that Kennedy had fallen victim to internal fighting over a joint plan between the US president and Soviet leader Nikita Khrushchev to replace Fidel Castro with a new communist leader in Cuba. The third explanation, which Oliver favored, was that "the Conspiracy ordered the assassination as part of systematic preparation for a domestic take-over. If so, the plan, of course, was to place the blame on 'right-wing extremists' (if I may use the Bolsheviks' codeword for informed and loyal Americans)." In other words, the blame would be shifted to the likes of the JBS and backers of Edwin Walker, including Revilo Oliver himself. Lee Harvey Oswald's fortuitous arrest had thwarted the conspiracy's pernicious plot.

"Marxmanship in Dallas" contained a great deal of talk about vermin, who were everywhere. There were the media vermin who "probably in obedience to general or specific orders issued in advance of the event" had spread "vicious lies about the 'radical right'" and its purported role in the assassination. There were the "showmen" who had turned Kennedy's funeral into "an orgy of bathos and irrationality," all to divert attention from the conspiracy. There was the "infamous Martin Luther King and other criminals engaged in inciting race war." There were the "'Liberal intellectuals' [who] try to conceal with all the contorted sophistries that they are perpetually devising to justify as 'social good' or 'progress' the murders and massacres that secretly fascinate and excite them." There was Jack Ruby—"Jakob Leon Rubenstein"—who had been in league with Oswald and other communists before acting on orders to liquidate the president's assassin. There was assorted scum within the Kennedy administration who had been covering up a "filthy scandal involving both sadistic sexual perversions and the use of government powers for the importation and distribution of hallucinatory narcotics."

Worst of all, there was John F. Kennedy himself, guilty of an appalling litany of treacherous sins. "So long as there are Americans, his memory will be cherished with distaste," Oliver wrote. (He originally had written "cherished with execration and loathing," but it seemed as though that was too much even for the JBS.)[44] Oliver continued: "If the United States is saved by the desperate exertions of patriots, we may have a future of true greatness and glory—but we shall never forget how near we were to total destruction in the year 1963.

And if the international vermin succeed in completing their occupation of our country"—something that Oliver warned still might very well happen in the very near future—then "Americans will remember Kennedy while they live, and will curse him as they face the firing squads or toil in a brutish degradation that leaves no hope for anything but a speedy death."

"Marxmanship in Dallas" was published in *American Opinion* in February 1964. It would rock the U of I in a way that that the campus had not experienced since the days of Leo Koch and his dashed-off letter on sex. And it would prompt U of I president David Henry to send former provost Gordon Ray a plaintive note: "Oliver and Koch in one decade are more than one institution should bear!"[45]

CHAPTER 6

Ungloriously Wrong

Back in 1960, it had taken a few weeks for the full furor to build over Leo Koch's letter on sex. There was no such delay in 1964 for Revilo Oliver's attack on John F. Kennedy. Almost immediately after the publication of "Marxmanship in Dallas," the story exploded in the news media. The Associated Press and United Press International distributed the news of Oliver's article nationwide and quoted extensively from it. The *New York Times* published its own story that cited John Birch Society (JBS) leader Robert Welch as saying that Oliver's article represented "superb commentary." *Newsweek* said of the article that its "intricately stitched plot makes secret agent James Bond's preposterous adventures read as soberly as the Federal budget." The *Daily Illini* was contacted by the Chicago newspapers and a Los Angeles radio station seeking reaction from Oliver's home university. (When the student paper tried to talk to Oliver himself, his wife Grace coolly replied that the "Daily Illini has not been kind to us" and that it had "smeared that great American Strom Thurmond" when he had spoken on campus three months previously.)[1]

Editorial outrage followed. "Shame!" thundered the *Chicago Sun-Times*. "Shame, Dr. Oliver, that you, a man engaged in teaching young people, should be unable to separate myth from fact; that you lend yourself to distortion and perversion of fact; shame that your venom runneth over and that your vitriol better qualifies you for association with Billingsgate fishwives than with the distinguished scholars who adorn the campus of this state's great university."

Similar comments appeared in newspapers across the country, with Oliver's article being called "revolting stuff," "vile" and "below the belt," a "repulsive piece of crankery," a "shameful, crackpot attack" that copied "the totalitarian method of the Big Lie," and "sick—seriously sick."[2] Oliver and the JBS were denounced by name on the floor of the US House of Representatives. There were furious letters to the University of Illinois ("I wish to formally express my profound *shock* and *grief*"), as well as to the *Daily Illini* editor: "Academic freedom is one thing, but offensive, libelous, slanderous rantings are another and should be dealt with accordingly." The president of the U of I Alumni Association called on Oliver to resign, adding that he had "considerable confidence that the vast majority of those who love the University of Illinois agree with me." And on the U of I campus itself, Revilo Oliver was hanged in effigy (just as President Henry had been hanged in effigy in response to the Koch case). The *Daily Illini* reported that Oliver's likeness was found on the main quadrangle "dangling by a noose of sheets from the branch of a locust tree in a pair of blue-striped pajamas. Attached was the sign: 'Revilo . . . hung by a birch.'"[3]

The sudden storm over Oliver caught University of Illinois administrators off guard, or at least as off guard as they could be in light of his past history. Classics department head John Heller was on sabbatical in England (likely to his relief), and President Henry said that he would withhold comment until he had read Oliver's article. That left it to Jack Peltason, the liberal arts and sciences dean and acting provost, to make the first administrative statement on Oliver. "He has the same rights as every other American to express his political views outside the classroom," Peltason said. "Personally, I find nothing of merit in the article, consider it in bad taste and offensive. However, this is irrelevant as far as my responsibilities as a dean are concerned." University public information director Charles Flynn took pains to separate the Oliver case from the Leo Koch case: Oliver had been speaking as a private citizen, said Flynn, whereas Koch had used his university position to aim his views at students. Samuel Gove, an official of the U of I chapter of the American Association of University Professors, called Oliver's article "a little irresponsible." But he added that should the university investigate the professor, the AAUP would "insist" that correct procedures be followed.[4]

David Henry drafted a formal statement that he first asked Jack Peltason and university counsel James Costello to review. Henry then announced that in his capacity as U of I president, he had no comment on Oliver's article. As a citizen, though, Henry viewed Oliver's "unreasoned and vitriolic attack on the character and patriotism of President Kennedy" as being "beyond the bounds of good taste in public comment and the normal proprieties of public debate." (The pending new university statutes—revised after the Koch case—would not take effect for another couple of years, but they would stipulate that when a faculty member said something inflammatory while speaking as a citizen, "the President may publicly disassociate the Board of Trustees and the University administration from, and express their disapproval of, such objectionable expressions.")[5]

Perhaps Henry hoped that his statement would put the matter to rest; but members of the U of I Board of Trustees, who themselves were being deluged with complaints over Oliver's piece, felt that more needed to be said and done. Even though the Oliver case was not on the agenda of the upcoming February board meeting, the president—after consulting with the trustees—used that meeting to issue an additional statement. Henry said that Oliver's "right to dissent, to express unorthodox views, and to criticize is not only recognized, it is protected by the tradition of academic freedom at the University of Illinois, in the academic world and by the Statutes governing the University." But the president added that "Mr. Oliver's expression raises questions as to whether he has complied with the expectations for professional responsibility." Saying that this was "a matter for professionals to consider," Henry announced that he would ask the campus academic freedom committee "to review the situation and give me their advice." The board unanimously endorsed Henry's new statement.[6]

With the specter of academic responsibility raised anew, it now seemed possible that Oliver could face formal university discipline for his extramural speech, just as Leo Koch had. Because Oliver held tenure (which Koch had not), it was highly unlikely that the classics professor would be fired. Regardless, the U of I law faculty issued its own statement protesting Henry's consultation with the academic freedom committee about Oliver's article: "If the encouragement of expression of ideas and individual views is to remain a meaningful principle, such expressions must not be subject to review and judgment by any University body nor cause for any disciplinary action."[7]

The law faculty were not the only individuals on campus concerned about what might happen to Oliver. So too were students who wrote for the *Daily Illini*, which maintained a lively editorial page under editor-in-chief Roger Ebert. The students' commentaries reflected a heightened political consciousness that had been shaped by the events of the past four years; they also displayed a keen understanding of just what was at stake in the Oliver case and others like it.

"A Strong and Free Society"

Roger Ebert himself addressed the case in his "Ars Gratia" column the day after the Oliver story first broke. He presciently noted that "Oliver's opinions, instead of resting unseen in the Birch magazine, will be the occasion of a brief national scandal. He will be attacked in editorials, and several citizens will doubtless call for his dismissal from the University." Ebert, who was a journalism major, questioned "why our newspapers are so quick to uncover and publicize irrelevant and extreme political opinions," which was exactly how he viewed Oliver's article: foolish and unworthy of notice. "Still, I must conclude that the American tradition provides for Professor Oliver the right to free public expression," Ebert wrote. "I see nothing wrong in his speaking out, particularly because by doing so he is disproving his charges. Only a strong and free society could permit Professor Oliver his own freedom." Ebert's editorial garnered him his first national attention as a writer. It was republished in full by the *St. Louis Post-Dispatch* (whose former editorial director, Irving Dilliard, was a U of I trustee); Ebert's comments also were picked up by the wire services and republished across the country (even though in some stories he was misidentified as "*Robert* Ebert").[8]

Ebert took up the Oliver case again after President Henry asked for advice on the matter from the academic freedom committee. Ebert said that the committee should be exceptionally cautious about restricting faculty speech on public issues: "My feeling is that if the line is drawn anywhere, the freedom of the academic community will be impaired. You can't put a picket fence around ideas, no matter how much you might want to sometimes." Ebert added that faculty should have "the right on occasion to be gloriously wrong," and the Oliver case was a test of whether the U of I had learned anything from the mishandling of the Leo Koch controversy: "In a way, it has to be seen as a trial of the things we say we believe about free speech. If truth will really prevail, then what are we so worried about?"[9]

Gary Porter, a political science major who served as a *Daily Illini* news analyst, compared the Koch and Oliver cases at length. Porter was unconvinced by the university's argument that the two cases were fundamentally different. If Koch was fired because he allegedly was encouraging students to partake in sex, then Oliver could just as easily be seen as encouraging people on the far right to partake in violence and "plan a coup against the 'unspeakable' gang of reds now entrenched in the executive department." According to Porter, the "University Administration stands accused of inconsistency, which is the cruelest wound to justice. University statutes were meant to prevent the arbitrary rule of officials over faculty and student[s], but we learn now, if we did not know before, that they are, after all, mere paper." If the university truly valued academic freedom, then it should not discipline Oliver for his speech, just as it should not have disciplined Koch.[10]

Daily Illini columnist Tony Burba took a similar stance. The notion that academic freedom did not apply to Leo Koch's letter because it had appeared in a student paper (as opposed to a national magazine such as *American Opinion*) made no sense: "Maybe that is supposed to mean that it's all right to say 'unpopular' things so long as you do it in a national publication rather than in The Daily Illini. After all, everyone knows that students are suckers for every half-baked idea that comes along, so their minds have to be protected." The real reason that Oliver seemed to warrant more protection than Koch was because the university understood that "taxpayers and coeds' parents would be far less likely to raise a stink over wild-eyed accusations of treason than they would over condoning sex.... Nobody has paid much serious attention to [Oliver's] outlandishly ridiculous ideas, so the administration can afford to let academic freedom prevail."[11]

On the other side of the debate was philosophy student Robert Jung, whose *Daily Illini* column would be remembered by Roger Ebert as being "somber and poetic about the big picture." While the Oliver controversy still was raging, Jung wrote of the power of ideas to spark "all kinds of little explosions down deep where people really live"; he also said that the "creation and exchange of ideas is the proper function of a university." For Jung, though, Oliver's ideas were "irrational to the point of paranoia," and therefore they fell beyond the protection of academic freedom. "Professors, whatever their private idiosyncrasies may be, are expected in their public actions to adhere to certain canons of lucidity, rationality, respect for evidence and truth," said Jung, and the classics professor had ignored those canons completely. "I have only sympathy for Oliver the private man," Jung concluded. "It is a tragedy when a trained mind falls victim to such wild and twisted thoughts. It is the public gesture of Prof. Oliver, the public man, which should be condemned by his associates in an old and respected profession."[12]

John Johnson, a student member of the U of I Conservative Coordinating Council, agreed with Jung to the extent that Oliver deserved pity; as Johnson put it, "this is a pathetic situation, not a damnable one." But he did not agree with the university president's decision to ask the academic freedom committee for advice on the case. "It appears that President Henry is trying to be all things to all people," Johnson wrote. "The taxpayers, unaware that Oliver has tenure blocking any Koch-type dismissal, will feel that Henry is following a public mandate; the faculty, always eager for administrative influence, will feel that he has recognized their omniscience; the trustees will be content that the responsibility for the Oliver episode has been removed from them." Johnson said that the university needed to remember that "serving the taxpayers, the state, and the students will best be accomplished by maintaining educational excellence and intellectual and political discourse and freedom."[13]

Then there was Liz Krohne, who chaired the U of I Liberal Discussion Group. She argued that too much attention was being paid to the likes of Koch and Oliver, saying that if the U of I "were indeed a forum for healthy and open discussion both by teachers and by students, we might have such a variety of controversy and honest, vital debate, that Kochs and Olivers would be thrown into the shadow. We might be so busy talking about important ideas that we would not have time to notice the ravings of a few academic mavericks." Krohne added that she was thankful that the mavericks had at least broken the campus monotony: "For monotony there is, and monotony there will continue to be as long as the university cares more for its precious public image than it does for the quality and vitality of the education it offers. And if we don't defend our Kochs and Olivers, chances are we will never have anyone more worth defending."[14]

Several months before the Free Speech Movement in Berkeley made national headlines in the fall of 1964, Krohne used her *Daily Illini* column to herald a "new American student movement. It is a movement which largely rejects the academic atmosphere. It attracts many who are deeply frustrated in their attempts to fulfill intellectual goals within the framework of the usual curriculum. The trend in the student movement is to leave the universities, to gravitate to the city streets of the north and the rural towns of the south, where ideas are alive because they have to be." Krohne argued that too often in a university setting "ideas become inert objects, stripped of dignity and force, swapped about like status symbols or sheltered like hothouse plants." Ideas instead needed to be mobilized toward effecting genuine social change, which was what the new student movement was seeking. "A university which cannot hold the people of the movement, which offers no scope to the creative searching in which they are engaged, is a sham," charged Krohne. "And the society which strangles and isolates them betrays its best hope."[15]

"Willing to Pay the Price"

While the U of I's student newspaper was debating the implications of the Koch and Oliver cases and the broader role of higher education, members of the campus academic freedom committee were struggling with how best to respond to President Henry's request for their advice. The existing university statutes—the same ones that had been in effect during the Koch case—made no provision for the president to consult with a faculty committee in such a case. (The pending new statutes *would* include such a provision, but again they would not take effect for another couple of years.) Furthermore, the academic freedom committee was charged with hearing complaints from faculty; should that committee advise Henry now concerning Oliver, it could compromise the committee's ability later to hear any complaint that Oliver might make.[16] The U of I law faculty was also about to go on record as saying that a professor's speech as a private citizen should be none of the university's business.

However, the committee members were loath to reject Henry's request out of hand. They were, after all, presumably the most qualified faculty on campus to provide advice on academic freedom questions. Henry had not made any such request for advice during the Koch case, and the result had been that the AAUP had censured the university. The policy committee of the U of I's AAUP chapter unanimously supported Henry's decision to seek counsel about Oliver now. "Ordinarily the expression of private views by a faculty member should not be subject to institutional scrutiny," the AAUP representatives said in a public statement, "but in this particular case the character of the statements made by Professor Oliver lead us to believe that his conduct is subject to review by those best able to evaluate it in light of the academic profession—namely, his faculty colleagues."[17]

The academic freedom committee met three times to consider the Oliver case; one of those meetings included President Henry, acting provost Jack Peltason, and university counsel James Costello. On March 6, a little more than two weeks after Henry had requested their input, the committee members sent their report to the president. "The exercise of academic freedom rights and privileges by a faculty is not without its price to a university, but the benefits greatly outweigh the costs," said the report. Noting that the public often did not understand why academic freedom was so important, the report said that universities were devoted to "developing and transmitting new ideas," and "in the search for the eternal verities, *administrative* restraint on the scholar searching for these truths must be avoided." Instead, judgment should be reserved for fellow professional faculty:

> [The scholar] must withstand the full glare of critical *professional* judgment and condemnation for unprofessional, undignified, unsupported, or offensive utterances. He must have the right to be as ungloriously wrong, and suffer the *professional* consequences thereof, as to be gloriously right and receive the acclaim of his *professional* colleagues therefor. Thus when abuses occur, and the *public* image of a great university is somewhat tarnished as a result thereof, it must be recognized that the larger gain is in the brighter image of the university presented to the scholarly world of an institution dedicated to the advancement of knowledge and learning, and one willing to pay the price for strict adherence to this ideal.[18]

The report ended by advising that no action be taken against Oliver. In defending the scholar's right to be "ungloriously wrong," the committee members had echoed one of Roger Ebert's commentaries on the Oliver case, consciously or not. They also had deleted a paragraph from the initial draft of their report. The omitted language had said that "the members of the Committee without exception feel that the article by Professor Oliver in *American Opinion*, February 1964, is so patently contrary to the truth that it tends to disparage the work of those staff members who are seeking the truth."[19]

When the U of I Board of Trustees met later in March to consider the Oliver case, President Henry said that he concurred with the academic freedom committee's report. He reiterated his earlier condemnation of Oliver's comments as violating the precepts of accuracy, forthrightness, and dignity; but the president added that "I do not believe that it is adequate grounds for my filing disciplinary charges against Mr. Oliver." The trustees then voted seven to one to approve Henry's recommendation of no action against the classics professor. Although trustee Harold Pogue voted with the majority, he announced that he wanted "to go on record as saying that I regard the statement made by Oliver with absolute loathing" and that "this is the most shameful thing that has ever happened to the reputation of the University of Illinois in my memory." Pogue viewed Oliver's attack on the late president Kennedy as being "as contemptible as the action of the killer was horrible." The trustee added that Oliver should resign—but Pogue knew that the professor never would do so, for his association with the university allowed him "to receive and achieve his widespread publicity."[20]

Irving Dilliard was the only trustee to vote against Henry's recommendation of no discipline against Oliver. Dilliard said that the academic freedom committee's report (on which the U of I president was basing his recommendation) was lacking in three aspects. It did not do enough to assert the university's devotion to free expression; it did not fully "disavow and disassociate" the university from Oliver's "disgraceful" attack on Kennedy; and it did not sufficiently stress "that a University of Illinois scholar, be his field Greek and Latin or current history and contemporary political science, has an obligation to back up his conclusions with weighed and tested facts."[21]

Even with that dissenting voice, it seemed that the university had achieved the best possible outcome from a deeply embarrassing situation. The U of I's commitment to academic freedom and to professional faculty oversight had been publicly reaffirmed, in stark contrast to the outcome of the Koch case; it was exactly the signal that the university needed to send at a time that it was trying to remove itself from the AAUP censure list. (At its national convention in April 1964, the AAUP praised the U of I's handling of the Oliver controversy, but it would not lift its censure of the university for another three years.) President Henry sent an effusive note to the academic freedom committee expressing his "profound thanks" for its work and advice. In response to a query from a fellow university president on the Oliver case, Henry observed that the U of I had no provisions "for 'discipline' short of dismissal" when it came to a faculty member. "In this case, both the Faculty Committee and I in effect issued a reprimand, without saying so," Henry said. "By so doing, and explaining academic freedom, I feel we strengthened the cause."[22]

Reprimand or not, if Henry and others at the university believed that Oliver would be chastened by the public tongue-lashing he had received and finally would begin restraining himself in his public speech, they quickly would be disabused of the notion.

Oliver the Celebrity

The same article that had made Oliver a pariah for so many people made him a hero among others. For those individuals, there was a second printing of ten thousand additional copies of the *American Opinion* issue containing "Marxmanship in Dallas." Grace Oliver said that her husband had received a thousand letters in response to the article, the overwhelming majority of which were laudatory. She added that "many others have said the same thing as Revilo has said, in different ways. But he's said it so well, and they thank God for him."[23]

As for Revilo himself, he declared that he was "not in the least astonished by the concerted campaign of defamation directed against me." He said that the campaign had begun five years earlier when he had warned that Fidel Castro was a communist and that Cuba would be turned into a Soviet missile base; although back then he had been vilified for those warnings, he was vindicated in the end. The same would prove true of his commentary about the Kennedy assassination and what it portended. "I take no pride in those predictions because no special talent was needed to make them," Oliver said. "They were merely logical deductions from known facts, and no more brilliant than a prediction that a man who drives northeast from Springfield, Illinois, on Route 66 will eventually reach Chicago." He added that he would "not be intimidated by the howling of our domestic enemies and the lamentable emotionalism of the innocent and uninformed persons who have been incited by them."[24]

Oliver followed up his original article of more than eight thousand words with a sequel of comparable length in the March 1964 *American Opinion*. "Marxmanship in Dallas: Part II" was even more vituperative than part one. "[Lee Harvey] Oswald was a young Communist punk, but, aside from his fortuitous notoriety, there was nothing unusual about him," wrote Oliver. "You have seen thousands like him, and you are paying taxes to breed or nourish swarms of them." There were "fledging Oswalds" any time "a loyal American is permitted to speak on or near a college campus," as presumably when Strom Thurmond had spoken at the University of Illinois and protestors had picketed him. Of such budding young assassins, Oliver said that it was "instructive to observe how many are deformed in body or feature as well as mind, and, if you approach near enough, you can see the hatred glistening in beady eyes. (For a close approach, a handkerchief sprinkled with ammonia will minimize the discomfort.)" Similar deviants had infested Congress, the churches, and the media: "Whether they are trying crudely or subtly to use the Communists' assassination of Kennedy to incite hatred against 'right-wing extremists,' you can no longer fancy that they are just ignorant 'intellectuals' with mixed-up ganglia. . . . You cannot mistake them when, in your very presence and with breath-taking effrontery, they discharge the diseased hatreds and homicidal lusts that fester in their gangrenous little minds."

Oliver asserted that loyal Americans' chief tasks needed to be "(a) preserving our national independence by recovering our federal government from the international vermin who have stealthily captured it, and (b) restoring as rapidly as may be—and that will be over a period of more than a decade—our Constitutional government that those vermin have all but totally subverted." It had yet to be determined who exactly were the masterminds behind the international communist conspiracy; all that was conclusively known was that "they must be phenomenally intelligent and unutterably evil." The loyal citizenry would have to expose those supervillains, for Congress never would do so: not when more than half the Senate was being "kept in line by blackmail made possible by highly-trained and expert 'call girls' operating, at the expense of American taxpayers, in collaboration with secret agents who installed concealed microphones and hidden cameras, including infra-red equipment." In conclusion, Oliver acknowledged that "apocalyptic visions of cosmic disaster are usually born of disordered imaginations." But apocalyptic and cosmic disaster was surely at hand, and "the fate of human civilization as we know it depends, I fear, on what we do this year." The ultimate question was "whether the world's most hated minority, the Christian West, shall be forever obliterated by the infinite barbarism of irrational hordes. Or, to put it in less general terms, the issue is whether your children will regret having been born."[25]

Even as the U of I Board of Trustees was deliberating Oliver's own fate, he was resuming his speaking engagements as part of the "Community Lecture Series" in Decatur, Illinois. The lectures were organized by Dale Scholz, a doctor from nearby Mt. Zion who denied that the series was a John Birch Society front even though he was a JBS member and all the speakers skewed toward a JBS point of view. Before Oliver's talk in Decatur, the publisher of a small-town weekly charged in his newspaper that the classics professor "probably did as much as any living human being to set the fires of hatred that spread into Lee Oswald's disordered brain," adding that the people who would attend Oliver's

Newspaper advertisement from March 1964 for a talk by Revilo Oliver in Decatur, Illinois. Oliver's talk coincided with the decision by the University of Illinois Board of Trustees not to take disciplinary action against him.

lecture were comparable to overfed dogs that "astonish their owners by lying down and rolling in the foulest corruption and filth they could find." For all that, the publisher—Bob Wilson of the *Prairie Post* in Maroa, Illinois—said that Oliver still had every right to speak. (Oliver was not placated, and he threatened a one-hundred-thousand-dollar libel suit against Wilson.)[26]

Publicity for Oliver's talk prominently listed his professional affiliation but also took pains to clarify that he would be speaking only for himself: "Professor Oliver's speeches and articles on Communism are his contribution as a loyal American to the preservation of his country. This is a burden voluntarily assumed as a private citizen and has, of course, no connection with his professional work in teaching and scholarly research in the field of Classical Philology at the University of Illinois." After Oliver took the podium in Decatur to cheers and a smattering of boos from an audience of at least five hundred people, he spoke for more than an hour. He raised questions that have been repeated by many other people over the years about the Kennedy assassination: Why was the president's motorcade routed directly past the Texas School Book Depository? Was there more than one shooter firing at Kennedy? Where was Oswald going when, as it was said, he shot and killed Dallas police officer J. D. Tippit? Did Oswald and Jack Ruby know each other? How could the Warren Commission be trusted to uncover and report the truth about the assassination?[27]

But the erudite professor's language during the speech was another matter entirely. According to one news account, "Oliver used the word 'vermin' six times, the word 'puke' four times and [he] made frequent use of 'spit' and 'vomit' in referring to anyone who did not share his views." He excoriated the "purulent pus" who dared criticize the JBS, "the finest Americans in our country." He sneered at Robert Kennedy for purportedly having arranged for Oswald's release from custody after the assassination attempt on Edwin Walker in Dallas, with Oliver even questioning "why Bobby himself not only remains silent but has refused an invitation to speak after me on a lecture series and to refute, if he can, anything that I have said." The professor made many other such assertions, often prefacing them by saying that although they had yet to be verified, they all came from unimpeachable sources: "I ask you to remember this if some 'Liberal' liepaper accuses me tomorrow of having made 'unsubstantiated allegations.'" Oliver also told his audience that the "puking" aimed at him would continue "unless the international Communist conspiracy decides to murder me, preferably in a fake accident." (He had been telling people for the past couple of years that he was on a communist hit list.)[28]

Oliver's Decatur talk was well received. "The audience seemed to enjoy his articulate delivery, freely sprinkled with salty words," said a reporter who

Revilo Oliver during his talk in Decatur on March 18, 1964. Hundreds of attendees cheered when he called his detractors "purulent pus." (Courtesy of the Champaign County Historical Archives, Urbana Free Library, Urbana, Illinois)

covered the lecture. While he was an adolescent, Oliver had passed the time watching "the holy men and holier women pitch the woo," as he put it; now he was preaching his own gospel in his own traveling show. One listener would say of Oliver that his "deep voice boomed and pulsed in a sort of oration which one imagines used to inhabit the Chautauqua tents and William Jennings Bryan."[29]

As 1964 progressed, according to historian Frank P. Mintz, Oliver "reveled in a growing sense of self-importance." His racism and anti-Semitism were now on regular, blatant display. In an August talk in Tucson, Arizona, he called three recently murdered civil-rights activists "cockroaches who crawled into the state of Mississippi to incite violence." That same month in Orange County, California, Oliver spoke of "the profound biological differences between human races," and he used a mock Yiddish accent to quote from a critical letter that he had received. Thirteen hundred people—consisting of what one journalist described as "middle-class businessmen and their stylishly dressed wives"— paid a dollar-fifty each to hear Oliver's California speech.[30]

Oliver's time in the spotlight peaked in September 1964 when he was subpoenaed to travel to Washington, DC, and give a deposition to the Warren Commission, a body that Oliver had claimed was "unconstitutional and illegal."[31] The commission wanted to determine whether there was any factual basis to the battery of allegations that Oliver had made in his writings and speeches. Oliver was interviewed for five hours by commission lawyer Albert Jenner, a U of I graduate. It quickly became evident that the brunt of Oliver's assertions had been grounded in presuppositions and hearsay. He had amassed snippets from articles and bulletins and tidbits from conversations with like-minded acquaintances; and from that material, he had drawn what seemed to him to be inescapable conclusions. For example, he had based his allegation that the Soviet Union had trained Lee Harvey Oswald to be an assassin on the fact that the Soviets had allowed Oswald to return to the United States and that all of Oswald's subsequent activities "were quite obviously in the Communist interest." But Oliver also acknowledged that "I had no personal knowledge that he was a Soviet agent."

Jenner asked Oliver about one of the professor's more hair-raising assertions: that John F. Kennedy's funeral had been rehearsed a full week before the president's assassination. Oliver had based that allegation on a Mississippi newspaper story about a such a rehearsal, which in fact had taken place—only it was for former president Herbert Hoover, who was then aged and gravely ill. "That is not a rehearsal for a funeral of President Kennedy a week in advance either of the funeral or of the assassination, is it?" Jenner asked Oliver. The professor denied implying that the rehearsal had been brazenly staged with advance knowledge of Kennedy's impending murder. "But it is certainly an inference that could be drawn from the facts," said Oliver. "I did not intend to exclude that possibility."[32]

After it was all over and the Warren Commission had issued its report, Jenner said that Oliver "did not produce a single item of evidence" and that his allegations had been "reckless and unfounded."[33] Oliver's star power on the JBS talk circuit was not dimmed in the slightest. Still to be seen was whether Oliver's professional standing would be diminished, which the U of I's academic freedom committee had implied might happen when it defended his right to be "ungloriously wrong and suffer the professional consequences." How would people outside JBS circles view the professor in light of all the controversy that he had generated? In particular, how would Oliver's faculty peers judge him?

Judging Oliver (or Not)

A key rationale for the university not having disciplined Oliver was that he had kept his political views out of the classroom. Oliver taught only small classes to advanced undergraduate and graduate students and, according to a handful of students who were willing to talk to the *Daily Illini*, he was a capable instructor. An undergraduate Latin major called him "a very brilliant man" and said that she had been unaware until recently that he was connected to the JBS. Other students allowed that he could be a "difficult" or "domineering" professor, but none said that his politics influenced his teaching.[34]

One potential concern about Oliver was that his speech outside the classroom might negatively influence impressionable young people, much as Leo Koch had been charged with irresponsibly encouraging young people to have premarital sex. Again, there was little evidence that such was the case. One student had regularly written letters to the *Daily Illini* back in 1961; the letters had vigorously defended Oliver and the JBS and attacked the campus NAACP and its integration efforts. In October of that year, an inflammatory flier purportedly from the NAACP was circulated on campus. It was quickly determined to be a forgery intended to rile up antiliberal and anti-Black sentiment. The university investigated and, coincidentally or not, the letters from the pro-Oliver student stopped.[35] Otherwise, students who identified as conservative seemed not to take Oliver especially seriously. In his *Daily Illini* column, John Johnson had said that the professor deserved pity. Jim Nowlan once was invited with other students to Oliver's home; he found Oliver "eccentric to say the least," and he was amused to hear talk that the professor had buried silver and other valuables in the yard to protect them against unnamed threats. After attending a speech by Oliver, Harrison Church wrote in a letter that the professor's language was so "plainly repulsive" that his warnings about the communist threat "will not only go unheeded, they will be ridiculed, as they are, in fact."[36]

The students' comments echoed those of conservatives with national reputations. Barry Goldwater called the JBS's attacks on the late president Kennedy "despicable," although Goldwater stopped short of disavowing JBS support. Russell Kirk, whose journal *Modern Age* had published Oliver's work, said that Oliver's screed against Kennedy was "silly." (Kirk added, "If every professor were expelled from the Academy who sometimes said something silly, college students would have to teach themselves.") Willmoore Kendall, who had recruited Oliver to *National Review*, wrote in his private correspondence that the U of I professor's speeches were "shameless beyond belief" and that the JBS was "the 1960s equivalent of the Know-Nothings" (although Kendall did agree with Oliver that the Soviets had been behind the Kennedy assassination). In his nationally syndicated column, William F. Buckley said that he held Oliver in the "highest affection and esteem," but the professor's thesis concerning Kennedy's murder was "disastrously wrongheaded." Buckley added that a "man who could correct the grammar of Horace is adrift in the seas of political solecism." The *National Review* founder soon received a package from Oliver in the mail. According to Buckley, the package contained "a tiny facsimile of a Florentine knife, and on the card: 'To stab your next friend in the back with, if you have another friend.'"[37]

So much for Oliver's friends. As for his professional peers, his department head, John Heller, had tried repeatedly to persuade him to tone down his extramural speech. The Department of Classics archives contain notes that Heller prepared before one of his many meetings with Oliver. The notes are undated, but they appear most likely to have come from the fall of 1964, after the publication of "Marxsmanship in Dallas" and after Oliver's more overtly anti-Semitic and racist pronouncements had been publicized. According to those notes, Heller planned to share with Oliver not an official statement of the department's views (although he had consulted with other departmental faculty); he was offering instead his "personal expression of very grave concern." The classics head believed that the university's recent decision not to take action against Oliver was "perfectly proper" in that "so far as public utterances in themselves are concerned, academic freedom extends to any mode of expression." Heller also acknowledged that the language in the university statutes on accuracy, forthrightness, and dignity was "only an admonition addressed to the teacher's conscience and good taste."

Yet Oliver had made it conspicuously clear that "your conscience is deaf to the admonition. You must expect to suffer the consequences—public disapproval, condemnation, ridicule. You delude yourself if you think the condemnation comes from a conspiracy. Just whose approval do you want to have, now and for all time? . . . So far, you are simply exposing yourself, and the spectacle is not edifying in the eyes of those whose good opinion you ought to value." Heller added that the only statutory requirements of Oliver were that he fulfill his "duties in the classroom, in the academic community, and as a scholar intent on seeking out the truth. As you know, your colleagues in the department, including me, were asked for their opinion on this question, and I am glad that their verdict

John L. Heller, longtime head of the University of Illinois Department of Classics. Heller repeatedly failed to persuade Revilo Oliver to tone down his extramural speech. (Courtesy of the University of Illinois Archives, Faculty, Staff and Student Portraits File, RS 39/2/26)

at the time was favorable to you. As I examine the present evidence, however, I have grave doubts about the accuracy of the judgment." Other documents in the departmental archives point to the evidence to which Heller was referring. Oliver's scholarly output declined markedly during the 1960s, with some years showing no academic publications at all; there also were concerns that Oliver's many speaking engagements were taking him away from the classroom and making his teaching more perfunctory than it once had been. Then, of course, there were Oliver's political writings, which, according to Heller, increasingly displayed "perversion of truth," "concealment of evidence," and "exhibitionism."[38]

Heller's meeting with Oliver appeared to be no more productive than any of their previous meetings. In March 1966, Heller told senior departmental faculty about two recent confrontations that he had had with their colleague. During an otherwise cordial phone conversation about a graduate seminar course, Oliver "suddenly changed his tone, accusing me, among various other complaints, of having threatened him with bodily harm." In a separate conversation on an unrelated departmental matter, the same thing occurred: "Again we conversed calmly and amicably until at the end he started on a still longer series of complaints and accusations.... His main point was that I had insulted him and indicated openly my disrespect for his views, and that I was engaged in a program of calculated 'harassment' in order to prevent his expressing them." Heller sounded resigned if not defeated about the whole matter, and at the end of the spring 1966 semester, he stepped down as classics department head after seventeen years in the position.[39]

Soon afterward, during the summer of 1966, Oliver made nationwide news for the final time. He told the New England Rally for God, Family and Country that a key objective of the civil-rights movement was "the complete destruction of the white race." He also said that people should dissuade themselves of the notion that if "only by some miracle all the Bolsheviks, or all the Illuminati, or all Jews were vaporized tomorrow, we should have nothing more to worry about." Oliver's incendiary remarks provoked a confrontation with JBS head Robert Welch, after which Oliver quit the JBS. He later claimed that the "B'Nai Birch" had become a "Jewish auxiliary, primarily used to keep the *goyim* confused and docile and to frustrate patriotic movements that had any potentiality of effectiveness."[40]

In subsequent years—as Oliver's claims about the JBS would indicate—the professor gravitated even more toward extremism. He became a hero to white nationalists, wrote for the anti-Semitic *Liberty Bell* magazine, and appeared on the masthead of the *Journal of Historical Review*, a publication devoted to Holocaust denial. He also prepared a promotional film for the far-right National Youth Alliance, one of whose members was William Pierce; Pierce's violently racist novel *The Turner Diaries* would help inspire Timothy McVeigh to bomb the Oklahoma City federal building in 1995. James von Brunn, a white supremacist who killed a guard at the Holocaust Museum in Washington, DC, in 2009, would point to Oliver as a key influence.[41]

Oliver did not keep his political activities secret even as he increasingly separated himself from his Department of Classics colleagues, spending the majority of his time on campus in an office in the university library.[42] Still, because he was appearing less often in the mainstream media, he did not create nearly the same degree of controversy or embarrassment that he once had done, and consequently he maintained professional respectability. *Pharos*—which calls itself an online "platform where classical scholars, and the public more broadly, can learn about and respond to appropriations of Greco-Roman antiquity by hate groups"—has documented how Oliver remained in the esteem of fellow classicists into the 1970s. For example, a longtime editor of *Classical Philology* wrote Oliver to say that he had read one of the U of I professor's scholarly articles "with intense interest and admiration," and a future president of the American Philological Association sent Oliver a letter in Latin that praised him as "a very distinguished man" and "a very learned man."[43]

Oliver also held the respect of at least one prominent scholar outside the classics, seemingly owing in part to Oliver's political views. Raymond Cattell was a widely published and cited U of I psychology professor; among his many other activities, he formulated a quasi-religious movement that he called "Beyondism." Social scientist Barry Mehler has charged that Beyondism embraced eugenics and was in fact a "neo-fascist contrivance" that was "striking for its extremism, racism, and virulent bias against the poor." In the preface to a book on Beyondism, Cattell acknowledged an intellectual debt to Revilo Oliver and cited two of his works. Another social scientist, William H. Tucker, notes that those works displayed Oliver's "single-minded focus on Jews as the underlying source of all contemporary social problems."[44]

In Oliver's home unit at the U of I, Miroslav Marcovich became the new classics department head in 1973. He seemed to try to placate Oliver, and the professor responded in kind. "Believe that we deeply appreciate all that you are doing for the department, which now has the prospect of becoming known again for scholarship instead of the antics of academic clowns," Oliver wrote to Marcovich. (It is possible that Oliver was taking a veiled swipe at Richard Scanlan, a U of I classics professor beloved by legions of undergraduates. Scanlan was renowned for dressing up as Apollo in front of his huge lecture classes and—in mock oracular fashion—predicting the scores of upcoming Illinois sporting events. Oliver previously had gone on record as vigorously opposing a promotion for Scanlan.) At a retirement dinner for Oliver and his wife Grace in April 1977, Marcovich hailed Oliver as "a great classical scholar and inspiring teacher" who had exemplified "the Golden Age of Illinois Classical Studies" and was indispensable for his "wisdom and insight" and his "enormous erudition and experience."[45]

As for top U of I administrators, they had continued to receive occasional complaints about Oliver, especially after his much-publicized break from the JBS over his remarks about Jews. "What in the world is an anti-Semitic teacher doing on the faculty of the University of Illinois?" a Connecticut newspaper asked in an editorial that was mailed to President Henry's office. "Are there no standards of decency applied by the academic community? Is a knowledge of Greek and Latin enough if a teacher violates the basic tenets of human rights?"

Letters to the president expressed similar sentiments: "We, of course, recognize the need for opposing views on matters, however Professor Oliver's position is a shame and discredit to the University's name. Do public funds have to support this neo-nazi?" In response to such queries, the U of I sent a form letter based on a template that the university had used for the past several years in connection with Oliver. The letter said that "as long as a member of the faculty meets the conditions of the accepted academic tradition, the University policy is to impose no restrictions." The letter added that "most members of the faculty would deplore [Oliver's] remarks, if asked to express themselves, but, at the same time, would defend him against institutional discipline."[46]

President Henry himself appears to have paid Oliver little heed after the storm over "Marxmanship in Dallas" back in 1964. In his memoirs, Henry briefly recapped the controversy and the decision not to take action against the professor. Then he provided a succinct conclusion: "The case of Mr. Revilo Oliver was thus closed and was soon forgotten."[47]

The Sixties Arrive

The debate over Oliver had dominated the first part of the spring 1964 semester at the U of I. The debate soon shifted back to other issues that had been percolating on campus since the start of the decade and that recently had become more contentious. In March 1964, a student sharply criticized the university disciplinary system when he was placed on probation for violating the campus housing guidelines (he had attempted to move off campus after contracting mononucleosis). The student said that the disciplinary committee had handled his case flippantly and never had made it clear what charges he was facing. Soon there were additional complaints. After a young man and young woman in an Urbana motel room were interrupted by a campus security officer, the young man said that he was no longer enrolled at the U of I and that the university should have no jurisdiction over what happened away from campus. Then a woman student was put on "informal conduct probation" for kissing her boyfriend in a parked car off campus. (The boyfriend also was a student, but he was not disciplined, indicative of the double standard at work.) The young woman protested that the incident had made her feel "cheap and ashamed" and that university regulations made it almost impossible for a couple to find any privacy.[48]

Those incidents sparked angry letters to the *Daily Illini*. "The curious doctrine of 'in loco parentis' has been elevated to a new height of absurdity," charged one such letter. "The odor is distinctly that of the police state and the contrast with the spirit of a great international center of learning is both obvious and unfortunate." The student paper compared the U of I's discipline policy with the policies at other Big Ten universities. A dean of students at the University of Wisconsin said that in loco parentis was "impossible to administrate and it involves the University in many things not connected with the educational purpose of the institution." The U of I would restructure its disciplinary system later in 1964, although student complaints about the system would continue for years to come.[49]

Civil rights was another issue of ongoing concern. In May 1964 students participated in a sit-in demonstration in Champaign. They were protesting the opposition of the National Association of Real Estate Boards to the civil-rights bill then before Congress. Fourteen students were taken into custody, including Connie Rolison, whose picture after her arrest appeared on the front page of the *Daily Illini*. Rolison was one of the relatively small number of African American students at the U of I at that time, and she would recall feeling a particular obligation to "represent and be active."[50]

The following summer was dubbed "Freedom Summer," as hundreds of college-age volunteers headed to Mississippi to register African Americans to vote. Liz Krohne joined them. She already had used her farewell column in the *Daily Illini* to call for "revolt against the unfreedom of the suburban bourgeoisie, an atmosphere in which most of us have been formed." In the South, Krohne worked for the *Mississippi Free Press*, and she witnessed the reaction of both White and Black people to the murders of the three civil-rights workers whom Revilo Oliver later would call "cockroaches." According to Krohne, White moderates were shocked by the murders, but "once the indignation was past, the episode could be repudiated and forgotten." For African Americans, "these tragedies are as inescapable as the pigmentation of one's skin." Krohne believed that White people suffered from their own lack of freedom in that they were imprisoned by "lack of introspection, and thus of personal identification with the issues of the whole community. . . . Few of them recognized their own profound loneliness." Krohne also said that she had come to recognize "the concrete truth in the truism that no man is free unless all men are free."[51]

In the fall of 1964, the Free Speech Movement erupted in Berkeley as University of California students protested campus restrictions on political speech. That October, U of I members of Students for a Democratic Society and Friends of the Student Nonviolent Coordinating Committee staged a small campus demonstration in solidarity with the Berkeley protesters. They also sent University of California president Clark Kerr a telegram: "We students at the University of Illinois protest your grave and irresponsible action in attempting to deny California students their constitutionally protected right to freedom of political expression and action." As the Berkeley demonstrations continued and several hundred students there were arrested, U of I students mounted another solidarity rally in December. "Liberty and democracy cannot survive where students aren't allowed to speak freely," said John Quirk of the Young Democrats.[52]

Roger Ebert joined the demonstrators. He was now a graduate student in English, and although he was no longer editor-in-chief of the *Daily Illini*, he maintained his "Ars Gratia" column. "This is the winter when, suddenly, we begin to see ourselves as student-citizens, and to have the imagination to act in that role," he wrote. "We are no longer willing to be the boobs and hicks in the constituency of our University." Ebert acknowledged that there still was "great, sullen apathy" among students, and he blamed it on the repressive paternalism of the university, which did not recognize that young people who "are arbitrarily ordered and punished are likely to rebel or sink into a shell of passive resentment." Ebert added that if students "accept without question the decisions of wise men who think they are acting benevolently for what they perceive to be our good, we are not scholars here, but only customers."[53]

One group of student-citizens asserted their right to political expression by rejecting the turn that the Free Speech Movement had taken. In a telegram, the U of I Young Republicans commended their Berkeley counterparts for having formally withdrawn from the movement after disagreement over the tactics that protesters were employing. The telegram praised the University of California Young Republicans "for recognizing that anarchy is not the answer to any problems, and that law and order is one of the basic foundations of American society." U of I student conservatives also helped welcome Republican presidential candidate Barry Goldwater when he stopped briefly in Champaign in October and spoke to a crowd of nine thousand people who both cheered and jeered him. Although Goldwater lost the election in a landslide, his U of I supporters were unbowed. A campus chapter of the Young Americans for Freedom was founded in December 1964 and given formal campus recognition the following month; its stance would be more militantly conservative than that of other such student groups in the past.[54]

During his campaign stop in Champaign, Barry Goldwater had accused President Lyndon Johnson of "trying to fool the people into thinking they are at peace when they are at war" in Vietnam. *Daily Illini* student news analyst Gary Porter already had been decrying the rapidly deteriorating situation in that country for the previous several months. In April 1964, he compared Johnson's Vietnam policy with that of Richard Nixon, who by then was returning to a preeminent position within the Republican Party. According to Porter, Nixon's policy asserted that "the winning of the Vietnamese War awaits only a slight change in tactics, which will issue from putting a tougher man in the White House. Johnson can only offer us a long, drawn-out war." Neither policy choice was palatable to Porter, who flatly predicted in another column the following month that the "war is unwinnable because of the fundamental and controlling fact that we are the foreigners there and not the Viet Cong." In July 1964, Porter wrote that "no one knows whether or not the President is actually ready to undertake the vastly dangerous venture implied in expanding the Vietnamese war. But if—as I suspect—he has doubts about it, he is making it ever more difficult to resist the pressures which will descend on him, when the time comes, to leave those doubts behind."[55]

That time did come soon after Johnson's election victory over Goldwater. In December 1964, about seventy-five U of I students and faculty gathered in front of the auditorium to protest US policy toward Vietnam. "Freedom cannot be won by bombs," said John Quirk of the Young Democrats, and U of I English professor Robert Welsh told the crowd, "We can call off the war in Vietnam now." The protesters were met by conservative student counter-protesters who waved signs reading "Young Americans for Freedom: Don't Negotiate Away the Life of 15 Million Vietnamese." While the antiwar demonstrators called for peace, the prowar demonstrators responded with taunts of "communists" and "appeasers."[56]

On February 10, 1965, the *Daily Illini*'s front page displayed a banner headline: "VIET NAM BATTLES RAGE." The United States had bombed North Vietnam; now there was ground fighting near Da Nang in South Vietnam with American casualties. An inside page of the newspaper carried an open letter to President Johnson from U of I members of the Young Democrats and Students for a Democratic Society. The letter called the bombing of North Vietnam a "blatant violation of international law," and it added, "It is incomprehensible that this extension of the war comes at a time when American public opinion runs more than 80 percent in favor of a cease-fire and negotiated settlement in Viet Nam." In that same issue of the paper was a column by student Tony Burba. He denounced the open letter against the war as being a "piece of trash," adding that campus "'liberals' are disgusting. They sit around on their ivory pedestals and blather about 'Great Societies' and Democratic Societies and expect to get all these things they prize so dearly for no work whatever." Burba agreed that Americans did not want war, but "talk at a negotiating table under the circumstances you 'liberals' propose would be worthless—because the Reds aren't willing to back up their talk with permanent peace, and they won't ever listen to us if we're not ready to move them out with guns if they won't go with words."[57]

The following month, in March 1965, the United States began sending ground troops into Vietnam, and the war escalated in earnest. The antiwar movement escalated as well—as did reaction against it—and pitched battles over free speech, Black Power, and the sexual revolution soon would follow at the University of Illinois and scores of other college campuses across the country. The age of student revolt had arrived, and the sixties, as they would be popularly remembered, had truly begun.[58]

CONCLUSION

Yeast and Ferment

Apart from being a year of dramatic change, the 1964–65 school year also marked the arrival of the first cohort of baby boomers at the University of Illinois. Enrollment at the Urbana campus stood at twenty-seven thousand students, up from a little more than twenty-one thousand just four years previously. That increase came at a cost. As the school year began, President David Henry in his annual state of the university report pointed to "the grim fact that for the first time in its history . . . the University of Illinois has denied enrollment to several thousand qualified students. Thus comes to reality the forecasts of the past decade." The president added that there were "grave overtones for our State and Nation as well. At a time when society demands more skills and knowledge on the part of more and more people, a condition of limitation on the development of human resources is a condition of limitation on the economic, social, and cultural health of our country." Henry said that the state of Illinois would need to increase funding in order for the U of I to meet the increased demands placed upon it.[1]

At about the same time that Henry was issuing his report, Abram L. Sachar was addressing U of I students in Assembly Hall. Sachar had been a U of I history professor and director of the Hillel Foundation before becoming the founding president of Brandeis University. He told the U of I students that "dissent, the very essence of critical thinking, must walk hand in hand with responsibility." According to Sachar, some student groups were irresponsibly displaying malice "in attacks on their elders, in arrogant questioning of the men and women who themselves fought for the very privileges of academic freedom today's students enjoy." He warned his audience that "unleashed invective is dangerous. We live in an era that lies at the very edge of violence. The climate of America is increasingly volcanic." And Sachar paraphrased the poem "Primer Lesson" by Illinois native Carl Sandburg in urging students to "look out how you use hard words, proud words. Nailed boots leave scars that never heal, and hard words wear nailed boots."[2]

U of I dean of women Miriam Shelden held a different perspective on contemporary college students. She told a 1964 meeting of the U of I Moms Association that a university was "a place of yeast and ferment where ideas are debated; where students try to sort out their own philosophies; where students rebel; where allegiances to social justice are pledged." Shelden said that students at the University of Illinois were struggling to establish their own individuality and independence; they were saying, "listen to me; I am a person, not a thing." They also increasingly were asserting that "their sexual behavior or misbehavior is their own business," an assertion with which Shelden did not agree. Yet she applauded their heightened interest in civil rights and economic inequality. "The University is not a quiet backwater; it is a throbbing, stirring place," Shelden said. She concluded by telling members of the Moms Association that they should "be not afraid. Yeast and ferment produce good bread, and from the University will go forth good students" who would "do their part to make it a better world."[3]

Shelden also regularly spoke to students themselves. Each fall, the dean told freshmen women that the ways in which they approached their college years would shape the rest of their lives. She asked the freshmen to try to visualize their futures: ten years hence, twenty years hence, and even sixty years hence in the unimaginably far-off 2020s, when the young women who were then still in their teens would be almost eighty years old. What would the world be like then?[4]

Now that we actually have reached the 2020s, we can look back six decades to the era of Shelden, Sachar, and Henry and reflect on the relevance of their words for our own times. We also can consider the implications of the Leo Koch and Revilo Oliver cases for our understanding of higher education history, as well as for contemporary debates over sex, politics, and academic freedom.

Higher Education Past and Present

The COVID-19 pandemic that hit the United States in 2020 only added to the problems already confronting higher education. Declines in enrollment have produced what one observer describes as a "death spiral"—a shortage of students compels many colleges and universities to cut programs, which in turn reduces student interest even more and creates even greater enrollment declines.[5] Gabriel Paquette recites a litany of other concerns: "the adjunctification of the professoriate; the proliferation of deans; the defunding of public universities; the depreciation of the humanities; the sharp rise in managerial salaries; the comparative stagnation of faculty and staff compensation; the conflation of a university's reputation with the fortunes of its athletic teams; and the asset-stripping that sometimes accompanies university partnerships with private enterprise."[6] There are persistent threats to cut university budgets over objectionable course content, controversies over provocative speakers on campuses, and questions about the true costs and benefits of a college education. Students are viewed—often mockingly—as having become "less resilient, or, at the least, more expressive of that lack," with a growing perception that "college is an unhealthy place," or conversely a place where student fragility is encouraged and indulged.[7]

It would be going too far to suggest that today's challenges are no different from those of the past; it is far preferable to turn students away because of high demand than it is to watch enrollments dwindle because of low demand. That said, U of I president David Henry's report from 1964 is a reminder that the challenges of the past were in fact formidable. He had pushed the university to pursue aggressive public outreach, as with the 1960 bond issue that was desperately needed to try to accommodate the coming surge of students. The ire stirred by Leo Koch and later by Revilo Oliver threatened to derail that outreach. Even after the U of I weathered those controversies and achieved passage of the bond issue, there still was not enough money for the university to do everything that it was expected to do, and rejecting qualified students was practically guaranteed to make a good number of tax-paying parents and appropriations-making lawmakers unhappy. The students already on campus also were cause for apprehension. Although members of the "silent generation" had been criticized for being too passive, they had grown sufficiently restive by 1964 to worry the likes of Abram Sachar. The concerns that he expressed about the nature of student dissent would become more pronounced and widespread in the "increasingly volcanic" years to come. Thus would University of California president Clark Kerr later say that "the 'golden years' between 1958 and 1968 were not free of difficulties" in higher education and that, although those difficulties "might not be identical to those confronted in the present," they "produced similar strains on institutions."[8]

The students whom Sachar admonished against becoming too arrogant or abusive were certainly not all activists. As late as 1966, Roger Ebert was charging in the *Daily Illini* that the majority of U of I undergraduates were "incapable of attending a demonstration, carrying a sign, or making a public speech on some current issue"; they seemed to be in college only "to get drunk, get laid, get their degree, and get out." Nor were the students of the first half of the 1960s a uniquely hardy lot. Experts and the news media fretted that they were "coddled" and "tormented" and that they suffered from "very much lowered self-esteem."[9] The students who wrote for the *Daily Illini* at the time of the Revilo Oliver case did display an admirable grasp of the importance of unfettered expression and academic freedom (indeed, they also highlighted the continuing importance of healthy, unfettered student news media).[10] In that regard, it may be tempting to draw unfavorable comparisons between the students of the past and the allegedly more ignorant and intolerant students of today. But it is worth remembering that the columnists and editorialists on the *Daily Illini* as of early 1964 were all White—they had not been subjected to the hate speech about "mongrels" and "cannibals" that Oliver brandished. For her part, Miriam Shelden was keenly aware of the challenges that African American students faced, and she tried to champion their cause even as she praised the growing social consciousness of many White students. That was precisely the kind of "yeast and ferment" that she wanted to see; and, by 1964, the progressive ideas being brewed on campuses were becoming increasingly potent: they did not suddenly emerge out of a vacuum in the latter part of the decade.

Sexual Mores Past and Present

One trend that Shelden did not approve of was students' growing insistence that their sexual behavior was their own business and not that of the university. "I cannot agree that society can give to each man or woman freedom without restraint," she told the U of I Moms Association. But the students seemed less focused on laying claim to unbridled sexual freedom than they were on freeing themselves from the arbitrary and inconsistent rules of the campus disciplinary system. By 1964, campus administrators were starting to recognize the problems with that system. As historian Beth Bailey observes, they "became increasingly aware that *in loco parentis* was a potential legal nightmare, with the universities' responsibility and liability undefined. By the time large numbers of students phrased their attacks in revolutionary terms, this system of sexual controls had already been weakened." The late-1960s "sexual revolution" had taken root during the first part of the decade, just as was the case with other significant social developments of the era.[11]

The sexual revolution reduced the stigma associated with premarital sex. There also is more acceptance of LGBTQ identities now and an greater awareness of issues relating to sexual assault and consent. But campus sex mores may be just as ritualized today as they were back in 1960 when Leo Koch wrote his infamous letter to the *Daily Illini*. "Students rarely are empowered to ask themselves, 'What do I want?' and 'What do I desire?' within a culture of hooking up," says Donna Freitas. "Instead, they spend most of their time asking, 'What am I allowed to do?' and 'What am I expected to do?' Students take the prescribed scripts and narratives that are handed down to them and do their best to perform them." Jennifer S. Hirsch and Shamus Khan assert that "a climate of shame and silence" still surrounds sex, with a message that sex is "potentially terrible and most certainly dangerous." They add, "Some people feel entitled to others' bodies, and others do not feel entitled to their own bodies."[12]

Hirsch and Khan outline a more comprehensive educational approach for young people that aims at developing "sexual citizenship," which they define as "the acknowledgment of one's own right to sexual self-determination" and recognition of "the equivalent right in others." Encouraging students to grapple with broad questions of self-determination, rights, and power is a key component of a college education; it is central to the process of what Miriam Shelden described as students "thinking, creating, [and] trying to determine their place in the world." It also advances higher education's public mission. "Universities are meant to be institutions that work for a better society and humanity, that work toward the 'common good,'" Donna Freitas argues. "Tearing down rape culture in order to build a culture of consent is one of those great common goods."[13] For all of those reasons, sex remains eminently worthy of open, vigorous discussion on college campuses.

Academic Freedom Past and Present

The continuing importance of sex as a public issue is another reason that the U of I was wrong to fire Leo Koch over his letter to the student newspaper. His view that sex should be condoned "among those sufficiently mature to engage in it without social consequences and without violating their own codes of morality and ethics" seems tame today compared with the way that it was viewed in 1960. The concepts of the "Overton window" and the "sphere of legitimate controversy" highlight the fact that public opinion on controversial matters can shift over time, with the "window" or "sphere" of what is considered to be socially or politically acceptable shifting as well.[14] Joan Wallach Scott notes that "there is nothing fixed about our social and political arrangements" and that they are "open to criticism and to change." Academic freedom allows scholars to question those prevailing arrangements and to call for the changes that they believe are needed. The same freedom extends into the classroom. "Universities should be places where novel, provocative, and even revolutionary ideas can be incubated and where students encounter views that challenge, confound, and even anger them," argues Suzanne Nossel. Back in 1960, Leo Koch's friend Harry Tiebout praised Koch for deliberately provoking "consternation, shock, dismay, and indignation" among students, thereby getting them "to think, and think hard, about serious issues." The university still fired Koch, allowing negative public opinion (and negative trustee opinion) to take precedence over professional faculty judgment.[15]

With the Revilo Oliver case of 1964, the U of I appeared to have learned its lesson. Again a faculty member expressed a politically unpalatable viewpoint: that the recently murdered John F. Kennedy was a loathsome traitor who had been liquidated by an international conspiracy. Public opinion has shifted enough over time to make highly negative views of Kennedy more acceptable; the opinion that a conspiracy killed the president is widely held (although there is considerable disagreement over what such a conspiracy may have involved). In Oliver's case, the university set aside transitory public sentiment about the late president in favor of professional judgment and the faculty member's right under the tenets of academic freedom to be "ungloriously wrong."

Of course, Oliver sounded off on much more than just the circumstances surrounding Kennedy's murder. He regularly said vile things about people of color and Jews and spouted wildly unhinged political fantasies. Those aspects of the Oliver case highlight complexities and contradictions within academic freedom, just as the Koch case does.

The concept of extramural speech can imply that when faculty speak as citizens, they are not speaking as academics; their public speech is supposedly distinct from their speech as teachers and scholars. That understanding worked to Revilo Oliver's advantage: as long as he was thought to be keeping his public utterances separate from his classroom duties and his classics scholarship, he was protected from university discipline. In contrast, Leo Koch identified himself as a U of I biology professor in his letter to the *Daily Illini*, which made him more vulnerable to charges that he was unacceptably blurring the lines between his role as a U of I faculty member and his role as a private citizen.

In considering questions about academic freedom, Joan Wallach Scott points to the "weakness of the notion that a full separation [is] in fact possible between thought and action, scholarship and politics." Koch and Oliver both serve as examples. Koch noted that he had intentionally appended his academic title to his controversial letter "to stress the fact that I was analyzing the subject from a particular perspective for which I felt myself qualified"—sex is after all a biological concern, among many other things. Koch's identity as a scientist was intertwined with his identity as a humanist; he believed that religion was being used unscientifically and inhumanely to repress young people's natural sexual desires. He also taught in a division of general studies, which originally had appealed to him because of his belief that "the relationship of science to society, and the implications of scientific method for the individual" were "the most important aspects of general education." In those ways, Koch's extramural speech in his letter to the editor was inseparable from his work as a teacher and a scholar.[16]

As for Oliver, his political speeches and writings ostensibly had little to do with his teaching or scholarship in the classics. But even though by 1964 publicity for his speeches was stressing that he was speaking only in his capacity as a citizen and not as a U of I professor, the publicity still was emphasizing that he held impeccable academic credentials, which implicitly added authority to his viewpoints. Furthermore, the *Pharos* website observes that Oliver "often invoked Classical antiquity to legitimize his views." For example, in "Marxmanship in Dallas," he compared President Kennedy to the "odious and despicable" Roman emperor Nero. In later writings (and in contrast to the nominally pro-Christian viewpoints that he previously had expressed), Oliver asserted that Christianity arose from an evil Jewish plot that had instigated "a moral decline" from "the established religions of the Graeco-Roman world." Nor has Oliver been alone in using the classics to justify far-right viewpoints. In her book *Not All Dead White Men*, Donna Zuckerberg notes that "white men who believe that white men are being oppressed" frequently argue that the White men of antiquity "gave us the beginnings of our philosophy, culture, and art. They—that is, we, their white male descendants, *deserve* to be in charge." They also want others to see the world in the same way. According to political scientist George Hawley, members of today's "alt-right" hope that "eventually a critical mass will come to share the movement's views on biological racial differences, multiculturalism, anti-Semitism, and the desirability of a white ethnostate." That is, they seek to make their views more mainstream, as has occurred over time with views about premarital sex.[17]

The idea that white supremacist talking points should enter the realm of permissible debate is profoundly disturbing to many observers. Dorothee Benz (borrowing a label from Bess Kalb) decries "Nazi-normalizing barf journalism." As she puts it, "corporate media have fallen over themselves to find acceptable ways to describe utterly unacceptable behavior, policies and decisions," thus serving to "normalize what should never be normalized." Benz argues that the US press regularly treated Donald Trump's invective as routine political news, overlooking how his branding of immigrants "as vermin who will 'infest our country'" could incite violence against them and also overlooking how his labeling of journalism as "fake news" was "one shade shy of Hitler's 'Lügenpresse' ('lying press')." In a like vein, Thomas Milan Konda has warned that "conspiratorial thinking, its increasing de facto linkage to right-wing and authoritarian politics, and the conspiracy-friendly imperatives of web-based communications have all combined in American politics to create a situation many people find extremely ominous" (and Konda was writing before the 2020 US presidential election and its aftermath).[18]

The authoritarianism and conspiracism that are manifest in contemporary politics display obvious parallels with the authoritarianism and conspiracism that were manifest in Revilo Oliver and the John Birch Society. JBS head Robert Welch claimed that democracy was "a deceptive phrase, a weapon of demagoguery, and a perennial fraud." Oliver spoke of "international vermin" who allegedly had captured the US government; he also called murdered civil-rights activists "cockroaches" and the news media "liepapers." Today's conspiracy-minded QAnon movement has been compared to "a kind of John Birch Society for the 4chan age." Political scientist Christopher Towler sees another parallel: "Just as the John Birch Society emerged in the midst of the civil rights movement, today's far-right movements formed as a reaction to the election of Barack Obama—a milestone for racial equality." A surge of far-right propaganda followed Obama's election as US president, with college campuses a key target.[19]

Therein lies an irony in the Revilo Oliver case. Back in 1964, the same year that Oliver's "Marxmanship in Dallas" was published, Abram Sachar told U of I students that "the essential purpose of the university" was "the search for truth, for the facts of the matter." He added that "the process of dissent is integral to the testing of ideas." And yet, Sachar said, "the bigoted shriek of the mob on the perimeter of legitimate dissent is a painful noise."[20] Revilo Oliver was a voice from the perimeter making an increasingly painful noise as the years passed. His version of the truth and his purported "facts of the matter" wilted under critical scrutiny. But he still maintained a national following as a speaker espousing the perspective of the JBS, a group that Oliver said constituted "the finest Americans in our country" (not unlike the time when Donald Trump spoke of "very fine people" on the side of violent white supremacist demonstrations in Charlottesville, Virginia, in 2017). Oliver did his best to push his extremist views toward the center of legitimate dissent. As for his academic peers—the ones entrusted by the precepts of academic freedom to condemn him for being "ungloriously wrong"—they largely seemed to look the other way, according to *Pharos*: "Oliver used his position as a member of the academy and as a professor of Classics in particular to legitimize his hateful politics up until his death in 1994, maintained professional correspondence with many distinguished scholars throughout the period of his most virulent political activism, and published in the most prestigious journals in Classics."[21]

In those ways, Revilo Oliver was normalized. He serves as a prime example of how academic freedom, far from protecting only liberal faculty, also can protect faculty who spew hate speech over a period of several decades. (It was in fact Leo Koch, the left-leaning professor, who was left unprotected at the U of I.) In addition, Oliver shows how academic freedom's self-regulating professionalism does not always challenge ideas that seem truly dangerous (as opposed to what Koch said years ago about sex, which today seems to represent conventional wisdom).

For all that, the U of I was right not to discipline Oliver, and it also was right to defer to the professional judgment of faculty, adhering to a principle that still must be upheld today even in the face of severe challenges to faculty autonomy. Higher education historian John R. Thelin observes that "a shrinking full-time tenured faculty [has] left a vacuum in providing checks and balances" on college administrators, and Christopher Newfield argues that "senior politicians and their business allies" have increasingly imposed privatization on higher education with the acquiescence of university leaders even as the general public has maintained support for education as a public good."[22]

In such a climate, as Thomas Milan Konda suggests, it is especially dangerous "to circumscribe free speech or have an authority designate which ideas are reasonable and which are conspiracist nonsense."[23] That is simply because that authority—whether it be an elected representative or a university president, trustee, or donor—may have a decidedly self-interested view on what is reasonable or nonsense. The same holds true of such concepts as academic responsibility (which was wielded against Leo Koch), responsible dissent (which was what Abram Sachar urged students to practice), or civility (which was the stated rationale for the U of I denying employment to Steven Salaita in 2014 after his "uncivil" tweets about Israel). "'Civility' is a laudable ideal, and many of us wish that American public life had more of it today," wrote the leadership of the American Historical Association in response to the Salaita case. "But imposing the requirement of 'civility' on speech in a university community or any other sector of our public sphere—and punishing infractions—can only backfire. Such a policy produces a chilling effect, inhibiting the full exchange of ideas that both scholarly investigation and democratic institutions need."[24]

The need for a full exchange of ideas strongly discourages putting limits on classroom expression or speech from outside campus speakers. At the same time, accusing today's students of being snowflakes or being more fragile than their predecessors is unfair and not supported by historical evidence. Nor is it reasonable to expect students—many of whom display a commitment to justice and equality at least as strong as that of students of the 1960s—to turn the other cheek to plainly bigoted speech, or to "suck it up" under the premise that it will toughen them (a premise that John Durham Peters has ironically characterized as "homeopathic machismo"). In Ulrich Baer's words, students who fight for equality reject turning "every neo-Nazi and hard-core pornographer into a free speech apostle defending our country's fundamental freedoms," while those students also resist being depicted themselves as "child-like, ignorant, or censorial traitors."[25]

Another scholar, Keith E. Whittington, is a staunch advocate of campus free speech, but he warns against "posing a false choice between inclusivity and free inquiry." Whittington says that along with freedom, universities also must nurture mutual tolerance and respect: "Universities are safe places for expressing often profound disagreements to the extent that they insist that members of the campus community tolerate such disagreements and recognize the right of even those very different from themselves to equally enjoy the benefits of the campus." Regarding unpopular speech on campuses, Suzanne Nossel notes that historically "the suppression of disfavored ideas has served to reinforce power structures and suppress dissent," whereas grappling "with objectionable viewpoints can help refine and strengthen the arguments against them." She recommends separating "the content of the speech from the speakers' right to express themselves—where appropriate reject the former while defending the latter." Nossel also suggests that university leaders "simultaneously affirm institutional values, show empathy toward those affronted by speech, and affirm the rights of the speaker."[26]

It is important to remember that despite all the rhetoric over the suppression of free speech in higher education, the open exchange of ideas takes place on campuses every day. In his treatise on academic freedom, Henry Reichman highlights the experiences of University of Wisconsin–Milwaukee professor Joel Berkowitz, who has observed that routine classroom interactions never make the news: "'Students With Diametrically Opposed Views Smile & Nod at One Another' is not a headline. But maybe it should be. Neither is 'Student Raises Voice in Heated Classroom Discussion, but No Harm Done, and People Learned Stuff.' The truly worrying classroom sessions . . . are when it's like pulling teeth to get anyone to participate at all. Maybe someone could endow a center to combat that sort of thing. Seriously, though, we already have that: it's called a university."[27] In sum, universities endure as places where the process of "yeast and ferment" and of ideas being formulated and tested continues unabated.

Coda

The sixties—the era of the antiwar movement and the reaction against it—were trying times for U of I president David Henry. "With acts of vandalism occurring with frequency, with hostile editorials an almost daily occurrence, with anonymous threats on personal safety, and with the presence of the National Guard [on campus] on two occasions, personal living was not without its apprehension and constraints," he recalled in his memoirs. He felt a growing disconnection between himself and students (one of whom would remember him as "a cipher, this invisible person"). Henry also recognized a growing disconnection between higher education and the public. "The universities today are at the vortex of a social storm," he said in 1968. "They are pulled and hauled from all sides, from the radical left, from the radical right and from the backlash on both of these. As the agents of the extremes try to 'radicalize' students, the latter in turn seek to use the universities as the agents of the 'reforms' as defined by them." But Henry still asserted that "the university is one of the few agencies in world society which stands for idealism, for the improvement of the human lot, for the advancement of knowledge and the encouragement of values essential to a civilization.... In spite of the fragile nature of a university, it has a thousand years of history. It has survived other times of unrest and unease, and it will again." Henry retired in the spring of 1971 and died in 1995. His *New York Times* obituary noted that he had been "frequently on the firing line" as U of I president, with the Leo Koch and Revilo Oliver cases cited as examples. The *Times* also eulogized Henry as "a quiet, forceful man who could energize a board meeting with cool, detached efficiency."[28]

Miriam Shelden had arrived at the U of I several years before Henry, and she still would be there when he departed. On occasion, she had fought frustrating battles with the university administration on behalf of the dean of women's office. ("It has been a year of overloads met by overwork by each of the staff," she wrote at the conclusion of one of her office's annual reports. "Yet we pick up and work again tomorrow.")[29] By the end of the 1960s, the dean of women's position had been eliminated altogether, and Shelden served instead as dean of student personnel and then as associate chancellor for affirmative action.

In the fall of 1971, Shelden delivered a campus talk titled "The University: A Man's World?" She began by recalling the patronizing attitudes toward women that she had encountered in the US Navy, and she added that she had found the situation to be little better at the U of I: "The University, like the Navy, still has its prejudices against women, still perpetuates the stereotypes, and is not yet a climate where women's abilities are sought and fully used, where expectancies for women students are still lower than those for men. The subtle, almost unconscious discrimination persists." Shelden cited statistics showing that women were grossly underrepresented on the faculty and especially in administrative positions (there was only one woman department head on the Urbana campus). She also compared the struggle for gender equality to that for racial equality: "Some people view the two struggles as an either/or proposition. I do not hold that view." Shelden saw Black people and women as similarly "seeking and demanding jobs that use their full talents, participation in decision-making, and the right to help shape future patterns of education"; both groups were "asking that they share the power now largely located in the white male in universities and elsewhere." She ended by saying that the "future is not rosy; there will be a long hard struggle." But she hoped that the university would one day be transformed from a White man's world into "a University of all of us." Shelden left the U of I on disability leave in 1973 and died of cancer two years later.[30]

Some of the African American women whom Shelden had helped mentor as students during the early 1960s returned to the U of I campus in 2018 for a reunion of their Delta Sigma Theta sorority chapter. Carol Easton Lee (also known as Safisha Madhubuti) had become an endowed professor at Northwestern University with a specialization in culture and literacy in education; other women at the reunion had assumed leadership positions in government and business. "These are the people that I am safe with," said Eleanor Saunders Towns of her U of I sorority sisters. "They know my secrets; I know theirs." Connie Rolison Corbett, who had been arrested during a 1964 sit-in protest in Champaign, reflected on her college years and what had not changed since then for young Black people: "I knew my parents, and their parents, and *their* parents—we for years and years and years had always been told, 'You'll have to be twice or three times as good.' And it was true then, and it's still true, unfortunately."[31]

Liz Krohne—who had left the U of I in the summer of 1964 to travel to Mississippi and who had written of hardships "as inescapable as the pigmentation of one's skin"—stayed in the South after Freedom Summer. She married an organizer for the Student Nonviolent Coordinating Committee, and they had two children together. After the marriage ended, she worked as a school social worker in Madison, Wisconsin, for many years, becoming known as Betsy Shirah and eventually remarrying. Her 2020 obituary observed that she had always "passionately loved justice" and had long fought "for the rights of children and families who were marginalized" and for environmental and labor causes. The obituary also quoted Roger Ebert's recollections of her from their days together at the *Daily Illini*: "As a writer she had a gift and a clear voice, and we thought her destined for remarkable things."[32]

While she was still at the U of I, Krohne had presented a student letter to the university Board of Trustees calling for the Leo Koch case to be reopened, which of course never happened. The following year, in 1964, Koch was living in New York City and working for the Sexual Freedom League, an organization that he had cofounded. "Freedom of expression truly exists only when the most despised person may express the most hated idea in the most obnoxious way," the league declared in one of its fliers. "Besides defending freedom of expression, we defend the right to engage in sexual activity—including the exhibition and viewing of erotic films. We consider breasts and sex organs to be far healthier than the sadistic violence which Hollywood prefers."[33] Koch also wrote several articles for nudist magazines (he later would say that they were the only publications that would print his work). After he divorced his wife Shirley, he remarried and moved to Rockland County, New York. Koch advocated legalizing marijuana and joined the antiwar movement, organizing a group of protesters to participate in the 1967 March on the Pentagon. Two years later, he attended the Woodstock festival, where his wife sold concessions.[34]

In March 1970, the *Daily Illini* marked the tenth anniversary of Koch's letter to the student newspaper by sending a reporter to New York to interview him. The formerly crew-cut, clean-shaven professor now sported long hair, a beard, and a black protest armband. He slept on the floor below a Viet Cong flag on the wall. "I in no way regret my decision to send the letter" back in 1960, Koch told the student reporter. "But my position today has changed. Instead of merely condoning sexual intercourse between mature individuals, I now strongly advocate it." Koch also had become chair of the Rockland County Liberal Party. A local newspaper noted that his "outspoken and sometimes eccentric advocacy of liberal causes made him a figure of scorn, amusement, abuse, and admiration." In August 1970 he abruptly quit his party post and left town. "He told me he was leaving not in victory but in disappointment," a friend said. "Things aren't getting any better around here, and he decided he'd be better off doing something he wanted to do"—which turned out to be moving his family to Arkansas and becoming a homesteader.[35] Koch lived the rest of his days out of the public eye, and he died in 1982.

Ira Latimer, who had instigated the campaign attacking Leo Koch and the U of I after the publication of Koch's letter, continued his self-described "ultra-conservative" activities. In 1968 he denounced the Kerner Commission report that condemned White racism and structural inequality in American society; according to Latimer, the report ignored the fact that communists controlled the civil-rights movement. Latimer also served as an executive of the American Federation of Small Businesses, which he characterized as a "conservative, anticommunist, antisocialist, pro-free market economy and pro-capitalism" organization. When Latimer died in 1985, though, his *Chicago Tribune* obituary highlighted his earlier work for the Chicago Civil Liberties Committee: a group that had "protested religious education in public schools, criticized police methods, served as a watchdog for the civil rights of defendants and sought equal opportunity in government jobs for blacks."[36]

Revilo Oliver and his wife Grace had befriended Latimer and fed him information about supposedly subversive faculty, administrators, and organizations on the U of I campus. After his 1977 retirement from the university, Oliver devoted himself to his political writings, warning readers that he would not "soothe [them] by retelling any of the fairy tales of which Americans seem never to tire" or appealing to "the personal wishes and emotional fixations that are commonly called 'faith' or 'ideals.'" The 1980 election of Ronald Reagan as US president—a triumph for longtime conservatives who back in the 1960s had enthusiastically supported Barry Goldwater—did not cheer Oliver in the least. Reagan had worked as an actor in Hollywood, which, according to Oliver, was controlled by Jews; Reagan also supported Israel. Such associations proved for Oliver that American conservatism was "finished." It had fallen prey to "dangerously antiquarian illusions" and ignored the "fundamental question [of] whether our race still has the will-to-live or is so biologically degenerate that it will choose extinction—to be absorbed in a pullulant and pestilential mass of mindless mongrels, while the triumphant Jews keep their holy race pure and predatory." In 1994, ill with cancer and fearing that his mind was failing, Oliver shot himself in the head, ending his own life just as his father had done sixty-five years earlier.[37]

Back when Oliver's "Marxmanship in Dallas" was published, Roger Ebert had commented on the resulting furor in his *Daily Illini* column. "The principle of freedom of speech, as written into the constitution, is nearly 200 years old now and should not be a surprise to any literate citizen," he had written then as a college senior. "Yet each new generation seems to discover it with mixed feelings. So many of us agree with freedom in general, but object to someone else's freedom when it causes us discomfort. Yet freedom cannot exist for us unless it exists, as well, for 'the other guy.' Freedom and tolerance, then, are like the proverbial horse and carriage: you can't have one without the other."[38]

Ebert left the U of I and his hometown of Urbana in 1966. The next year, he was hired as the film critic for the *Chicago Sun-Times*. He won a Pulitzer Prize in 1975, and subsequently he became arguably the most famous movie critic in the country, joining fellow Chicago critic Gene Siskel in hosting a long-running syndicated television series that reviewed current movies. After grappling with alcoholism for years, Ebert quit drinking in 1979. He married Chaz Hammelsmith in 1992, later saying that "she saved me from the fate of living out my life alone, which was where I seemed to be heading."[39] In 1999 he helped start an annual film festival called Ebertfest in Champaign-Urbana. A recurrence of salivary gland cancer robbed him of his ability to talk in 2006, but he persevered in writing about the movies and the world.

"I know it is coming, and I do not fear it," wrote Ebert about death not long before it came to him in 2013. He had kept the social values of his Catholic upbringing, but not the theology. "All I require of a religion is that it be tolerant of those who do not agree with it," Ebert said. He summarized his political beliefs as being centered on kindness: "To make others unhappy is where all crime starts. We must try to contribute joy to the world. That is true no matter what our problems, our health, our circumstances. We must try. I didn't always know this and am happy I lived long enough to find it out."[40]

The circumstances that higher education now faces are difficult, and its problems are many. It may be challenging at times to maintain one's faith and ideals, items on the lengthy list of things that Revilo Oliver held in contempt. There is no point in longing for an idealized past that never existed.

Nevertheless, we should keep faith in the ideal that Miriam Shelden called "a university of *all* of us," and try to realize it: a "stirring place where ideas fight for the supremacy of truth," and a place that shapes young people who are "resolved to do their part to make it a better world." Such a university remains one of our best hopes of propagating freedom, tolerance, kindness, and joy.

Notes

Introduction

1. David D. Henry memoirs, David D. Henry Papers, University of Illinois at Urbana-Champaign (U of I) Archives, Series No. 2/12/20 [hereafter, Henry memoirs], box 25; David D. Henry to Gordon Ray, April 22, 1964, Henry memoirs, box 28.

2. See, for example, Christopher Newfield, *The Great Mistake: How We Wrecked Public Universities and How We Can Fix Them* (Baltimore, MD: Johns Hopkins University Press, 2016); Donna Freitas, *Consent on Campus* (New York: Oxford University Press, 2018); Henry Reichman, *The Future of Academic Freedom* (Baltimore, MD: Johns Hopkins University Press, 2019); Richard E. Vatz, "Fighting for Conservatives under Attack in Academe," *InsideHigherEd.com*, November 25, 2020, https://www.insidehighered.com/views/2020/11/25/higher-education-doesnt-adequately-support-conservatives-and-their-academic-freedom; Ulrich Baer, *What Snowflakes Get Right: Free Speech, Truth, and Equality on Campus* (New York: Oxford University Press, 2019); "ADL: White Supremacist Propaganda Distribution Hit All-Time High in 2019," *ADL.org*, February 12, 2020, https://www.adl.org/news/press-releases/adl-white-supremacist-propaganda-distribution-hit-all-time-high-in-2019.

3. See, for example, Megan Brenan, "Birth Control Still Tops List of Morally Acceptable Issues," *Gallup.com*, May 29, 2019, https://news.gallup.com/poll/257858/birth-control-tops-list-morally-acceptable-issues.aspx; Art Swift, "Majority in U.S. Still Believe JFK Killed in a Conspiracy," *Gallup.com*, November 15, 2013, https://news.gallup.com/poll/165893/majority-believe-jfk-killed-conspiracy.aspx; Beth Bailey, *Sex in the Heartland* (Cambridge, MA: Harvard University Press, 1999), 1–2; Kathryn

S. Olmsted, *Real Enemies: Conspiracy Theories and American Democracy, World War I to 9/11* (New York: Oxford University Press, 2009), 111–48.

4. Bailey, *Sex in the Heartland*, 76; Leo F. Koch, "Advice on Sex" (letter to the editor), *Daily Illini*, March 18, 1960, 8; Revilo P. Oliver, "Marxmanship in Dallas," *American Opinion*, 7, no. 2 (February 1964), 17, http://archive.org/stream/MarxmanshipIn Dallas/MarxmanshipInDallas_djvu.txt; Susan J. Douglas, *Where the Girls Are: Growing Up Female with the Mass Media* (New York: Times Books, 1994), 23.

5. Leo Koch Papers, Biographical Material, box 1, folder 1, Wisconsin Historical Society, Madison; Koch, "Advice on Sex," 8.

6. Richard Dudman, *Men of the Far Right* (New York: Pyramid, 1962), 85; Eric Cavaliero, "Slain Rights Workers Called 'Cockroaches,'" *Tucson Daily Citizen*, August 25, 1964, 3; Revilo P. Oliver, "Postscripts," *Liberty Bell*, February 1985, 3–4. In his 1985 article (which quoted from his 1966 speech), Oliver denied actually having advocated vaporizing Jews, but he also scorned what he called "the world-conquering Sheenies who have occupied and rule what was once a White Man's country."

7. Stanley Fish, *Versions of Academic Freedom: From Professionalism to Revolution* (Chicago: University of Chicago Press, 2014), 1–18.

8. Matthew W. Finkin and Robert C. Post, *For the Common Good: Principles of American Academic Freedom* (New Haven, CT: Yale University Press, 2009), 7; McGuire quoted in Reichman, *Future of Academic Freedom*, 274.

9. Finkin and Post, *For the Common Good*, 154; Reichman, *Future of Academic Freedom*, 174; Joan Wallach Scott, *Knowledge, Power, and Academic Freedom* (New York: Columbia University Press, 2019), 49, 80.

10. John Karl Wilson, "A History of Academic Freedom in America" (PhD diss., Illinois State University, 2014), 19–20, https://ir.library.illinoisstate.edu/etd/257; Henry memoirs; Finkin and Post, *For the Common Good*, 42–43.

11. Wilson, "History of Academic Freedom," 25, 28, 43. See also John Durham Peters, *Courting the Abyss: Free Speech and the Liberal Tradition* (Chicago: University of Chicago Press, 2005), 166; Steven Helle, "A Theoretical Framework for Media Law Courses," *Journalism Educator* 46, no. 2 (Summer 1991): 7.

12. Ellen W. Schrecker, *No Ivory Tower: McCarthyism and the Universities* (New York: Oxford University Press, 1986), 341; Vatz, "Fighting for Conservatives"; Reichman, *Future of Academic Freedom*, 105–35.

13. See Scott, *Knowledge, Power, and Academic Freedom*, 69–93; Reichman, *Future of Academic Freedom*, 20–22, 74–76; John K. Wilson, "Academic Freedom and Extramural Utterances: The Leo Koch and Steven Salaita Cases at the University of Illinois," *AAUP Journal of Academic Freedom* 6 (2015), https://www.aaup.org/JAF6/academic-freedom-and-extramural-utterances-leo-koch-and-steven-salaita-cases-university#.Xy7muol7lBy.

14. See Robert Mackey, "Professor's Angry Tweets on Gaza Cost Him a Job," *New York Times*, September 12, 2014, https://nyti.ms/1qQEHoP.

15. Peters, *Courting the Abyss*, 155; Mari J. Matsuda, "Public Response to Racist Speech: Considering the Victim's Story," *Michigan Law Review* 87, no. 8 (1989): 2323; Baer, *What Snowflakes Get Right*, xiii, xv, xxi.

16. Reichman, *Future of Academic Freedom*, 174; John K. Wilson, "An Interview with Henry Reichman on the Future of Academic Freedom," *Academeblog.org*, April 16, 2019, https://academeblog.org/2019/04/16/an-interview-with-henry-reichman-on-the-future-of-academic-freedom/. See also Jennifer Ballengee, "Academic Freedom and Responsibility," *InsideHigherEd.com*, December 16, 2020, https://www.insidehighered.com/views/2020/12/16/academic-freedom-and-diversity-higher-education-opinion.

17. Scott, *Knowledge, Power, and Academic Freedom*, 19, 118.

18. John R. Thelin, *Going to College in the Sixties* (Baltimore, MD: Johns Hopkins University Press, 2018), Kindle, chap. 1.

19. See, for example, David Lance Goines, *The Free Speech Movement* (Berkeley, CA: Ten Speed, 1993).

20. Scott, *Knowledge, Power, and Academic Freedom*, 121; David F. Labaree, *A Perfect Mess: The Unlikely Ascendancy of American Higher Education* (Chicago: University of Chicago Press, 2017), 142.

21. Brian Ward, ed., introduction to *The 1960s: A Documentary Reader* (Malden, MA: Wiley-Blackwell, 2010), 6–7.

22. Bailey, *Sex in the Heartland*, 1; Andrew Hartman, *A War for the Soul of America: A History of the Culture Wars* (Chicago: University of Chicago Press, 2015), 2.

23. Roger L. Geiger, *American Higher Education since World War II* (Princeton, NJ: Princeton University Press, 2019), 129; John R. Thelin, *A History of American Higher Education*, 3rd ed. (Baltimore, MD: Johns Hopkins University Press, 2019), Kindle, chap. 7; David D. Henry, *Challenges Past, Challenges Present: An Analysis of American Higher Education since 1930* (San Francisco: Jossey-Bass, 1975), 112; Clark Kerr, foreword to Henry, *Challenges Past*, ix.

24. Labaree, *Perfect Mess*, 142, 150; Thelin, *Going to College*, chap. 3.

25. Ward, introduction, 7, 9; Bailey, *Sex in the Heartland*, 11–12.

26. Michael V. Metz, *Radicals in the Heartland: The 1960s Student Protest Movement at the University of Illinois* (Urbana: University of Illinois Press, 2019), Kindle, preface; Rose K. Goldsen, Morris Rosenberg, Robin M. Williams Jr., and Edward A. Suchman, *What College Students Think* (Princeton, NJ: D. Van Nostrand, 1960), 199; Morton M. Hunt and Rena Corman, "The Tormented Generation," *Saturday Evening Post*, October 12, 1963, 30; Rita Hoffmann, "Swept with Confused Alarms: Psychological Climate on Campus," *Mademoiselle*, August 1964, 261; Marti Sauer, "Eth[ical] Values Relate to Student Sex," *Daily Illini*, March 5, 1963, 5. (The printed headline accompanying the Sauer article contained the error "*Ethnic* Values.")

27. Hunt and Corman, "Tormented Generation," 30; Sauer, "Eth[ical] Values," 5; Douglas, *Where the Girls Are*, 25; Bailey, *Sex in the Heartland*, 11.

28. See Thelin, *Going to College*, chaps. 3–4.

29. Rebecca E. Klatch, *A Generation Divided: The New Left, the New Right, and the 1960s* (Berkeley: University of California Press, 1999), 30; Roger Ebert, ed., *An Illini Century* (Urbana: University of Illinois Press, 1967), 188.

30. Thelin, *Going to College*, chap. 1.

31. Hanna Rosin, *The End of Men: And the Rise of Women* (New York: Riverhead, 2012), 17–21; Vanessa Grigoriadis, *Blurred Lines: Rethinking Sex, Power, and Consent on Campus* (Boston: Houghton Mifflin Harcourt, 2017), Kindle, introduction.

32. Koch, "Advice on Sex," 8; Dick Hutchison and Dan Bures, "Sex Ritualized," *Daily Illini*, March 16, 1960, 6; Freitas, *Consent on Campus*, 78–79.

33. Leo Koch class notes on humanism and religion, January 1960, in Harry M. Tiebout Papers, U of I Archives, Series No. 15/16/21, box 15; Revilo P. Oliver, "The Conspiracy against America," *American Mercury*, May 1960, 14–15.

34. Hartman, *War for the Soul of America*, 6–7.

35. George Hawley, *The Alt-Right* (New York: Oxford University Press, 2019), 1–38; Damon T. Berry, *Blood and Faith: Christianity in American White Nationalism* (Syracuse, NY: Syracuse University Press, 2017), 19.

36. Jeremy Bauer-Wolf, "White Nationalist Defies Auburn," *InsideHigherEd.com*, April 19, 2017, https://www.insidehighered.com/news/2017/04/19/white-nationalist-backed-court-order-appears-auburn; Heidi Beirich, "Holocaust Museum Shooter Had Close Ties to Prominent Neo-Nazis," Southern Poverty Law Center, June 10, 2009, https://www.splcenter.org/hatewatch/2009/06/10/holocaust-museum-shooter-had-close-ties-prominent-neo-nazis; Thomas Milan Konda, *Conspiracies of Conspiracies* (Chicago: University of Chicago Press, 2019), 162, 330.

37. See Dorothee Benz, "Nazi-Normalizing Barf Journalism: A Brief History," *Fairness and Accuracy in Reporting*, November 1, 2019, https://fair.org/home/nazi-normalizing-barf-journalism-a-brief-history/; Hawley, *Alt-Right*.

38. Henry memoirs; "Is Case of Unusual Interest," *Paxton* (IL) *Record*, November 6, 1919, 1.

39. Robert Jung, "Cabbages and Kings," *Daily Illini*, March 4, 1964, 6.

Chapter 1. Tidal Wave

1. Michael V. Metz, *Radicals in the Heartland: The 1960s Student Protest Movement at the University of Illinois* (Urbana: University of Illinois Press, 2019), Kindle, conclusion; *Illini Years: A Picture History of the University of Illinois* (Urbana: University of Illinois Press, 1950), 115–18.

2. Winton U. Solberg and Robert W. Tomilson, "Academic McCarthyism and Keynesian Economics: The Bowen Controversy at the University of Illinois," *History of Political Economy* 29, no. 1 (1997): 56–57, 63, 67.

3. Robert M. MacIver, *Academic Freedom in Our Time* (New York: Columbia University Press, 1955), 63; Ellen W. Schrecker, *No Ivory Tower: McCarthyism and the Universities* (New York: Oxford University Press, 1986), 340.

4. Nicholas Wisseman, "Falsely Accused: Cold War Liberalism Reassessed," *Historian* 66, no. 2 (Summer 2004): 321.

5. Wisseman, "Falsely Accused," 324, 327; Walter Gellhorn, ed., *The States and Subversion* (Ithaca, NY: Cornell University Press, 1952), 78; "University Ban on Political Speakers," in Harry M. Tiebout Papers, University of Illinois at Urbana-Champaign (U of I) Archives, Series No. 15/16/21, box 8; "An Act to Prohibit the University of Illinois from Extending the Use of Its Facilities to Subversive, Seditious, and Un-American Organizations," Robben W. Fleming Papers, U of I Archives, Series No. 14/2/21, box 1.

6. Wisseman, "Falsely Accused," 329–30. Stoddard also had become embroiled in an unlikely controversy over a cancer nostrum promoted by a top U of I administrator; Stoddard's pronounced skepticism toward the nostrum pitted him against a number of lawmakers and trustees (George D. Stoddard, *"Krebiozen": The Great Cancer Mystery* [Boston: Beacon, 1955]).

7. Jim Large, "Unidentified Board Member Explains Trustees' Views," *Daily Illini*, July 28, 1953, 4; "Crime and Punishment," *Daily Illini*, July 28, 1953, 6; "Morey Honored, Opinionated," *Daily Illini*, October 1, 1965, 9. See also Metz, *Radicals in the Heartland*, chap. 1.

8. David D. Henry memoirs, David D. Henry Papers, U of I Archives, Series No. 2/12/20, box 25 [hereafter, Henry memoirs].

9. Ibid. See also Metz, *Radicals in the Heartland*, chap. 2.

10. Schrecker, *No Ivory Tower*, 341; Henry memoirs; "People: The Younger Generation," *Time*, November 5, 1951, http://content.time.com/time/subscriber/article/0,33009,856950,00.html.

11. See William Strauss and Neil Howe, *Generations: The History of America's Future, 1584 to 2069* (New York: William Morrow, 1991), 279–94.

12. Gail Sheehy, *New Passages* (New York: Ballantine, 1995), 29; William Manchester, *The Glory and the Dream: A Narrative History of America, 1932–1972* (Boston: Little, Brown, 1973), 580.

13. "People: The Younger Generation"; William Sloane Coffin Jr., "Heirs to Disillusion," *Nation*, May 16, 1959, 449; "Tension beneath Apathy," *Nation*, May 16, 1959, 440; Dorothy Barclay, "The 'Silent Generation' Speaks Up," *New York Times Magazine*, May 15, 1960, 96.

14. Philip E. Jacob, *Changing Values in College* (New York: Harper and Row, 1957), 1–12; Rose K. Goldsen, Morris Rosenberg, Robin M. Williams Jr., and Edward A. Suchman, *What College Students Think* (Princeton, NJ: D. Van Nostrand, 1960), 2.

15. Otto Butz, ed., *The Unsilent Generation* (New York: Rinehart, 1958), 8–12.

16. Bob Perlongo, "Off the Cuff," *Daily Illini*, January 8, 1955, 4.

17. Edward D. Eddy Jr., "Paradox in Parenthesis," *Nation*, May 16, 1959, 443; Robb K. Burlage, "The Silent Faculty," *Nation*, May 16, 1959, 444–45.

18. Eddy, "Paradox in Parenthesis," 441; Barclay, "Silent Generation," 96; Jacob, *Changing Values*, 4.

19. Sheehy, *New Passages*, 32.

20. "Things to Watch," *Daily Illini*, September 13, 1955, 12.

21. Henry memoirs.

22. Ibid. After long and heated debate, the University of Illinois opened a new Chicago campus just west of downtown in 1965.

23. Lex Tate and John Franch, *An Illini Place: Building the University of Illinois Campus* (Urbana: University of Illinois Press, 2017), 47; David D. Henry, *Challenges Past, Challenges Present: An Analysis of American Higher Education since 1930* (San Francisco: Jossey-Bass, 1975), 99. See also Roger L. Geiger, *American Higher Education since World War II* (Princeton, NJ: Princeton University Press, 2019), 129–36.

24. Geiger, *American Higher Education*, 133; John R. Thelin, *Going to College in the Sixties* (Baltimore, MD: Johns Hopkins University Press, 2018), Kindle, chap. 2. See also Henry, *Challenges Past*, 99–103.

25. Henry, *Challenges Past*, 103; Tate and Franch, *Illini Place*, 39; Jan Johnson, "Opinions on T-Dorm Life Voiced by House Officers," *Daily Illini*, January 5, 1956, 5; Toni Greene, "Housing Director Announces Plans for Permanent Housing Facilities," *Daily Illini*, September 26, 1959, 3.

26. Bond issue promotional materials in Universities Bond Issue Referendum 1959–60 folder, Dean of Men Administrative Subject File, U of I Archives, Series No. 41/2/31, box 5 [hereafter, Bond issue promotional materials]; "Facilities for College of Education Cover Campus—From End to End," *Daily Illini*, October 29, 1959, 9.

27. See Dick Icen, "Ma-Wan-Da Tree in Danger," *Daily Illini*, June 18, 1956, 13; Tom Barber, "Disease Destroys Noted Landmark, Ma-Wan-Da Elm," *Daily Illini*, July 24, 1958, 1; "Shade's Gone; 1,000 Stumps Line UI Walks," *Daily Illini*, September 19, 1959, 5; Kathy Gauen, "Okay Tree Planting Fund," *Daily Illini*, January 12, 1962, 3; Tate and French, *Illini Place*, 13, 55. These sources estimate the number of affected U of I elms as ranging from about eighteen hundred to about twenty-four hundred.

28. Henry, *Challenges Past*, 113; "Henry Defines 10-Year Needs," *Daily Illini*, July 31, 1958, 1.

29. Henry memoirs.

30. Bond issue promotional materials.

31. Tom Barber, "Democrats Urge Bond Defeat," *Daily Illini*, October 15, 1958, 1; Gauen, "Okay Tree Planting Fund"; Tate and French, *Illini Place*, 46–63; Henry memoirs.

32. Bonnie Byrns, "Stall Building Plan," *Daily Illini*, September 17, 1959, 1. See also "Steel Shipments Unavailable, Assembly Hall Awaits Cold," *Daily Illini*, November 21, 1959, 3; "No Hope for Immediate Settlement of University Construction Strike," *Daily Illini*, May 4, 1960, 4.

33. Henry memoirs.

34. Bond issue promotional materials; Bonnie Byrns, "Staff to Back Bond Issue," *Daily Illini*, March 29, 1960, 2; "UI Instructors Receive Plea for Donations," *Daily Illini*, April 19, 1960, 4; Gene Bryerton, "Senate Favors Bond Issue; Creates New Travel Bureau," *Daily Illini*, January 7, 1960, 3; Bob Adams, "Students Help UI Bond Issue,"

Daily Illini, September 28, 1960, 3; Mary Conour, "Plan Bond Issue Marathon," *Daily Illini*, October 11, 1960, 1; "80,000 Alumni Receive Letters on Bond Issue," *Daily Illini*, May 11, 1960, 9.

35. Bond issue promotional materials.

36. Ibid.

37. Ibid.

38. Report on Ira Latimer in Wayne A. Johnston Papers, U of I Archives, Series No. 1/20/3, box 4; "Ira Latimer, Battled for Civil Rights," *Chicago Tribune*, February 17, 1985, https://www.chicagotribune.com/news/ct-xpm-1985-02-17-8501090867-story.htm.

39. Report on Ira Latimer; "Ira Latimer, Battled for Civil Rights"; Joseph Raphael Demartini, "Student Protest during Two Periods in the History of the University of Illinois: 1867–1894 and 1929–1942" (PhD diss., University of Illinois at Urbana-Champaign, 1974), 361–68, ProQuest; Gordon Melvin Patric, "The Impact of the McCollum Decision Particularly in Illinois" (PhD diss., University of Illinois at Urbana-Champaign, 1957), 22–37, ProQuest; "Inter-Racial Group Calls Meeting," *Daily Illini*, August 31, 1946, 1.

40. Report on Ira Latimer; "Latimer Denied Teaching Post in Illinois Schools," *Chicago Tribune*, June 9, 1949, part 2, 9; "The U.N. Spokesman in Chicago," *Chicago Tribune*, October 28, 1950, 8.

41. Report on Ira Latimer; "Latimer Lists 50 Lawyers As Chicago Reds," *Chicago Tribune*, April 27, 1956, part 1, 17.

42. Frank Hughes, "The Case of Ira Latimer," *National Review*, February 16, 1957, 154–55.

43. Ralph E. Ellsworth and Sarah M. Harris, *The American Right Wing* (Urbana: University of Illinois Graduate School of Library Science, 1960), 22; Carl T. Bogus, *Buckley: William F. Buckley and the Rise of American Conservatism* (New York: Bloomsbury, 2011).

44. Harry T. Everingham, "Man's Shortcomings Mustn't Be Forgotten," *Indianapolis Star*, June 27, 1960, 12; Ellsworth and Harris, *American Right Wing*, 15.

45. Unidentified news clipping, c. February 1960, Ira Latimer Papers, Chicago History Museum Research Center, box 87.

46. Clippings from *Champaign-Urbana Courier* and *News-Gazette* (Champaign, IL), c. February 1960, Latimer Papers, boxes 27 and 87. See also Victor Stone obituary, *News-Gazette.com*, November 28, 2010, updated June 13, 2019, https://www.news-gazette.com/obituaries/victor-stone/article_4f4f67f7-8426-5f8a-ad8f-8e03407ceaa1.html.

47. Ira Latimer letter to Howard Barham, February 8, 1960; and Ira Latimer letter to Revilo and Grace Oliver, February 9, 1960; both in Latimer Papers, box 87.

48. Clippings from *Champaign-Urbana Courier*, c. February 1960, Latimer Papers, box 87.

49. Unidentified clipping, c. February–March 1960, Latimer Papers, box 87.

50. Tom Shilgalis, "Philbrick Warns of Reds," *Daily Illini*, February 27, 1960, 1.

51. Ira Latimer letter to unidentified correspondents in Champaign-Urbana, c. March 1960; Ira Latimer letter to Howard Barham, March 4, 1960; Howard Barham

letter to Ira Latimer, March 6, 1960; and Ira Latimer letter to Howard Barham, March 8, 1960; all in Latimer Papers, box 87.

52. See Metz, *Radicals in the Heartland*, chap. 3. See also clippings, fliers, and index cards in Latimer Papers, boxes 27 and 87.

53. Seymour "Cy" Kaplan, "All in All," *Chicago Sentinel*, April 5, 1945, 27; index cards in Latimer Papers, box 87.

54. Ira Latimer letter to Otto E. Brunkow, March 11, 1960; Grace Oliver letter to Ira Latimer, January 27, 1960; and Ira Latimer letter to unidentified correspondent, March 13, 1960; all in Latimer Papers, box 87.

55. Ira Latimer letter, March 25, 1960, Administrative and Personnel Actions File, U of I Archives, Series No. 2/15/10, box 5. (Latimer's letter originally was addressed to the *Daily Illini* student newspaper; after the paper declined to print it, the letter was sent to parents of women students.)

Chapter 2. Sex Ritualized

1. "Autobiography of Leo Koch" and "Autobiographical Sketch," Leo Koch Papers, box 1, folder 1, Wisconsin Historical Society, Madison [hereafter, Koch Papers]. For information on the International Foundation for Advanced Study, see John Markoff, *What the Dormouse Said: How the Sixties Counterculture Shaped the Personal Computer Industry* (New York: Viking, 2005).

2. "Autobiography of Leo Koch."

3. Ibid.

4. See Roger L. Geiger, *American Higher Education since World War II* (Princeton, NJ: Princeton University Press, 2019), 16–28, 168–75; Judy Osterbach, "General Curriculum Offers Chance to Explore LAS," *Daily Illini*, April 25, 1968, 3. The University of Illinois eventually would eliminate its Division of General Studies in 1968 (the division would be resurrected many years later in a different format).

5. Unless otherwise noted, information on Koch's years at the U of I (including his letters to the editor and his school board campaign) comes from the Leo Koch personnel file, Administrative and Personnel Actions File, Series No. 2/15/10, University of Illinois at Urbana-Champaign (U of I) Archives, box 5.

6. James M. McCrimmon and Otto E. Kugler to Lyle H. Lanier, April 12, 1960, Koch personnel file. Information about Koch's reported lack of cooperation with DGS program chores comes from Committee on Academic Freedom, "Memorandum on the Koch Case," Faculty Organizations/AAUP file, U of I Archives, Series No. 48/1/5, box 3.

7. Leo F. Koch letters to the *Champaign-Urbana Courier*, *Daily Illini*, and *News-Gazette*, c. 1958–59, Koch personnel file.

8. Leo Francis Koch, "Vitalistic-Mechanistic Controversy," *Scientific Monthly*, November 1957, 254; Oscar Riddle, *The Unleashing of Evolutionary Thought* (New York: Vantage, 1954), 195.

9. Ron Szoke, interview by author, Champaign, IL, March 2, 2020; Leo F. Koch, "Religious Manifesto," February 24, 1960, in Harry M. Tiebout Papers, U of I Archives, Series No. 15/16/21, box 15; Leo F. Koch, "Science Teaching" (letter to the editor), *Science*, July 17, 1959, 188.

10. Dick Hutchison and Dan Bures, "Sex Ritualized," *Daily Illini*, March 16, 1960, 6.

11. Paula A. Treichler, "Isabel Bevier and Home Economics," in *No Boundaries: University of Illinois Vignettes*, ed. Lillian Hoddeson (Urbana: University of Illinois Press, 2004), 33–39. The Woman's Building is now known as the English Building.

12. Paula A. Treichler, "Alma Mater's Sorority: Women and the University of Illinois, 1890–1925," in *For Alma Mater: Theory and Practice in Feminist Scholarship*, ed. Paula A. Treichler, Cheris Kramarae, and Beth Stafford (Urbana: University of Illinois Press, 1985), 6; Paula S. Fass, *Outside In: Minorities and the Transformation of American Education* (New York: Oxford University Press, 1989), 156–88; Barbara Miller Solomon, *In the Company of Educated Women* (New Haven, CT: Yale University Press, 1985), 194.

13. Linda Eisenmann, *Higher Education for Women in Postwar America, 1945–1965* (Baltimore, MD: Johns Hopkins University Press, 2006), 41–42. See also Elaine Tyler May, *Homeward Bound: American Families in the Cold War Era*, rev. ed. (New York: Basic Books, 2008).

14. Jessica Weiss, *To Have and to Hold: Marriage, the Baby Boom, and Social Change* (Chicago: University of Chicago Press, 2000), 223.

15. Carl Binger, "The Pressures on College Girls Today," *Atlantic*, February 1961, 41–42.

16. Ibid., 42; Rose K. Goldsen, Morris Rosenberg, Robin M. Williams Jr., and Edward A. Suchman, *What College Students Think* (Princeton, NJ: D. Van Nostrand, 1960), 58.

17. Regina Markell Morantz, "The Scientist as Sex Crusader: Albert C. Kinsey and American Culture," in *Procreation or Pleasure?: Sexual Attitudes in American History*, ed. Thomas L. Altherr (Malabar, FL: Robert E. Krieger, 1983), 151–54; Gloria Steinem, "The Moral Disarmament of Betty Coed," *Esquire*, September 1962, 153.

18. Beth Bailey, *Sex in the Heartland* (Cambridge, MA: Harvard University Press, 1999), 78; Winston W. Ehrmann, "The Variety and Meaning of Premarital Heterosexual Experiences for the College Student," *Journal of the National Association of Women Deans and Counselors* 26, no. 2 (January 1963): 27; Nora Johnson, "Sex and the College Girl," *Atlantic*, November 1959, 60.

19. Roger Ebert, "Making Out Is Its Own Reward," *SunTimes.com*, January 12, 2010, https://web.archive.org/web/20100116153852/http://blogs.suntimes.com/ebert/2010/01/making_out_is_its_own_reward.html; Martin Abramson, "Campus Romance: A Degree in Divorce," *Cosmopolitan*, September 1963, 51; Roger Ebert, *Life Itself: A Memoir* (New York: Grand Central, 2011), 351.

20. Bailey, *Sex in the Heartland*, 77; Ebert, *Life Itself*, 345–50; Ebert, "Making Out Is Its Own Reward."

21. Bailey, *Sex in the Heartland*, 11; Irving B. Tebor, "Male Virgins: Conflicts and Group Support in American Culture," *Family Life Coordinator* 9, nos. 3–4 (March–June 1961): 42; Gael Greene, *Sex and the College Girl* (New York: Dial, 1964), 140–43.

22. For background on the significance of the song "Will You Love Me Tomorrow" and the movie *Where the Boys Are* for young women of the early 1960s, see Susan J. Douglas, *Where the Girls Are: Growing Up Female with the Mass Media* (New York: Times Books, 1994), 61–95; Lynn Peril, *College Girls* (New York: W. W. Norton, 2006), 303–8.

23. Johnson, "Sex and the College Girl," 60; Greene, *Sex and the College Girl*, 188–89.

24. Clifford Kirkpatrick and Eugene Kanin, "Male Sex Aggression on a University Campus," *American Sociological Review* 22, no. 1 (February 1957): 52–58; Phyllis and Eberhard Kronhausen, *Sex Histories of American College Men* (New York: Ballantine, 1960), 208–14.

25. Roger Ebert, "Charge Coed, Local Man in Deaths," *Daily Illini*, February 6, 1962, 2; Don Henry, "UI Coed Still Faces Murder Charge," *Daily Illini*, February 7, 1962, 1; Peg Richardson, "Charges Reduced," *Daily Illini*, May 22, 1962, 3.

26. Wade Freeman, "Shoots Coed, Then Self," *Daily Illini*, November 9, 1961, 1–2; Ken Viste and Dave Young, "'They Began to Drift Apart . . .'" *Daily Illini*, November 9, 1961, 3; Roger Ebert, "Mautz Profile: Active, Stormy," *Daily Illini*, November 10, 1961, 3; reports and correspondence dated November 1961, Susan L. Stout file, Administrative and Personnel Actions File, U of I Archives, box 5.

27. Correspondence dated from November 1961 to September 1962, Stout file.

28. Robert Schwartz, *Deans of Men and the Shaping of Modern College Culture* (New York: Palgrave Macmillan, 2010), 27; *Illini Years: A Picture History of the University of Illinois* (Urbana: University of Illinois Press, 1950), 47; Treichler, "Alma Mater's Sorority," 24–32.

29. Kelly Morrow, "Sex and the Student Body: Knowledge, Equality, and the Sexual Revolution, 1960 to 1973" (PhD diss., University of North Carolina at Chapel Hill, 2012), 35, ProQuest; Ebert, *Life Itself*, 349–50.

30. Letter to David D. Henry, April 11, 1960, Administrative and Personnel Actions File, U of I Archives, box 10; Ebert, *Life Itself*, 351, Greene, *Sex and the College Girl*, 21. See also Bailey, *Sex in the Heartland*, 45–74.

31. Ebert, *Life Itself*, 351–52. See also Schwartz, *Deans of Men*, 113–40.

32. Jana Nidiffer, *Pioneering Deans of Women* (New York: Teachers College Press, 2000), 1–2; Tony Burba, "Dear Granny," *Daily Illini*, April 10, 1964, 8.

33. "UI's Dean Miriam Shelden Dies at 62," *News-Gazette* (Champaign, IL), May 13, 1975, sec. 1, 3; Miriam Shelden, "Changing Patterns in the Lives of Women," May 7, 1960, in Miriam A. Shelden Papers, U of I Archives, Series No. 41/3/21 [hereafter, Shelden Papers].

34. Shelden, "Changing Patterns," Shelden Papers; "Girls Are Told of Dual Roles in Life Today," *Chicago Tribune*, May 8, 1960, part 1, 30; Fass, *Outside In*, 173.

35. "Dean Calls for New Hours," *Daily Illini*, November 28, 1961, 2; Miriam A. Shelden, "Yeast and Ferment," May 1, 1964, Shelden Papers; Marti Sauer, "Eth[ical] Values

Relate to Student Sex," *Daily Illini*, March 5, 1963, 5 (an error gave the headline as "*Ethnic Values*"); Larry Finley, "Dean Traces Morality," *Daily Illini*, October 12, 1963, 2.

36. Dean of Women's office annual report, 1959–60, in Student Affairs/Dean of Students file, U of I Archives, Series No. 41/1/30, box 2; Finley, "Dean Traces Morality," 2; Arthur S. Adams, "The Role of the Dean of Women on the College Campus," *Journal of the National Association of Women Deans and Counselors* 26, no. 1 (October 1962): 23; Kate Hevner Mueller, "The Role of the Counselor in Sex Behavior and Standards," *Journal of the National Association of Women Deans and Counselors* 26, no. 2 (January 1963): 4.

37. Institute for Sex Research, *Sexual Behavior in the Human Female* (Philadelphia: W. B. Saunders, 1953), 14–15; Morantz, "Scientist as Sex Crusader," 148–49, 156–57.

38. Morantz, "Scientist as Sex Crusader," 154; Marion Hilliard, "Why Premarital Sex Is Always Wrong," *Ladies' Home Journal*, September 1958, 56, 160–62; Margaret Mead, "Sex on Campus: The Real Issue," *Redbook*, October 1962, 8.

39. Robert A. and Frances R. Harper, "Are Educators Afraid of Sex?" *Marriage and Family Living* 19, no. 3 (August 1957): 244; Steinem, "Moral Disarmament of Betty Coed," 157; John T. Rule, "Must the Colleges Police Sex?" *Atlantic*, April 1964, 57; Milton I. Levine and Maya Pines, "Sex: The Problem Colleges Evade," *Harper's*, October 1961, 130; Lester A. Kirkendall, "Sex on the Campus," *Nation*, February 17, 1964, 166; Greene, *Sex and the College Girl*, 246.

40. "With a Capital 'F,'" *Daily Illini*, September 18, 1959, 14; Gene Lemon, "Campus Scout," *Daily Illini*, January 20, 1960, 4; "Campus Serves as Habitat for 100 Queens," *Daily Illini*, November 25, 1959, 3; Bob Adams, "Keep Campus Queens," *Daily Illini*, May 26, 1960, 1. Percentages on the male-female breakdown of the undergraduate student body come from Shelden Papers.

41. Bill Stephens, "Condemn Obscene Magazines," *Daily Illini*, January 7, 1960, 1; "Turk's Head Painting Called Obscene," *Daily Illini*, November 24, 1959, 2; "Tumor—Malignant Outgrowth," *Daily Illini*, October 20, 1959, 8; *College Tumor* file, Student Affairs, U of I Archives, Series No. 41/67/942. Movie listings and descriptions for the Illini Theater come from the *Daily Illini*, 1959–60.

42. Bill Stephens, "Here We Go Again! Students Stage Water Fight Encompassing Entire Campus," *Daily Illini*, April 18, 1958, 1; "UI Dismisses 19 Students," *Daily Illini*, April 30, 1958, 1. See also Bailey, *Sex in the Heartland*, 45–48.

43. Bob Adams, "'Fair Play' Issue—Where It Stands after Months of Debate," *Daily Illini*, February 13, 1960, 8; Margie Molitor, "Senate Supports Sit-Ins," *Daily Illini*, March 1, 1960, 1–2; Bob Adams, "Liberal Group Forms to Kill Apathy at UI," *Daily Illini*, February 20, 1960, 1; Bob Adams, "Liberal Group Plans against Discrimination," *Daily Illini*, February 27, 1960, 1; "Liberalism Not Dead," *Daily Illini*, February 24, 1960, 6.

44. Margie Schaefer, "Coeds Question WRH [Women's Residence Hall] Discipline," *Daily Illini*, March 12, 1960, 4.

45. "Sex Slate Puzzles Committee," *Daily Illini*, February 11, 1960, 14; "Ever since Adam," *Daily Illini*, February 13, 1960, 8.

46. Dan Bures, "Views of UI Student Who Started It All," *Champaign-Urbana Spectator*, February 20, 1961, 1.

47. Dick Hutchison and Dan Bures, "Sex Ritualized," *Daily Illini*, March 16, 1960, 6.

48. Ibid.; Bailey, *Sex in the Heartland*, 10.

49. Unless otherwise noted, Koch's memories of reading "Sex Ritualized," writing his subsequent letter to the editor, and experiencing fallout from the letter come from Speeches and Writings, Koch Papers, boxes 12 and 13. See also Polly Anderson, "AAUP Censured University," *Daily Illini*, March 14, 1970, 11, 14.

50. "More Equal Than Others?" *Daily Illini*, March 16, 1960, 6.

51. Leo F. Koch, "Advice on Sex" (letter to the editor), *Daily Illini*, March 18, 1960, 8; Koch Papers, boxes 12–13.

52. Richard Archbold, "Illini Editor Tells Story of Letter," *News-Gazette* (Champaign, IL), June 14, 1960, 3; Rich Archbold, "Editor Defends Koch Opinion," *Daily Illini*, March 21, 1961, 7.

53. Rich Archbold, telephone interview by author, February 20, 2020; Koch Papers, boxes 12–13.

54. Archbold, "Illini Editor Tells Story," 3. Other items come from the *Daily Illini*, March 18, 1960.

55. Koch Papers, boxes 12–13.

Chapter 3. Seriously Prejudicial

1. Leo F. Koch, "Advice on Sex" (letter to the editor), *Daily Illini*, March 18, 1960, 8; Michael N. Soltys, "Sex Is Not Evil" (letter to the editor), *Daily Illini*, March 19, 1960, 8; Robert Bookstein, "Clarifies Koch's Position" (letter to the editor), *Daily Illini*, March 23, 1960, 6.

2. Brian Wallen, "Unadulterated Trash" (letter to the editor), *Daily Illini*, March 23, 1960, 6; James R. Hine, "Rev. Hine Answers" (letter to the editor), *Daily Illini*, March 23, 1960, 6.

3. Carolyn Daily, "Coles Sound Off on Sex," *Daily Illini*, March 22, 1960, 3; "Universal Topic," *Daily Illini*, March 29, 1960, 6; Leo Koch, "Academic Freedom and the Minister," c. 1961, Leo Koch Papers, box 13, folder 6, Wisconsin Historical Society, Madison [hereafter, Koch Papers].

4. Bob Adams, "Liberals May Demonstrate for Koch," *Daily Illini*, April 2, 1960, 1; Dillon E. Mapother notes on interview with member of the Committee for Liberal Action, April 4, 1960, Administrative and Personnel Actions File, University of Illinois at Urbana-Champaign (U of I) Archives, Series No. 2/15/10, box 8.

5. Information on Latimer's campaign against alleged subversion at the University of Illinois comes from the Ira Latimer Papers, Chicago History Museum Research Center, Chicago, Illinois, boxes 27 and 87.

6. Ira Latimer letter, March 25, 1960, Administrative and Personnel Actions File, U of I Archives, box 5.

7. Ibid. See also Bonnie Bryns, "Loyalty Oath Receives Censure of UI Trustees," *Daily Illini*, January 21, 1960, 1; Michael V. Metz, *Radicals in the Heartland: The 1960s Student Protest Movement at the University of Illinois* (Urbana: University of Illinois Press, 2019), Kindle, chap. 3.

8. Eloise E. Mount letter, April 2, 1960, Administrative and Personnel Actions File, U of I Archives, box 11. See also "Students Back Free Sex Prof," *Chicago Tribune*, April 12, 1960, 1; "School Board at Argenta Meets Legion," *Decatur Daily Review* (IL), May 1, 1956, 24.

9. Documents and correspondence, April 1960, Wayne A. Johnston Papers, U of I Archives, Series No. 1/20/3, box 4 [hereafter, Johnston Papers].

10. "U. of I. Moss Expert Gathers Verbal Stones for Love Views," *Chicago Daily News*, April 5, 1960, 5. See also Lynn Ludlow, "Suspended for Sex Views, U.I. Biologist Will Appeal," *Champaign-Urbana Courier*, April 8, 1960, 1; "Students Back Free Sex Prof," 1.

11. Frances B. Watkins to David D. Henry, March 20, 1960, Administrative and Personnel Actions File, U of I Archives, box 9. A written note on the letter indicates that the president's office called Watkins back a few days later.

12. Frances B. Watkins to Wayne A. Johnston, March 22, 1960, Johnston Papers, box 4; Wayne A. Johnston to David D. Henry, March 23, 1960, Administrative and Personnel Actions File, U of I Archives, box 9.

13. David D. Henry memoirs and notebook in David D. Henry Papers, U of I Archives, Series No. 2/12/20, boxes 25 and 28 [hereafter, Henry Papers]; David D. Henry to Ralph S. Lesemann, March 14, 1961, in Administrative and Personnel Actions File, U of I Archives, box 9.

14. James M. McCrimmon to Lyle H. Lanier, April 5, 1960, Koch Papers, box 5, folder 1; Otto E. Kugler to Lyle H. Lanier, April 13, 1960, Administrative and Personnel Actions File, U of I Archives, box 5.

15. James M. McCrimmon to Leo F. Koch, March 25, 1960, Koch Papers, box 5, folder 1.

16. Report to David D. Henry from Urbana-Champaign Senate Committee on Academic Freedom, May 13, 1960; Lyle H. Lanier to David D. Henry, April 7, 1960; and Lyle H. Lanier to Leo F. Koch, April 11, 1960; all in Koch Papers, box 5, folder 1.

17. Extract from University of Illinois Statutes effective September 1, 1957, Leo Koch personnel file, Administrative and Personnel Actions File, U of I Archives, box 5.

18. American Association of University Professors, "1940 Statement of Principles on Academic Freedom and Tenure," https://www.aaup.org/report/1940-statement-principles-academic-freedom-and-tenure; Hans-Joerg Tiede, "Extramural Speech, Academic Freedom, and the AAUP: An Historical Account," in *Challenges to Academic Freedom*, ed. Joseph C. Hermanowicz (Baltimore, MD: Johns Hopkins University Press, forthcoming).

19. David D. Henry to Lyle H. Lanier, April 7, 1960, Koch Papers, box 5, folder 1.

20. Ludlow, "Suspended for Sex Views," 1; Rich Archbold, "University Fires Koch: Is Not Sorry He Sent Letter," *Daily Illini*, April 8, 1960, 1.

21. "President Henry Hanged in Effigy," *Champaign-Urbana Courier*, April 8, 1960, 1; Margie Molitor, "Liberals Censure Henry; Koch Appeals to UI Senate," *Daily Illini*, April 9, 1960, 1–2.

22. Details of the pro-Koch rally come from news clippings, April 1960, Koch Papers, box 4, folders 8–9.

23. Bob Adams, "Senate Bill Asks for Koch Appeal," *Daily Illini*, April 12, 1960, 1–2; "Somebody Has to Lose," *Daily Illini*, April 9, 1960, 8; "Letters to the Editor: Editor's Note," *Daily Illini*, April 21, 1960, 6; "Koch Sex Views Hit in Illini Poll, but Firing Held Unfair," *Chicago's American*, April 23, 1960, 1–2; "An Open Letter to the President and Board of Trustees," *Daily Illini*, May 4, 1960, 12.

24. News clippings, c. April 1960, Koch Papers, box 4, folders 8–12; "Oust Prof for Sex Views," *Chicago Tribune*, April 8, 1960, 1, 10; "Academic Freedom?" (reprint from *Cincinnati Enquirer*), *Chicago Tribune*, April 28, 1960, pt. 1, 16.

25. Letters to President Henry's office and to *Champaign-Urbana Courier*, April–June 1960, Administrative and Personnel Actions File, U of I Archives, boxes 9–10; news clippings, c. April 1960, Koch Papers, box 4, folders 8–12.

26. Letters to President Henry's office, April–June 1960, Administrative and Personnel Actions File, U of I Archives, boxes 9–10; "Koch Firing Protested in Oslo," *Daily Illini*, May 24, 1960, 6. See also "The Limit," *Time*, April 18, 1960, 48; "The Professor Was Fired," *Newsweek*, April 18, 1960, 30.

27. "Iowa Protests Firing," *Daily Illini*, May 10, 1960, 6; "Koch's Views 'Not Obscene,'" *Daily Illini*, May 4, 1960, 1; "Victorian in Urbana" (reprint from *Harvard Crimson*), *Daily Illini*, April 29, 1960, 12.

28. David J. Armor to Leo F. Koch, May 4, 1960, in Koch Papers, box 5, folder 4; "U. C. Students Get Warning on 'Defiance,'" *Oakland Tribune*, May 16, 1960, 21; Leo F. Koch, "Illini Incident: Academic Sex," September 1960, Koch Papers, box 12, folder 9; David Lance Goines, *The Free Speech Movement* (Berkeley, CA: Ten Speed, 1993), 68–70.

29. Harry M. Tiebout Jr. to L. H. Lanier, April 11, 1960, Harry M. Tiebout Papers, U of I Archives, Series No. 15/16/21, box 2.

30. News clippings and Koch private comments, c. April 1960, Koch Papers, box 4, folders 8–9 and 13; Leo Koch, "The Dimensions of the Koch Case," c. 1960, Koch Papers, box 12, folder 8; Leo F. Koch to Glenn W. Salisbury, April 8, 1960, Koch Papers, box 5, folder 1; "Date Set for Koch Hearing," *Daily Illini*, May 18, 1960, 2.

31. John Karl Wilson, "A History of Academic Freedom in America" (PhD diss., Illinois State University, 2014), 227, https://ir.library.illinoisstate.edu/etd/257.

32. Report to David D. Henry from Urbana-Champaign Senate Committee on Academic Freedom, May 13, 1960, Koch Papers, box 5, folder 1.

33. "No Koch Report: Henry," *Daily Illini*, May 28, 1960, 1; David D. Henry, "Memorandum to the Members of the Board of Trustees," c. June 1960, Koch Papers, box 5, folder 1.

34. Lynn Ludlow, "U. I. Counsel Rips Prof. Koch's Letter," *Champaign-Urbana Courier*, June 14, 1960, 3; Lynn Ludlow, "U. I. Board Fires Biology Teacher," *Champaign-Urbana Courier*, June 15, 1960, 1, 3; Wilson, "History of Academic Freedom," 235–36.

35. Quotes from the transcript of the hearing come from Board of Trustees Secretary's File, U of I Archives, Series No. 1/1/6, box 31. See also Ludlow, "U. I. Counsel"; Thom Weidlich, *Appointment Denied: The Inquisition of Bertrand Russell* (Amherst, NY: Prometheus, 2000).

36. Henry memoirs.

37. Coleman R. Griffith to David D. Henry, April 25, 1960, Henry Papers, box 28; Coleman R. Griffith letter, June 28, 1960, Coleman R. Griffith Papers, U of I Archives, Series No. 5/1/21, box 12; Fran Myers, "Senate View on Freedom is Told," *News-Gazette* (Champaign, IL), June 16, 1960, 25; "Faculty Members Censure Trustees," *Daily Illini*, July 21, 1960, 1–2.

38. Wilson, "History of Academic Freedom," 231. Information on the national AAUP's investigation of the Koch firing comes from Administrative and Personnel Actions File, U of I Archives, box 7, and Faculty Organizations/AAUP file, U of I Archives, Series No. 48/1/5, boxes 3–4.

39. "Academic Freedom and Tenure: The University of Illinois," *AAUP Bulletin*, Spring 1963, 34.

40. Ibid., 36–39.

41. Ibid., 40–43.

42. Henry memoirs. See also "Faculty Letter from the Office of the President," May 16, 1963, Administrative and Personnel Actions File, U of I Archives, box 11; David D. Henry to Lyle Lanier, May 29, 1963, Administrative and Personnel Actions File, U of I Archives, box 7; David D. Henry to William P. Fidler, June 29, 1963, Faculty Organizations/AAUP file, U of I Archives, box 3.

43. Extracts from the University of Illinois Statutes, June 1, 1966, Faculty Organizations/AAUP file, U of I Archives, box 4. The new statutes also said that a faculty member could be removed for illegally advocating the overthrow of the US government by force.

44. Wilson, "History of Academic Freedom," 233–34; Brian Braun, "AAUP Removes UI Censure," *Daily Illini*, February 28, 1967, 2; Henry memoirs.

45. Joan Wallach Scott, *Knowledge, Power, and Academic Freedom* (New York: Columbia University Press, 2019), 61–62.

46. Wilson, "History of Academic Freedom," 19–20, 38–41, 241–42; Tiede, "Extramural Speech." See also AAUP, "1940 Statement"; Matthew W. Finkin and Robert C. Post, *For the Common Good: Principles of American Academic Freedom* (New Haven, CT: Yale University Press, 2009), 144–46; Henry Reichman, *The Future of Academic Freedom* (Baltimore, MD: Johns Hopkins University Press, 2019), 55–57.

47. Leo F. Koch to AAUP Academic Freedom Fund, June 19, 1961, Koch Papers, box 4, folder 6; David P. Ausubel to Contributor to the Koch Fund, May 5, 1961, Charles

B. Hagan Papers, U of I Archives, Series No. 15/18/25, box 1; Leo F. Koch to William P. Fidler, August 29, 1961, Koch Papers, box 4, folder 6; Felix Morrow to Paul Edwards, July 26, 1961, Koch Papers, box 5, folder 3.

48. Leo F. Koch to Louis Joughin, March 5, 1967; U of I AAUP members to Sanford H. Kadish, June 20, 1967; and Sanford H. Kadish to U of I AAUP members, October 24, 1967; all in Koch Papers, box 4, folder 6. See also Wilson, "History of Academic Freedom," 234.

49. Koch v. Board of Trustees, January 22, 1963, https://casetext.com/case/koch-v-board-of-trustees. Other information about Koch's legal fight against the University of Illinois comes from Administrative and Personnel Actions File, U of I Archives, box 8.

50. Leo F. Koch, "Autobiography of Leo Koch," Koch Papers, box 1, folder 1.

51. See Jon Elliston, "Cruel Summer: The Attack on Camp Summerlane," September 20, 2010, *Mountain Xpress* (Asheville, NC), https://mountainx.com/news/community-news/cruel_summer_the_attack_on_camp_summerlane_a_four-part_story/.

52. David Allyn, *Make Love, Not War* (London: Routledge, 2016), 43–44; Leo Koch, notes for interview with *Newsweek*, c. 1963–64, Koch Papers, box 5, folder 4.

53. Leo F. Koch, "Advice on Sex" (letter to the editor), *Daily Illini*, March 18, 1960, 8; Koch, "Dimensions of the Koch Case"; David Harris Cole, "Freedom and Responsibility on the College Campus," April 24, 1960, Koch Papers, box 5, folder 4.

54. Koch, "Illini Incident."

Chapter 4. Storm Coming

1. "Baptist Unit Raps Rule by Catholic," *Des Moines Tribune*, April 20, 1960, 35.

2. TJ Blakeman, "Senator John F. Kennedy Campaigns in Champaign on October 24, 1960," *ChampaignHistory.com*, August 4, 2018, updated March 14, 2020, https://www.champaignhistory.com/post/john-f-kennedy-visit-october-24-1960; Anthony J. Janata to William L. Obriecht, June 24, 1957, Harry M. Tiebout Papers, University of Illinois at Urbana-Champaign (U of I) Archives, Series No. 15/16/21, box 8 [hereafter, Tiebout Papers]; Wade Freeman, "Controversial Speakers Issue May Start Popping Here Again," *Daily Illini*, March 3, 1962, 7; Bill Stephens, "Lodge Seeks Local Vote," *Daily Illini*, September 16, 1960, 1.

3. Bonnie Dictor, "Kennedy Hearers Push, Shove," *Daily Illini*, October 25, 1960, 9; Gene Lemon, "Campus Scout," *Daily Illini*, October 28, 1960, 8.

4. Blakeman, "Senator John F. Kennedy."

5. Deirdre Lynn Cobb-Roberts, "Race and Higher Education at the University of Illinois, 1945 to 1955" (PhD diss., University of Illinois at Urbana-Champaign, 1998), 121–22, http://hdl.handle.net/2142/80240; Roger Ebert, "Last 2 Weeks Tested Student Ideals," *Daily Illini*, February 16, 1963, 8.

6. Carol Easton Lee (Safisha Madhubuti) oral history, Voices of Illinois Oral History Project, May 22, 2018, https://www.library.illinois.edu/voices/collection-item

/carol-easton-lee/; David D. Henry to Irving Dilliard, February 11, 1963, David D. Henry Papers, U of I Archives, Series No. 2/12/20, box 28. See also Joy Ann Williamson, *Black Power on Campus: The University of Illinois, 1965–75* (Urbana: University of Illinois Press, 2003).

7. Carol Easton Lee oral history; Beverly Effort Biggs oral history, May 22, 2018, Voices of Illinois Oral History Project, https://www.library.illinois.edu/voices/collection-item/beverly-effort-biggs/; Connie Rolison Corbett oral history, May 22, 2018, Voices of Illinois Oral History Project, https://www.library.illinois.edu/voices/collection-item/connie-rolison-corbett/; "To the Editor," *Daily Illini*, January 15, 1960, 6. See also Bob Adams, "'Fair Play' Issue—Where It Stands after Months of Debate," *Daily Illini*, February 13, 1960, 8.

8. "Penney Picketing Campaign," https://localwiki.org/cu/Penney_Picketing_Campaign; Harry Tiebout, "Pickets Were 'Secret Weapon,'" *Champaign-Urbana Spectator*, May 6, 1961, 1. Other information about antidiscrimination campaigns against J. C. Penney's, local barbers, and the Coca-Cola bottling company comes from Tiebout Papers, U of I Archives, boxes 7–8.

9. Lew Collens, telephone interview by author, March 4, 2020; Harry Tiebout, "UI Confuses Discrimination," *Daily Illini*, March 3, 1962, 6; Marilyn Skor, "CSA Passes Anti-discrimination Bill," *Daily Illini*, October 13, 1961, 1; Kathy Gauen, "Trustees Pass CSA Measure to End Housing Discrimination," *Daily Illini*, February 22, 1962, 1; "Fraternities Will Sign," *Daily Illini*, May 22, 1962, 1.

10. Dave Young, "Students Attack ROTC, City Police," *Daily Illini*, March 2, 1961, 2; Martin Cobin, "Urges ROTC Orientation" (letter to the editor), *Daily Illini*, February 15, 1961, 7; Don Henry, "Henry Supports Change in Compulsory ROTC," *Daily Illini*, June 17, 1963, 1–2; Mike Van de Kerckhove, "Compulsory ROTC Tradition Ends," *Daily Illini*, July 9, 1964, 3.

11. "Volunteers Swamp Corps," *Daily Illini*, March 4, 1961, 13; "UI Leaders Present Peace Corps," *Daily Illini*, April 11, 1961, 1.

12. "Picket UI on Fallout Shelters," *Daily Illini*, October 10, 1961, 5; John Dolan, "Local Student Peace Union Protests Recent Russian Atomic Bomb Test," *Daily Illini*, October 25, 1961, 1; Joe Tuchinsky, "20th Century's Great Debate: Peace," *Daily Illini*, January 16, 1962, 7; Joe Tuchinsky, "At the Brink of a University Doctorate, a Time for Solemn Soul-Searching," *Daily Illini*, October 6, 1962, 7; Stu Cohn, "Reflect Cold War Tensions," *Daily Illini*, October 25, 1961, 7.

13. Mary Conour, "Smythe Asks Breakthrough in 'Thought Barrier' at Forum," *Daily Illini*, November 12, 1960, 9; Mary Conour, "Smythe, Dawn Summarize Series on Breaking Barriers to Survival," *Daily Illini*, April 22, 1961, 3; James Carey in conversation with Lawrence Grossberg, "From New England to Illinois: The Invention of (American) Cultural Studies," in *Thinking with James Carey*, ed. Jeremy Packer and Craig Robertson (New York: Peter Lang, 2006), 25.

14. William F. Brewer, "Charles Osgood: The Psychology of Language," in *No Boundaries: University of Illinois Vignettes*, ed. Lillian Hoddeson (Urbana: University of Illinois

Press, 2004), 216–17; "Professor Denies Accusation of Appeasing Reds in Essay," *Daily Illini*, March 30, 1962, 7.

15. Nan Lundberg, "Rabinowitch on World Peace," *Daily Illini*, November 17, 1961, 1; Bruce Bowen, "Lewis Scoffs Idea of Post-atom Life," *Daily Illini*, November 18, 1961, 1; "University Faculty Members Question Fallout Shelter Idea," *Daily Illini*, January 5, 1962, 2; "An Open Letter to President Kennedy," *Daily Illini*, May 13, 1961, 12.

16. Roger Ebert, "Ars Gratia...," *Daily Illini*, October 24, 1962, 6; Harlan Berk, "Opinions on Cuba Vary," *Daily Illini*, October 24, 1962, 5; Richard Synnestvedt, "CD Officials Call Response to Alert Good Wednesday," *Daily Illini*, October 25, 1962, 2; John Keefe, "Local Opinion Sharply Divided," *Daily Illini*, October 23, 1962, 1; Dallas Smythe, "The Agonizing Cuban Question: A Study in American Motives," *Daily Illini*, October 27, 1962, 10.

17. Dixie Cowan, "Illini Rally behind Kennedy—but List Some Reservations," *Daily Illini*, October 25, 1962, 5; "We Give Support to Kennedy's Action," *Daily Illini*, October 25, 1962, 6; Don Henry, "The Last Word," *Daily Illini*, October 25, 1962, 6.

18. Dallas Smythe, *Counterclockwise: Perspectives on Communication*, ed. Thomas Guback (Boulder, CO: Westview, 1994), 56; "Think Long and Deep about This 'Victory,'" *Daily Illini*, October 31, 1962, 12.

19. "A New Twist to Christmas" (photo), *Daily Illini*, December 15, 1961, 16; "Ah... Ah... Snoot Boot!" *Daily Illini*, December 12, 1961, 3; Carol Hamilton, "It's All Over! UI Talkathon Champ Again," *Daily Illini*, November 20, 1962, 1; "37 Out for Waterfight—More Come," *Daily Illini*, June 19, 1961, 6; Dave Young, "Water Fight—It Never Happened," *Daily Illini*, June 1, 1962, 1–2.

20. Angela Jordan, "Campus Folksong Club," U of I Archives, December 3, 2012, https://archives.library.illinois.edu/blog/campus-folksong-club/; Jim Weaver, "Audience Taps White Concert Huge Success," *Daily Illini*, December 8, 1960, 1; Roger Ebert, "Rambling Jack Rambles Here, Leaves Folk Songs, Anecdotes," *Daily Illini*, November 21, 1962, 2; Harvey Hoffswell, "Odetta Talent, Gentle Humor Win Audience," *Daily Illini*, February 10, 1962, 1; Roger Ebert, "PP&M Sing, Preach and Entertain," *Daily Illini*, October 10, 1963, 1; Roger Ebert, "Joan Baez Quiet, Human: Says Singing 'Part of Life,'" *Daily Illini*, November 30, 1962, 1.

21. Robert D. Novak, "Campus Ferment," *Wall Street Journal*, November 20, 1961, 1; "Campus Conservatives," *Time*, February 10, 1961, 34–35.

22. Jim Nowlan, telephone interview by author, February 22, 2020; David Young and Robert Auler, "Fresh Wind in Illinois," *National Review*, June 18, 1963, 495; M. Stanton Evans, *Revolt on the Campus* (Chicago: Henry Regnery, 1961), 22, 108–24.

23. Jane Phillips, "'Great Debates' Begin Tonight," *Daily Illini*, February 22, 1962, 3; Roger Ebert, "2 Debaters Agree: We Lag behind Reds," *Daily Illini*, May 4, 1962, 1–2; "Conservatives Down Liberals," *New Voice*, April 1963, 1, Student Organizations Publications file, U of I Archives, Series No. 41/6/840, box 21.

24. Roger Ebert, "Awesome Struggle! Liberals, Conservatives Plan Basketball Game," *Daily Illini*, January 11, 1963, 2; Rennie Davis, "UI Campus 'Cries' for Controversy," *Daily*

Illini, September 22, 1962, 5, 13; Garry Winter, "Trustees Accept Letter on Koch; Deny Discussion of Student View," *Daily Illini*, March 21, 1963, 1; Tony Fuller, "Senate Blocks JFK Telegram; Krohne Quits," *Daily Illini*, May 9, 1963, 1; Liz Krohne, "Why a Senator Quit," *Daily Illini*, May 10, 1963, 6; Roger Ebert, *Life Itself* (New York: Grand Central, 2011), 98.

25. Students for a Democratic Society, *The Port Huron Statement* (New York: Students for a Democratic Society, 1964), 7, http://www.progressivefox.com/misc_documents/PortHuronStatement.pdf; Paul Goodman, "For a Reactionary Experiment in Education," *Harper's*, November 1962, 69, 72 (emphasis in original); Ebert, *Life Itself*, 98. See also Bob Threlkeld, "SDS Organizes UI Chapter," *Daily Illini*, May 29, 1963, 5; Paul Goodman, *Growing Up Absurd* (New York: Vintage, 1960).

26. Ebert, *Life Itself*, 98; Charlene Segal, "Urbana Youngsters to Help Policemen; Applicants Register for Junior Police," *Daily Illini*, October 24, 1950, 4.

27. Ebert, *Life Itself*, 84; *Rosemary*, Urbana [IL] High School yearbook, 1960, Ancestry.com.

28. Ebert, *Life Itself*, 91, 96, 100; Roger Ebert, "He Saw a Generation Growing Up Absurd," *RogerEbert.com*, December 21, 2011, https://www.rogerebert.com/reviews/paul-goodman-changed-my-life-2011.

29. Ebert, *Life Itself*, 97–98; "New Student Paper to Appear, 'Spectator' on Sale Monday," *Daily Illini*, February 16, 1961, 12; Roger Ebert, "Post-war Generation: Parasites on Past?" *Champaign-Urbana Spectator*, February 27, 1961, 4.

30. Roger Ebert, "Ars Gratia . . .," *Daily Illini*, July 20, 1961, 6; Roger Ebert, "Henry Miller: Big Bad Man . . . with a Dirty Mind?" *Daily Illini*, October 28, 1961, 9; Roger Ebert, "Ars Gratia . . .," *Daily Illini*, December 6, 1961, 6.

31. Quotes are from Roger Ebert's "Ars Gratia . . ." column in *Daily Illini*, March 27, 1963, 4; October 17, 1962, 6; November 7, 1962, 6; and November 14, 1962, 6; and also from Barry Goldwater, "Letter from Goldwater," *Daily Illini*, November 2, 1962, 6.

32. Quotes are from Roger Ebert's "Ars Gratia . . ." column in *Daily Illini*, February 13, 1963, 6, and January 24, 1962, 6.

33. William F. Gavin, "Young Americans for Nothing," *America*, April 28, 1962, 113; Rita Hoffmann, "Swept with Confused Alarms: Psychological Climate on Campus," *Mademoiselle*, August 1964, 261; Morton M. Hunt and Rena Corman, "The Tormented Generation," *Saturday Evening Post*, October 12, 1963, 34 (emphasis in original).

34. John R. Thelin, *Going to College in the Sixties* (Baltimore, MD: Johns Hopkins University Press, 2018), Kindle, chap. 4.

35. "Only Authorized Picketing: Henry," *Daily Illini*, March 7, 1961, 1; "'Damn Pickets' Go Home," *Daily Illini*, May 23, 1961, 3; Ellen Filurin, "Continue Picket Policy Discussion," *Daily Illini*, September 15, 1961, 5.

36. Freeman, "Controversial Speakers Issue," 7; Roger Ebert, "Fight Local Speakers Ban," *Daily Illini*, March 16, 1962, 1; Royce Rowe, "Senate to Study Speakers Policy," *Daily Illini*, March 29, 1962, 1. See also Michael V. Metz, *Radicals in the Heartland: The*

1960s Student Protest Movement at the University of Illinois (Urbana: University of Illinois Press, 2019).

37. Roger Ebert, "American Nazi Leader's Speech Here Cancelled," *Daily Illini*, October 9, 1962, 1; Roger Ebert, "Liberals Keep Us Away," *Daily Illini*, October 10, 1962, 1; Bennett Reimer letter to the editor, *Daily Illini*, October 17, 1962, 6.

38. Undergraduate student code, c. 1963, Tiebout Papers, U of I Archives, box 2; Larry Miller, "UI's Student Senate Saw a 'Year of Breakthrough,'" *Daily Illini*, August 1963 (back-to-school issue), 27; Dave Young, "The Folly," *Daily Illini*, December 11, 1962, 6; Lois Levy, "Weaknesses Exist: Young," *Daily Illini*, January 12, 1963, 5; "Slow Progress," *Daily Illini*, April 4, 1962, 8; Cliff Steward, "Civil, Criminal Laws Inadequate?" *Daily Illini*, November 17, 1962, 11; Tony Fuller, "Discipline Bill Calls for Reform, Definition," *Daily Illini*, February 21, 1964, 2.

39. Philip Martin email to author, March 27, 2020; David D. Henry, "State of the University: Challenges for 1963," *Daily Illini*, January 12, 1963, 8; Clark Kerr, "The Multiversity: Are Its Several Souls Worth Saving?" *Harper's*, November 1963, 38. See also Thelin, *Going to College in the Sixties*, chap. 4.

40. Philip Martin, "State of the University: A Sober Student View," *Daily Illini*, February 16, 1963, 5.

41. Dave Reed, "Was Phil Martin Right? 'No Comment,'" *Daily Illini*, February 19, 1963, 1; Martin email to author; Charles A. Knudson, "UI Has Many Messages," *Daily Illini*, February 23, 1963, 5; Irving Dilliard, "Dilliard Shows Concern over Criticism of UI," *Daily Illini*, March 1, 1963, 6.

42. Karen Lucas Petitte, telephone interview by author, March 18, 2020; "The Daily Illini's Editorial Platform," *Daily Illini*, February 12, 1963, 10.

43. Petitte interview; Ebert, *Life Itself*, 95, 100–105; Ron Szoke, interview by author, Champaign, IL, March 2, 2020.

44. Miriam Shelden, "The Education of Women—the Counselor's Role," c. October 1964, Miriam A. Shelden Papers, U of I Archives, Series No. 41/3/21, box 1; Eleanor Saunders Towns oral history, *Voices of Illinois Oral History Project*, May 22, 2018, https://www.library.illinois.edu/voices/collection-item/eleanor-saunders-towns/.

45. Susan Stevens, "Talks at Noon by Clergymen," *Daily Illini*, September 17, 1963, 1; Roger Ebert, "Protest Vigils Catch On," *Daily Illini*, September 18, 1963, 1–2; Rudy Frank, "Millions for Charity . . ." (letter to the editor), *Daily Illini*, September 25, 1963, 6; Earl Wordlaw, "Years at Illinois: Lonely, Sterile," *Daily Illini*, October 26, 1963, 5. Wordlaw's series "The Revolution of 1963" appeared in the *Daily Illini* from November 19 to November 22, 1963.

46. "Senate Approves Treaty!" *Daily Illini*, September 25, 1963, 1; "What's Going On?" *Daily Illini*, September 12, 1963, 10; "The Tightrope," *Daily Illini*, November 5, 1963, 6.

47. Gary Porter, "Thurmond Talk Rambling," *Daily Illini*, November 9, 1963, 1; Barb Whiteside, "Thurmond to Receive an Apology," *Daily Illini*, November 14, 1963, 1.

48. "The Apology," *Daily Illini*, November 15, 1963, 8; Richard Schwarzlose, "The Meaning of Political Debate," *Daily Illini*, November 13, 1963, 6; J. A. Donaldson,

"Disagrees with Thurmond" (letter to the editor), *Daily Illini*, November 12, 1963, 6; Gary Porter, "Free Speech: Principle or Whim?" *Daily Illini*, November 16, 1963, 6.

49. Roger Ebert, "University Arrests McMullin," *Daily Illini*, November 19, 1963, 1; Roger Ebert, "In the Desert," *Daily Illini*, November 20, 1963, 6; "Bible Dispenser Arrested; U. of I. in Furor," *Chicago Sun-Times*, November 22, 1963, 3; Ebert, *Life Itself*, 104.

50. Ebert, *Life Itself*, 104–5; Larry Finley, "Gloomy Friday Recalled," *Daily Illini*, November 22, 1966, 3; Roger Ebert, ed., *An Illini Century* (Urbana: University of Illinois Press, 1967), 197; "Horrible News Hits 'Like a Bomb' Here," *Champaign-Urbana Courier*, November 22, 1963, 1, 5; Fran Myers, "Candidate Kennedy Was an Exciting Visitor at UI," *News-Gazette* (Champaign, IL), November 23, 1963, 3.

51. Finley, "Gloomy Friday Recalled," 3; Paula Peters, "11,500 Attend U. I. Rites for President Kennedy," *Champaign-Urbana Courier*, November 25, 1963, 3; Roger Ebert, "The Loud Silence," *Daily Illini*, November 26, 1963, 6; Bill Schwarz, "Kennedy Assembly Hall" (letter to the editor), *Daily Illini*, November 27, 1963, 5.

52. Ebert, *Life Itself*, 106–8; Dave Reed, "Ecstatic Fans Fell Goal Posts," *Daily Illini*, January 3, 1964, 1; "Football Team Welcomed," *Daily Illini*, January 3, 1964, 3.

53. Ebert, *Life Itself*, 105.

Chapter 5. International Vermin

1. Revilo P. Oliver to Fred W. Decker, November 12, 1978, Donald L. Kemmerer Papers, University of Illinois at Urbana-Champaign (U of I) Archives, Series No. 9/5/32, box 10; *The Biographical Record of Livingston and Woodford Counties, Illinois* (Chicago: S. J. Clarke, 1900), 420–22.

2. "The Oliver Family," *Chatsworth Illinois Memories*, https://sites.google.com/site/chatsworthillinoismemories/chatsworth-history/the-oliver-family; "Old But Frisky," *Streator Daily Free Press*, June 22, 1881, 1; "A Fine Point," *Bloomington Daily Leader*, January 31, 1887, 8.

3. *Biographical Record*, 421–22; "Afflicted with the Muse," *Bloomington Pantagraph* (reprint from *Piper City Journal*), April 1, 1898, 4.

4. "Search for a Wife," *Daily Leader* (Bloomington, IL), October 26, 1897, 1; "Wants a Divorce," *Times* (Streator, IL), October 28, 1897, 2; "The Oliver Case Again," *Bloomington Pantagraph*, November 5, 1897, 8; "Now That the Burning Passion . . ." *Streator Free Press*, December 10, 1897, 7; "Is Case of Unusual Interest," *Paxton Record*, November 6, 1919, 1. Some sources give Barlow's first name as "Maud." The junior Revilo Oliver would give his birth year as 1908, but if 1910 census data from *Ancestry.com* is accurate, the correct birth year is 1909.

5. "Is Case of Unusual Interest," 1; "Probe Aged Man's Death," *Murphysboro Daily Independent*, March 19, 1929, 2; "Revilo Oliver Commits Suicide in Springfield," *Paxton Record*, March 21, 1929, 1; "Mrs. Flora Oliver Bankrupt, Husband Was Landowner," unidentified news clipping, January 18, 1931, *Ancestry.com*.

6. Oliver to Decker; *Spectrum*, Compton [CA] High School yearbook, 1926, *Ancestry.com*. Springfield city directories indicate that Oliver had returned to live at home with his parents by 1927.

7. Dale Putnam, "Oliver's College Days Related," *Bloomington Pantagraph*, February 27, 1964, 5.

8. "The Wrong Time," *Daily Illini*, May 12, 1935, 4.

9. Andrea Lynn, "U. of I. Classics Department Celebrating 100th Year," University of Illinois News Bureau, November 4, 2005, https://news.illinois.edu/view/6367/207137; Michael Armstrong, "A German Scholar and Socialist in Illinois: The Career of William Abbott Oldfather," *Classical Journal* 88, no. 3 (1993): 240n25, 249.

10. Revilo P. Oliver to William A. Oldfather, January 25, 1938, William A. Oldfather Papers, U of I Archives, Series No. 15/6/20, box 4.

11. Frank P. Mintz, *The Liberty Lobby and the American Right* (Westport, CT: Greenwood, 1985), 164.

12. Oliver to Decker; correspondence in Oldfather Papers, U of I Archives, box 4; Armstrong, "A German Scholar," 250–51; correspondence in Revilo P. Oliver File, U of I Archives, Series No. 15/6/5; "John Lewis Heller," *Illinois Classical Studies* 8, no. 1 (Spring 1983): 168–72.

13. Oliver to Decker; "Carriage Owner Has Troubles," *Champaign-Urbana Courier*, February 24, 1954, 6; Carl T. Bogus, *Buckley: William F. Buckley Jr. and the Rise of American Conservatism* (New York: Bloomsbury, 2011), 183.

14. Revilo P. Oliver, *America's Decline* (London: Londinium, 1981), 5, 8, 12, 52–54; Oliver to Decker.

15. Donna Zuckerberg, *Not All Dead White Men: Classics and Misogyny in the Digital Age* (Cambridge, MA: Harvard University Press, 2018), 22–24; "Revilo Oliver: The White Supremacist Within," *Pharos*, September 6, 2019, http://pages.vassar.edu/pharos/2019/09/06/revilo-oliver-the-white-supremacist-within/. See also Page duBois, *Trojan Horses: Saving the Classics from Conservatives* (New York: New York University Press, 2001).

16. Revilo P. Oliver, "A Standard Pronunciation of Latin," *Classical Journal* 44, no. 4 (January 1949): 267; Oliver, "Modern Latin," *Classical Weekly*, March 12, 1951, 193–94; Oliver, "A Voice in the Wilderness," in *Classical, Mediaeval, and Renaissance Studies in Honor of Berthold Louis Ullman*, ed. Charles Henderson Jr. (Rome: Edizioni di Storia e Letteratura, 1964): 515–35, quote on 516. See also Ernest H. Wilkins, "On the Nature and Extent of the Italian Renaissance," *Italica* 27, no. 2 (June 1950): 67.

17. "Clabaugh's AYD Bill Made Law by Governor," *Daily Illini*, August 9, 1947, 1; Walter Gellhorn ed., *The States and Subversion* (Ithaca, NY: Cornell University Press, 1952), 136.

18. William F. Buckley Jr., *God and Man at Yale* (Chicago: Regnery, 1951), 141, 181, 190; Nicholas Buccola, *The Fire Is upon Us: James Baldwin, William F. Buckley Jr., and the Debate over Race in America* (Princeton, NJ: Princeton University Press, 2019), 53; Oliver to Decker; William F. Buckley Jr., *Cruising Speed* (New York: Putnam, 1971), 111.

19. Buccola, *Fire Is upon Us*, 2, 69; Damon T. Berry, *Blood and Faith: Christianity in American White Nationalism* (Syracuse, NY: Syracuse University Press, 2017), 31–32; John O'Donnell, "Capitol Stuff," *New York Daily News*, September 18, 1957, 4C. Oliver's reviews appeared in *National Review* in 1957 and 1958.

20. Oliver to Decker; "DAR Hears Prof. Oliver," *Champaign-Urbana Courier*, November 15, 1957, 6.

21. Donald R. McNeil, "America's Longest War: The Fight over Fluoridation," *Wilson Quarterly*, Summer 1985, 140–53; "Fluoridationists Blasted," *Champaign-Urbana Courier*, May 3, 1957, 9; "Anti's Hit Fluoridation in Tuscola," unidentified news clipping, c. 1957, Oliver File.

22. Arnold Forster and Benjamin R. Epstein, *Danger on the Right* (New York: Random House, 1964), 17–22; Alvin Felzenberg, "The Inside Story of William F. Buckley Jr.'s Crusade against the John Birch Society," *NationalReview.com*, June 20, 2017, https://www.nationalreview.com/2017/06/william-f-buckley-john-birch-society-history-conflict-robert-welch; Lynn Ludlow, "Prof. Oliver Tells How He Helped Start Birch Group," *Champaign-Urbana Courier*, March 28, 1961, 3, 10; "Senators Rap Birch Society for Calling Eisenhower Red," unidentified news clipping, c. March 1961, Oliver File; Colin E. Reynolds, "The Not-So-Far Right: Radical Right-Wing Politics in the United States, 1941–1977" (PhD diss., Emory University, 2016), 95, ProQuest.

23. R[evilo] P. Oliver, "The Decay of the Academy," *Modern Age*, Fall 1959, 340–41; Revilo P. Oliver, "Conservatism and Reality," *Modern Age*, Fall 1961, 402.

24. "Americans Speak Out!" *American Mercury*, January 1960, 126; "Prof. Oliver Claims Red 'Cells' at U. I.," *Champaign-Urbana Courier*, April 6, 1959, 8; Gilbert Moore, "Taxpayers Group Hears of Communist 'Plot,'" *Galesburg Register-Mail*, May 15, 1959, 2; "Weekend Review," *Galesburg Register-Mail*, May 16, 1959, 4.

25. Correspondence from Charles Morrow, James S. Spencer, and R. E. Pettit to U of I president David Henry's office, May 1959, Administrative and Personnel Actions File, U of I Archives, Series No. 2/15/10, box 4.

26. Lyle H. Lanier to Gordon N. Ray, June 9, 1959, and Gordon N. Ray to David Henry, June 11, 1959, Administrative and Personnel Actions File, box 4; John Heller notes on meetings with Revilo Oliver, April–June 1959, Oliver File. (Heller's notes are dated 1960; that appears to be an error.)

27. Lanier to Ray.

28. Grace Oliver to Ira Latimer, January 27, 1960, and form letters from John L. Heller and David D. Henry, c. 1959, Ira Latimer Papers, Chicago History Museum Research Center, box 87.

29. Dick Icen, "A Biased View," *Daily Illini*, October 18, 1960, 8; Howard Barham to Wayne Johnston, April 13, 1960, Wayne A. Johnston Papers, U of I Archives, Series No. 1/20/3, box 4; Wayne A. Johnston to David D. Henry (accompanied by clippings), September 26, 1960, Administrative and Personnel Actions File, box 9; Lew Collens, telephone interview by author, March 4, 2020.

30. Gordon N. Ray to Mary Nolan, December 22, 1959, Administrative and Personnel Actions File, box 4; John Heller notes and correspondence, c. February 1960, Oliver File.

31. Mintz, *Liberty Lobby*, 167–68; Ludlow, "Prof. Oliver," 3, 10; "Birch Officer Says Kennedy Has Weak Aids," *Chicago Tribune*, April 4, 1961, part 1, 8.

32. "Who Points a Finger?" *Springfield Leader and Press* (MO), April 5, 1961, 12; "Society Condemnation," *Daily Illini*, April 6, 1961, 6; "Henry Disclaims Responsibility for Oliver's Right-Wing Views," *Daily Illini*, April 8, 1961, 2; John L. Heller, "Views Unshared" (letter to the editor), *Daily Illini*, April 8, 1961, 6.

33. John Heller notes on meeting with Revilo Oliver, April 1961, Oliver File.

34. Alan F. Westin, "The John Birch Society: 'Radical Right' and 'Extreme Left' in the Political Context of Post World War II (1962)"; Daniel Bell, "The Dispossessed (1962)"; and Richard Hofstadter, "The Pseudo-Conservative Revolt (1955)"; all in *The Radical Right*, 3rd ed., ed. Daniel Bell (New Brunswick, NJ: Transaction, 2002), 8, 16, 75–76, 240–41.

35. David L. Chappell, "The Triumph of Conservatives in a Liberal Age," in *A Companion to Post-1945 America*, ed. Jean-Christophe Agnew and Roy Rosenzweig (Malden, MA: Blackwell, 2006), 307; William F. Buckley Jr., *Up from Liberalism* (New York: McDowell, Obolensky, 1959), 61; "The Question of Robert Welch," *National Review*, February 13, 1962, 88. See also Bogus, *Buckley*, 375–76n26; Felzenberg, "Inside Story."

36. Bogus, *Buckley*, 375–76n26; Buckley, *Cruising Speed*, 112–13.

37. Henry Lowenthal and John Glass, "Refute Views of Professor" (letter to the editor), *Daily Illini*, April 13, 1961, 7; William K. Wyant Jr., "The Rev. Billy James Hargis's Crusade Viewed As One of Most Significant of Anti-red Groups," *St. Louis Post-Dispatch*, February 27, 1962, 1C; "Prof. Oliver Takes Aim," *Champaign-Urbana Courier*, April 29, 1962, 44.

38. John Heller notes on meetings with Revilo Oliver and Jack W. Peltason, March 1962, and J. W. Peltason to Robert M. Derman, March 5, 1962, Oliver File.

39. John Heller to J. W. Peltason, April 17, 1963, Administrative and Personnel Actions File, box 4; Mintz, *Liberty Lobby*, 168–71; "Birch Society Sets Seminar," *Times and Democrat* (Orangeburg, SC), November 5, 1963, 8; Buckley, *Cruising Speed*, 112.

40. Richard Hofstadter, "The Paranoid Style in American Politics," *Harper's*, November 1964, 77–86, https://harpers.org/archive/1964/11/the-paranoid-style-in-american-politics/.

41. Bill Minutaglio and Steven L. Davis, *Dallas 1963* (New York: Twelve, 2013), 74–79, 240–51, 267–94.

42. These quotes and the ones that follow come from Revilo P. Oliver, "Marxmanship in Dallas," *American Opinion* 7, no. 2 (February 1964): 13–28, http://archive.org/stream/MarxmanshipInDallas/MarxmanshipInDallas_djvu.txt.

43. 109 Cong. Rec. 23331 (1963) (statement of Rep. Ashbrook). In "Marxmanship in Dallas," Oliver lists a different page number in the *Congressional Record* that makes no mention of Oswald.

44. The original draft of Oliver's article is at http://www.revilo-oliver.com/rpo/Marxmanship1.html. (Readers are cautioned that this website contains white supremacist and anti-Semitic material.)

45. David D. Henry to Gordon Ray, April 22, 1964, David D. Henry Papers, U of I Archives, Series No. 2/12/20, box 28.

Chapter 6. Ungloriously Wrong

1. Peter Kihss, "Kennedy Target of Birch Writer," *New York Times*, February 11, 1964, 18; "Birch View of JFK," *Newsweek*, February 24, 1964, 29–30; John Keefe, "UI Professor's Article Says JFK Was Red Collaborator; Stirs National Controversy," *Daily Illini*, February 12, 1964, 1–2; "No Comment," *Daily Illini*, February 12, 1964, 1.

2. "Shame!" *Chicago Sun-Times*, February 13, 1964, 35; "Antidote to Poison," *St. Louis Post-Dispatch*, February 23, 1964, 4; Lee Merriman, "Libel, 'Academic Freedom,' & Shame," *Pasadena Independent*, February 18, 1964, 14; "A Repulsive Piece of Crankery," *Chicago's American*, February 14, 1964, Samuel K. Gove Papers, University of Illinois at Urbana-Champaign (U of I) Archives, Series No. 21/1/20, box 26; "Birchers Do the Impossible: Manage to Reach New Low," *Philadelphia Daily News*, February 13, 1964, 33; "Kennedy the Communist," *World* (Coors Bay, OR), February 13, 1964, 4.

3. 110 Cong. Rec. A717–18 (1964) (statement of Rep. Senner); Sammy R. Danna to J. L. Heller, February 12, 1964, Revilo P. Oliver File, U of I Archives, Series No. 15/6/5; Mel E. Miles, "Oliver a Fanatic?" (letter to the editor), *Daily Illini*, February 14, 1964, 9; "Pogue Asks That Oliver Leave U. I.," *Champaign-Urbana Courier*, February 22, 1964, 3; "Hanging on Quad," *Daily Illini*, February 14, 1964, 1.

4. Marge Slavin, "Oliver's Opinions His Own: Peltason," *Daily Illini*, February 13, 1964, 1–2; Keefe, "UI Professor's Article," 1–2.

5. Frances Dickman to Jack Peltason and James Costello, February 12, 1964, Administrative and Personnel Actions File, U of I Archives, Series No. 2/15/10, box 4; "Oliver's Outburst Was Unreasoned, Vitriolic: Henry," *Daily Illini*, February 14, 1964, 1; extract from the University of Illinois Statutes, June 1, 1966, Faculty Organizations/AAUP File, U of I Archives, Series No. 48/1/5, box 4.

6. Documents in Administrative and Personnel Actions File, box 4; Anda Korsts, "Henry Requests Advice from Urbana Senate," *Daily Illini*, February 20, 1964, 1.

7. "Text of Statement," *Daily Illini*, February 28, 1964, 10.

8. Roger Ebert, "Why It Isn't True," *Daily Illini*, February 12, 1964, 4; Roger Ebert, "Contemptible—but Free," *St. Louis Post-Dispatch*, February 22, 1964, 4A. For one example of Ebert being misidentified as "Robert," see "Prof's Attack on JFK Brings Gripes of Wrath," *Philadelphia Daily News*, February 13, 1964, 16.

9. Roger Ebert, "Plain Talk," *Daily Illini*, February 26, 1964, 6.

10. Gary Porter, "The Cases of Oliver and Koch: What Boundaries on Free Speech?" *Daily Illini*, February 15, 1964, 5.

11. Tony Burba, "Bad Eggs," *Daily Illini*, February 28, 1964, 8.

12. Roger Ebert, *Life Itself* (New York: Grand Central, 2011), 103; Robert Jung, "Cabbages and Kings," *Daily Illini*, March 4, 1964, 6; Robert Jung, "Says Oliver's Article Unethical," *Daily Illini*, February 14, 1964, 8.

13. John Johnson, "Let Oliver Speak!" *Daily Illini*, February 18, 1964, 6; John Johnson, "At the Crossroads," *Daily Illini*, February 25, 1964, 6.

14. Liz Krohne, "The Holy Region," *Daily Illini*, February 27, 1964, 6.

15. Liz Krohne, "Time for a Change," *Daily Illini*, February 20, 1964, 6.

16. Documents and correspondence in Harold W. Hannah Papers, U of I Archives, Series No. 8/4/34 [hereafter, Hannah Papers], box 5.

17. Barbara Whiteside, "AAUP Backs Henry's Stand," *Daily Illini*, February 21, 1964, 1.

18. Urbana-Champaign Senate Committee on Academic Freedom and Tenure to David D. Henry, February 28, 1964, Hannah Papers, box 5.

19. Documents and correspondence in Hannah Papers, box 5; "Text of Statement on Oliver Case," *Daily Illini*, March 20, 1964, 10.

20. Anda Korsts, "No Action on Oliver: Trustees," *Daily Illini*, March 19, 1964, 1–2; "Two Trustees Rap Oliver," *Champaign-Urbana Courier*, March 18, 1964, 3.

21. Korsts, "No Action on Oliver," 1–2.

22. Barb Whiteside, "AAUP Upholds Censure," *Daily Illini*, April 11, 1964, 1; David D. Henry to E. B. McNatt, March 19, 1964, Hannah Papers, box 5; David D. Henry to Charles E. Odegaard, March 30, 1964, David D. Henry Papers, U of I Archives, Series No. 2/12/20 [hereafter, Henry Papers], box 28.

23. "2nd Printing for Article By Oliver," *Champaign-Urbana Courier*, February 20, 1964, 3.

24. Revilo P. Oliver, "Dr. Oliver Replies," circular distributed by Community Lecture Series, Mt. Zion, IL, c. March 1964, Champaign County Historical Archives, Urbana, IL.

25. Revilo P. Oliver, "Marxmanship in Dallas: Part II," *American Opinion*, March 1964, 65–78, http://archive.org/stream/MarxmanshipInDallas/MarxmanshipInDallas_djvu.txt.

26. Richard H. Icen, "Dr. Scholz Denies Lecture Series Is Front for John Birch Society," *Decatur Herald*, March 4, 1964, 1; "Let Him Speak!" *Prairie Post* (Maroa, IL), March 5, 1964, Decatur Public Library, Decatur, IL; "$100,000 Libel Suit Pondered by Oliver," *News-Gazette* (Champaign, IL), March 17, 1964, 3.

27. Revilo P. Oliver, "The Aftermath of the Assassination," and accompanying circular distributed by Community Lecture Series, Mt. Zion, IL, c. March 1964, Champaign County Historical Archives; Richard H. Icen, "Says Insider Aided Oswald," *Champaign-Urbana Courier*, March 19, 1964, 3, 10; Paul A. Driscoll, "Oliver Claims Opponents Make Him Smear Victim," *News-Gazette* (Champaign, IL), March 19, 1964, 3. See also Kathryn S. Olmsted, *Real Enemies: Conspiracy Theories and American Democracy, World War I to 9/11* (New York: Oxford University Press, 2009), 111–48.

28. Henry Hanson, "Birch Professor's Right Wing Thundering Stuns Decatur," *Press and Sun-Bulletin* (Binghamton, NY), March 30, 1964, 6; Oliver, "Aftermath of the

Assassination"; Driscoll, "Oliver Claims Opponents," 3; Hugh Hough, "Road to Far Right Leads U. of Illinois Professor into Difficulty," *Star Tribune* (Minneapolis, MN), February 23, 1964, 13A.

29. Driscoll, "Oliver Claims Opponents," 3; Revilo P. Oliver to Fred W. Decker, November 12, 1978, Donald L. Kemmerer Papers, U of I Archives, Series No. 9/5/32, box 10; Larry Finley, "'Obey Him!'" *Daily Illini*, March 4, 1965, 4.

30. Frank P. Mintz, *The Liberty Lobby and the American Right* (Westport, CT: Greenwood, 1985), 172; Eric Cavaliero, "Slain Rights Workers Called 'Cockroaches,'" *Tucson Daily Citizen*, August 25, 1964, 3; Julius Duscha, "California Crowd Hears Harangue by Bircher," *Washington Post*, August 30, 1964, A19.

31. "Oliver Wants New Probe," *Champaign-Urbana Courier*, April 3, 1964, 3.

32. "Revilo Oliver 'Deposition' to Be Public," *Champaign-Urbana Courier*, September 11, 1964, 3; Dorothy Williams, "What Oliver Told Warren Commission: Its Questions, His Answers," *Champaign-Urbana Courier*, December 10, 1964, 3, 15; "Testimony of Revilo Pendleton Oliver," *Hearings before the President's Commission on the Assassination of President Kennedy*, vol. 15 (Washington, DC: United States Government Printing Office, 1964), 709–44, https://www.govinfo.gov/content/pkg/GPO-WARRENCOMMISSIONHEARINGS-15/pdf/GPO-WARRENCOMMISSIONHEARINGS-15.pdf.

33. "Oliver Had No Evidence: Jenner," *Champaign-Urbana Courier*, November 19, 1964, 3; Diana Dupin, "Lawyer Defends Warren Probe," *Daily Illini*, November 19, 1964, 3.

34. Dixie Cowan, "Call Oliver 'Excellent,'" *Daily Illini*, February 26, 1964, 3.

35. See Dave Young, "Young's Folly," *Daily Illini*, October 24, 1961, 6.

36. Johnson, "Let Oliver Speak!"; Jim Nowlan, telephone interview by author, February 22, 2020; Harrison Church to Francis G. Wilson, April 28, 1964, Francis G. Wilson Papers, U of I Archives, Series No. 15/18/24, box 1.

37. "Barry: Attack on JFK Despicable," *News-Gazette* (Champaign, IL), February 13, 1964, 3; Russell Kirk, "Academic Freedom Is Worth Keeping," *Daily Press* (Newport News, VA), March 5, 1964, 4; Willmoore Kendall to Francis G. Wilson, c. February 1963, c. March 1963, and c. March 1964, Wilson Papers, box 3; William F. Buckley Jr., "Two Who Were Smeared," *Boston Globe*, February 28, 1964, 15; William F. Buckley Jr., *Cruising Speed* (New York: Putnam, 1971), 113–14.

38. John Heller notes for meeting with Revilo Oliver, c. fall 1964, and note on Oliver scholarly output, c. 1969, Oliver File.

39. John Heller to senior members of the classics department, March 5, 1966, Oliver File.

40. Stephen Zorn, "Rally for God and Country Finds Subversion Rampant," *Boston Globe*, July 3, 1966, 6; Thomas Buckley, "A Birch Society Founder Quits; Pressure by Welch Is Reported," *New York Times*, August 16, 1966, 23; Revilo P. Oliver, *America's Decline* (London: Londinium, 1981), 333–34.

41. See Damon T. Berry, *Blood and Faith: Christianity in American White Nationalism* (Syracuse, NY: Syracuse University Press, 2017), 19–43; Mintz, *Liberty Lobby*, 172–79; "Revilo

Oliver: The White Supremacist Within," *Pharos*, September 6, 2019, http://pages.vassar.edu/pharos/2019/09/06/revilo-oliver-the-white-supremacist-within/; Heidi Beirich, "Holocaust Museum Shooter Had Close Ties to Prominent Neo-Nazis," *Southern Poverty Law Center*, June 10, 2009, https://www.splcenter.org/hatewatch/2009/06/10/holocaust-museum-shooter-had-close-ties-prominent-neo-nazis.

42. "About Revilo P. Oliver," newsroom notes from *Champaign-Urbana Courier*, c. 1971, Champaign County Historical Archives.

43. "Revilo Oliver," *Pharos*. See also *Pharos*'s mission statement at http://pages.vassar.edu/pharos/.

44. Barry Mehler, "Beyondism: Raymond B. Cattell and the New Eugenics," Institute for the Study of Academic Racism, January 1998, http://www.ferris-pages.org/ISAR/bios/Cattell/genetica.htm; William H. Tucker, *The Cattell Controversy: Race, Science, and Ideology* (Urbana: University of Illinois Press, 2009), 132.

45. Revilo Oliver to Miroslav Marcovich, October 20, 1973; Revilo P. Oliver to John J. Bateman, December 5, 1969; and Miroslav Marcovich, "The Dinner for Revilo and Grace Oliver," April 28, 1977; all in Oliver File. See also Tim Mitchell, "Life Remembered: Popular Classics Prof Was 'Legendary,'" *News-Gazette.com*, June 22, 2009, https://www.news-gazette.com/news/life-remembered-popular-classics-prof-was-legendary/article_011aa26e-2f3c-59d9-a8ff-6edcc75dd188.html.

46. "Not Fit to Teach," *Bridgeport Post*, c. August 1966; Seymour B. Dill to office of the president, August 16, 1966; and A. J. Janata to Aaron Freedman, August 23, 1966; all in Administrative and Personnel Actions File, box 4.

47. David D. Henry memoirs, Henry Papers, box 25.

48. Tony Fuller, "Student Blasts Disciplinary Policy," *Daily Illini*, March 5, 1964, 2; Tony Fuller, "Former Student Criticizes Security Office," *Daily Illini*, March 12, 1964, 1; Tony Fuller, "Coed Kisses, Gets Squad Car Ride," *Daily Illini*, March 17, 1964, 1.

49. "Police State Odor" (letter to the editor), *Daily Illini*, March 18, 1964, 7; Tony Fuller, "Other Colleges Vary on Discipline," *Daily Illini*, March 25, 1964, 1, 3; Tony Fuller, "Discipline Restructured," *Daily Illini*, July 23, 1964, 1. See also Michael V. Metz, *Radicals in the Heartland: The 1960s Student Protest Movement at the University of Illinois* (Urbana: University of Illinois Press, 2019).

50. Bob Strohm, "Arrest 14 Students in Demonstration," *Daily Illini*, May 20, 1964, 1; Connie Rolison Corbett oral history, Voices of Illinois Oral History Project, May 22, 2018, https://www.library.illinois.edu/voices/collection-item/connie-rolison-corbett/.

51. Liz Krohne, "Brass Tacks," *Daily Illini*, May 28, 1964, 4; Liz Krohne, "In Jackson: Between Two Worlds," *York Daily Record* (reprint from *Southern Patriot*), October 2, 1964, 25.

52. "Students Telegram Berkeley," *Daily Illini*, October 9, 1964, 6; Dixie Cowan, "Students Protest Berkeley Policy," *Daily Illini*, December 5, 1964, 3. See also David Lance Goines, *The Free Speech Movement* (Berkeley, CA: Ten Speed, 1993).

53. Roger Ebert, "Motives," *Daily Illini*, November 25, 1964, 4.

54. "Illinois YRs Praise Berkeley Chapter," *Daily Illini*, December 17, 1964, 3; Tony Burba, "Barry Train Stops Here: GOP Nominee Greets 9,000, Raps Jeers, Pro-LBJ Signs," *Daily Illini*, October 3, 1964, 1; "CSA Grants UI Recognition to New Conservative Group," *Daily Illini*, January 8, 1965, 3.

55. Burba, "Barry Train Stops Here," 1; Gary Porter, "Viet Nam Follies," *Daily Illini*, April 23, 1964, 6; Gary Porter, "Too Late," *Daily Illini*, May 14, 1964, 6; Gary Porter, "Danger Words," *Daily Illini*, July 2, 1964, 6.

56. Vicki Packer, "CCC Jeers Speakers during Protest Rally," *Daily Illini*, December 19, 1964, 1.

57. "Viet Nam Battles Rage"; "YDs, SDS Letter to Johnson"; and Tony Burba, "Viet Nam"; all in *Daily Illini*, February 10, 1965, 1, 4, 5.

58. See Metz, *Radicals in the Heartland*; Joy Ann Williamson, *Black Power on Campus: The University of Illinois, 1965–75* (Urbana: University of Illinois Press, 2003); Patrick D. Kennedy, "Reactions against the Vietnam War and Military-Related Targets on Campus: The University of Illinois as a Case Study, 1965–1972," *Illinois Historical Journal* 84, no. 2 (Summer 1991): 101–18.

Conclusion

1. David D. Henry, "State of the University: Time of Achievement," *Daily Illini*, September 19, 1964, 7.

2. Abram L. Sachar, "Hard Words Wear Nailed Boots: The Role of Responsible Dissent," September 20, 1964, University of Illinois Library, Urbana. See also Carl Sandburg, "Primer Lesson," https://allpoetry.com/Primer-Lesson.

3. Miriam A. Shelden, "Yeast and Ferment," May 1, 1964, Miriam A. Shelden Papers, University of Illinois at Urbana-Champaign (U of I) Archives, Series No. 41/3/21.

4. Miriam A. Shelden, "A Charge to Women," September 15 and 18, 1964, Shelden Papers.

5. Adam Harris, "Here's How Higher Education Dies," *Atlantic*, June 5, 2018, https://www.theatlantic.com/education/archive/2018/06/heres-how-higher-education-dies/561995/.

6. Gabriel Paquette, "Bashing Administrators While the University Burns," *Chronicle of Higher Education*, May 29, 2020, https://www.chronicle.com/article/bashing-administrators-while-the-university-burns.

7. Vimal Patel, "The New 'In Loco Parentis,'" *Chronicle of Higher Education*, February 17, 2019, https://www.chronicle.com/article/why-colleges-are-keeping-a-closer-eye-on-their-students-lives/.

8. Clark Kerr, foreword to David D. Henry, *Challenges Past, Challenges Present: An Analysis of American Higher Education since 1930* (San Francisco: Jossey-Bass, 1975), ix.

9. Roger Ebert, "Out of the Herd," *Daily Illini*, April 8, 1966, 6; Rita Hoffmann, "Swept with Confused Alarms: Psychological Climate on Campus," *Mademoiselle*, August 1964,

261; Morton M. Hunt and Rena Corman, "The Tormented Generation," *Saturday Evening Post*, October 12, 1963, 30; Carl Binger, "The Pressures on College Girls Today," *Atlantic*, February 1961, 41–42.

10. See John K. Wilson, "Freedom of the Press on Campus," National Center for Free Speech and Civic Engagement, University of California, 2020, https://freespeechcenter.universityofcalifornia.edu/fellows-19-20/wilson-research/.

11. Shelden, "Yeast and Ferment"; Beth Bailey, *Sex in the Heartland* (Cambridge, MA: Harvard University Press, 1999), 8.

12. Donna Freitas, *Consent on Campus* (New York: Oxford University Press, 2018), 77–78; Jennifer S. Hirsch and Shamus Khan, *Sexual Citizens* (New York: W. W. Norton, 2020), xvii–xix, 239.

13. Hirsch and Khan, *Sexual Citizens*, xvi; Shelden, "Yeast and Ferment"; Freitas, *Consent on Campus*, 192.

14. Leo F. Koch, "Advice on Sex" (letter to the editor), *Daily Illini*, March 18, 1960, 8. See also Maggie Astor, "How the Politically Unthinkable Can Become Mainstream," *New York Times*, February 26, 2019, https://nyti.ms/2TiP44d; "Hallin's Spheres," *Wikipedia.org*, https://en.wikipedia.org/wiki/Hallin%27s_spheres.

15. Joan Wallach Scott, *Knowledge, Power, and Academic Freedom* (New York: Columbia University Press, 2019), 99; Suzanne Nossel, *Dare to Speak: Defending Free Speech for All* (New York: Dey Street, 2020), 53; Harry M. Tiebout Jr. to L. H. Lanier, April 11, 1960, in Harry M. Tiebout Papers, U of I Archives, Series No. 15/16/21, box 2.

16. Scott, *Knowledge, Power, and Academic Freedom*, 64; Leo Koch Papers, Speeches and Writings, boxes 12 and 13, Wisconsin Historical Society, Madison; Leo Koch personnel file, U of I Archives, Series No. 2/15/10, box 5.

17. "Revilo Oliver: The White Supremacist Within," *Pharos*, September 6, 2019, http://pages.vassar.edu/pharos/2019/09/06/revilo-oliver-the-white-supremacist-within/; Donna Zuckerberg, *Not All Dead White Men: Classics and Misogyny in the Digital Age* (Cambridge, MA: Harvard University Press, 2018), 24; George Hawley, *The Alt-Right* (New York: Oxford University Press, 2019), 27.

18. Dorothee Benz, "Nazi-Normalizing Barf Journalism: A Brief History," *Fairness and Accuracy in Reporting*, November 1, 2019, https://fair.org/home/nazi-normalizing-barf-journalism-a-brief-history/; Thomas Milan Konda, *Conspiracies of Conspiracies* (Chicago: University of Chicago Press, 2019), 330. See also Hannah Allam, "Right-Wing Embrace of Conspiracy is 'Mass Radicalization,' Experts Warn," *NPR.org*, December 15, 2020, https://www.npr.org/2020/12/15/946381523/right-wing-embrace-of-conspiracy-is-mass-radicalization-experts-warn.

19. Alvin Felzenberg, "The Inside Story of William F. Buckley Jr.'s Crusade against the John Birch Society," *National Review*, June 20, 2017, https://www.nationalreview.com/2017/06/william-f-buckley-john-birch-society-history-conflict-robert-welch; Revilo P. Oliver, "Marxmanship in Dallas: Part II," *American Opinion*, March 1964, 65–78, http://archive.org/stream/MarxmanshipInDallas/MarxmanshipIn

Dallas_djvu.txt;' Eric Cavaliero, "Slain Rights Workers Called 'Cockroaches,'" *Tucson Daily Citizen*, August 25, 1964, 3; Kevin Roose, "Think QAnon Is on the Fringe? So Was the Tea Party," *New York Times*, August 13, 2020, https://nyti.ms/3kLJouG; Christopher Towler, "The John Birch Society Is Still Influencing American Politics, 60 Years after Its Founding," *The Conversation*, December 6, 2018, https://theconversation.com/the-john-birch-society-is-still-influencing-american-politics-60-years-after-its-founding-107925; "ADL: White Supremacist Propaganda Distribution Hit All-Time High in 2019," *ADL.org*, February 12, 2020, https://www.adl.org/news/press-releases/adl-white-supremacist-propaganda-distribution-hit-all-time-high-in-2019.

20. Sachar, "Hard Words."

21. Revilo P. Oliver, "The Aftermath of the Assassination," Community Lecture Series, Mt. Zion, IL, c. March 1964, Champaign County Historical Archives, Urbana, IL; Glenn Kessler, "The 'Very Fine' People at Charlottesville: Who Were They?" *Washington Post*, May 8, 2020, https://www.washingtonpost.com/politics/2020/05/08/very-fine-people-charlottesville-who-were-they-2/; "Revilo Oliver: The White Supremacist Within."

22. John R. Thelin, *A History of American Higher Education*, 3rd ed. (Baltimore, MD: Johns Hopkins University Press, 2019), Kindle, chap. 10; Christopher Newfield, *The Great Mistake: How We Wrecked Public Universities and How We Can Fix Them* (Baltimore, MD: Johns Hopkins University Press, 2016), Kindle, part 2, stage 1.

23. Konda, *Conspiracies of Conspiracies*, 330.

24. Jan Goldstein, Vicki Ruiz, and Kenneth Pomerantz, "An Open Letter to Chancellor Wise of the University of Illinois," American Historical Association, October 1, 2014, https://www.historians.org/publications-and-directories/perspectives-on-history/october-2014/an-open-letter-to-chancellor-wise-of-the-university-of-illinois.

25. John Durham Peters, *Courting the Abyss: Free Speech and the Liberal Tradition* (Chicago: University of Chicago Press, 2005), 142–80; Ulrich Baer, *What Snowflakes Get Right: Free Speech, Truth, and Equality on Campus* (New York: Oxford University Press, 2019), 107.

26. Keith E. Whittington, *Speak Freely: Why Universities Must Defend Free Speech* (Princeton, NJ: Princeton University Press, 2018), 72–75; Nossel, *Dare to Speak*, 62.

27. Burkowitz quoted in Henry Reichman, *The Future of Academic Freedom* (Baltimore, MD: Johns Hopkins University Press, 2019), 191–92.

28. David D. Henry memoirs, David D. Henry Papers, U of I Archives, Series No. 2/12/20, box 25; Michael V. Metz, *Radicals in the Heartland: The 1960s Student Protest Movement at the University of Illinois* (Urbana: University of Illinois Press, 2019), Kindle, chap. 2; Robert Mcg. Thomas Jr., "David D. Henry, 89, President of Illinois U. in Time of Tumult," *New York Times*, September 7, 1995, B17. Metz's *Radicals in the Heartland* provides a comprehensive history of the student movement at the U of I from 1965 to 1970.

29. Dean of Women's office annual report, 1963–64, in Student Affairs/Dean of Students file, U of I Archives, Series No. 41/1/30, box 2.

30. Miriam A. Shelden, "The University: A Man's World?" October 15, 1971, Shelden Papers; "UI's Dean Miriam Shelden Dies at 62," *News-Gazette* (Champaign, IL), May 13, 1975, sec. 1, 3.

31. Eleanor Saunders Towns oral history, Voices of Illinois Oral History Project, May 22, 2018, https://www.library.illinois.edu/voices/collection-item/eleanor-saunders-towns/; Connie Rolison Corbett oral history, Voices of Illinois Oral History Project, May 22, 2018, https://www.library.illinois.edu/voices/collection-item/connie-rolison-corbett/.

32. Liz Krohne, "In Jackson: Between Two Worlds," *York Daily Record* (reprint from *Southern Patriot*), October 2, 1964, 25; Elizabeth C. "Betsy" Shirah obituary, Gunderson Funeral and Cremation Care, July 2020, http://www.gundersonfh.com/obituaries/Elizabeth-C-Betsy-Shirah?obId=17258632#/obituaryInfo. See also Roger Ebert, *Life Itself* (New York: Grand Central, 2011), 98.

33. "We Protest Raids on Films," Sexual Freedom League flier, c. March 1964, Samuel K. Gove Papers, U of I Archives, Series No. 21/1/20, box 21. The original name of the organization was the New York City League for Sexual Freedom.

34. Biographical note in Leo Koch Papers finding aid, Wisconsin Historical Society; Kathy Reinbolt, "The Case of Leo F. Koch," *Daily Illini*, March 14, 1970, 11–12, 14.

35. Reinbolt, "The Case of Leo F. Koch," 11; David Corcoran, "Dr. Koch Trades Liberal Party Post for Life on Farm," *Record* (Hackensack, NJ), August 14, 1970, B-1, B-3.

36. Ande Yakstis, "Unauthorized Group Solicits Funds for GOP," *Alton Evening Telegraph*, March 12, 1968, 1–2; "Ira Latimer; Battled for Civil Rights," *Chicago Tribune*, February 17, 1985, https://www.chicagotribune.com/news/ct-xpm-1985-02-17-8501090867-story.html.

37. Revilo P. Oliver, *America's Decline* (London: Londinium Press, 1981), 4, 338–39; Damon T. Berry, *Blood and Faith: Christianity in American White Nationalism* (Syracuse, NY: Syracuse University Press, 2017), 39. Details of Oliver's suicide come from the *Vanguard News Network Forum*, November 2005, https://vnnforum.com/showthread.php?t=25453. (Readers are cautioned that this website contains white supremacist and anti-Semitic material.)

38. Roger Ebert, "Why It Isn't True," *Daily Illini*, February 12, 1964, 4.

39. Ebert, *Life Itself*, 361.

40. Ibid., 412–14.

Index

Page numbers in *italics* refer to photographs.

AAUP. *See* American Association of University Professors
Abt, John, 132
academic freedom, 1–16, 163–69; and extramural speech, 4–8, 69, 83, 150–51, 164–65; free speech versus, 4–8, 163–69; and Leo Koch case, 1–16, 64–86, 122, 163–69; and McCarthyism, 6, 17–19, 21; models of, 4–6, 83; and Revilo Oliver case, 1–16, 120–28, 135–43, 150–54, 163–69; professional oversight of, 4–8, 80–83, 140–43, 163–69; and responsibility, 5–8, 75–76, 80–83, 136–43, 167; and Steven Salaita case, 6, 167; and Statement of Principles on Academic Freedom and Tenure, 69, 75, 81, 83
ACLU (American Civil Liberties Union), 34, 35, 77, 84
Adams, Arthur S., 54
African Americans. *See* civil rights movement; college students; University of Illinois

alt-right, 12–13, 165. *See also* white supremacy
America (magazine), 101
American Association of University Professors (AAUP), 4–8, 15; and extramural speech, 4–8, 69, 83; and Leo Koch, 76, 80–84; and Revilo Oliver, 122, 136, 141–43; and Steven Salaita case, 6; and Statement of Principles on Academic Freedom and Tenure, 69, 75, 81, 83; and Statement on Extramural Utterances, 83; and University of Illinois censures, 2, 6, 15, 80–84, 142–43; University of Illinois chapter, 35, 76, 80–84, 136, 141
American Federation of Small Businesses, 172
American Historical Association, 167
American Opinion, 16, 120, 124, 129; and "Marxmanship in Dallas," 132–34, 139, 142, 143–44. *See also* John Birch Society
American Philological Association, 153
Anti-Communist League (Champaign-Urbana, IL), 34, 35–36, 123–24

Archbold, Rich, 60–61
Armstrong, Michael, 114–15
Army Security Agency (US), 115
Ashbrook, John M., 132
Associated Press, 135
Association of American Colleges, 69
Atlantic, 45
Auburn University, 13
Auler, Robert (Bob), 96, 106

baby boom generation, 2, 14, 21, 24–30, 159–62
Baer, Ulrich, 6–7, 168
Baez, Joan, 95–96
Bailey, Beth, 3, 9–10, 46–47, 58, 162
Bakersfield College, 40
Bardeen, John, 79
Barham, Howard, 34–36, 73, 121, 123
Barlow, Maude, 112–13, 195n4
Begando, Joseph, 29
Bell, Daniel, 15, 126
Benz, Dorothee, 165–66
Berkeley, CA. *See* University of California
Berkowitz, Joel, 168–69
Berry, Damon T., 119
Beyondism, 153
Binger, Carl, 45
Biondi, Dick, 95
Birmingham, AL, 97, 107
bond issue referendums, *29*; campaigns for in Illinois, 2, 14–15, 26–30, 79, 161; and Leo Koch, 14–15, 37–38, 65, 70–73, 123; and Revilo Oliver, 121
Bowen, Howard, 18
Brandeis University, 159
Broyles commission (Illinois), 18–19, 118
Buccola, Nicholas, 118, 119
Buckley, William F., Jr.: and conservatism's critics, 127; and *God and Man at Yale*, 118; and John Birch Society, 127, 129; and *National Review*, 12, 15, 33, 118–19, 127; and Revilo Oliver, 12–15, 33, 118–19, 127–29, 150; University of Illinois visit of, 97, 100, 127; and Young Americans for Freedom, 96
Bulletin of Atomic Scientists, 94
Burba, Tony, 139, 157–58
Bures, Dan, 57–60

Burlage, Robb K., 23
Butkus, Dick, 110
Butz, Otto, 22

Carey, James, 93–94
Castro, Fidel, 94, 133, 143
Cattell, Raymond, 153
Chalmers, W. Ellison, 123
Champaign-Urbana Courier, 34, 109; and Leo Koch, 42, 71–72; and Revilo Oliver, 116, 124
Channing Murray Foundation (Urbana, IL), 103, 106
Chappell, David L., 127
Chicago Civil Liberties Committee, 32, 34, 172
Chicago Daily News, 66, 72
Chicago's American, 72
Chicago Sun-Times 73, 109, 135, 173
Chicago Tribune, 32, 72, 124–25, 172
Church, Harrison, 149
City College of New York, 78
civil rights movement, 2, 52, *92*, 100, 160; and Birmingham, AL, 97, 107; and Freedom Summer, 16, 155, 170; and Ira Latimer, 14, 32, 172; and March on Washington, 106–7; and Revilo Oliver, 4, 133, 147–48, 152, 166; and Miriam Shelden, 52, 106–7, 160, 162, 169–70; and sit-ins, 56, 59, 155; at University of Illinois, 11–15, 56–57, 90–92, 106–8, 155
Clabaugh Act (Illinois), 18–19, 102–3, 118
Clark, Thomas Arkle, 50, 51. *See also* deans of students
Classical Philology, 153
Cobb, Deirdre Lynn, 90
Cobin, Martin, 93
Cohen v. California, 6
Cohn, Stu, 93
Cold War, 2, 9, 15, 30, 92–95. *See also* McCarthyism; Vietnam War
Cole, David Harris, 85–86
Cole, William and Doris, 57, 60–61, 64
college students: activism and discontent of, 10–11, 56–57, 102–9, 154–62, 168–69; and African Americans, 56–57, 90–92, 106–7, 155, 170; and baby boom generation, 2, 14, 21, 24–30, 159–62;

critiques of in 1950s and 1960s, 2, 10, 21–24, 101–2, 159–62; critiques of today, 1, 6–7, 159–62, 168–69; and Free Speech Movement, 8, 16, 74, 140, 155–56; and in loco parentis, 10, 50–57, 103–6, 154–55, 162; and silent generation, 2, 14, 21–24, 101–2, 161–62; and women, 10–12, 14, 44–61, 90, 169–70
College Tumor, 56
Collens, Lew, 91, 123–24
Columbia University, 125, 126
Committee for Liberal Action (University of Illinois), 56–57, 64, 71
Community Lecture Series (Decatur, IL), 144, *145*, 146–47
Compton (CA) High School, 113
Congressional Record, 132
Consent on Campus (Freitas), 11–12
Conservative Coordinating Council (University of Illinois), 96, 139
conspiracism, 103; academic critiques of, 13, 125–27, 166–67; and communism fears, 33–38, 120–34, 143–50; and fluoridation, 15, 119–20, 121; and free speech, 163–69; and John F. Kennedy assassination, 3, 131–34, 143–49, 164; and "Paranoid Style of American Politics," 129–30, 132; and politics today, 13, 166–67. *See also* John Birch Society; Latimer, Ira; Oliver, Revilo
Costello, James, 136, 141
Council for Community Integration (Champaign-Urbana, IL), 91
COVID-19, 1, 160
Cuba, 30; and Bay of Pigs invasion, 94; and Cuban missile crisis, 15, 94–95; and Revilo Oliver, 3, 127–28, 133, 143
culture wars, 12
Curley, Dan, 99–100

Daily Californian, 74
Daily Illini, 49, 55–57, 95, 97, 123; and civil rights, 59, 90–91, 107, 155, 162; and Cold War, 93–95; Roger Ebert as columnist and reporter, 46, 100–102, 156, 161–62, 172; Roger Ebert as editor-in-chief, 2, 15, 99–100, 106–10, 139; and free speech, 103, 108–9, 137–40, 162, 172; and David Henry, 24; and in loco parentis, 57, 104, 154–55; and John F. Kennedy, 88, 109–10; and Leo Koch dismissal, 63–72, 77–78, 85, 163–65, 171; and Leo Koch letters to the editor, 2–3, 11, 14, 42–43, 57–61; and Liz Krohne, 106, 140, 155, 171; and Karen Lucas, 106; and Philip Martin, 104–5; on Revilo Oliver 1964 and later, 16, 135–40, 149, 162, 172; on Revilo Oliver pre-1964, 114, 125, 149; and "Sex Ritualized," 43–44, 57–61, 77–78; and silent generation, 22–23; and George Stoddard, 19; and Strom Thurmond, 108, 135; and University of Illinois facilities, 25–27; and Vietnam, 107–8, 156–58
Dallas, TX, 109, 130–32, 146
Dallas Morning News, 130
Danelski, David, 77–78
Dangerfield, Royden, 36, 102
Daughters of the American Revolution (DAR), 19, 119, 121
Davis, Rennie, 97
deans of students, 50–55. *See also* Clark, Thomas Arkle; Shelden, Miriam; Turner, Fred
Dewey, John, 23, 34, 118; and Leo Koch, 12, 43; and Revilo Oliver, 12, 118, 120–21
Dilliard, Irving, 105, 138, 142
discipline on campus. *See* in loco parentis; sex
Douglas, Paul, 64–65, 124
Douglas, Susan J., 3, 10
Dutourd, Jean, 119

Easton, Carol, 90, 170
Ebert, Chaz Hammelsmith, 173
Ebert, Roger, 11, *99*; and Cuban missile crisis, 94; and Daniel Curley, 99–100; as *Daily Illini* columnist and reporter, 46, 100–102, 156, 161–62, 172; as *Daily Illini* editor-in-chief, 2, 15, 99–100, 106–10, 139; early life of, 98–100; family relationships of, 47, 98–99, 173; and film criticism, 100, 106, 173; and free speech, 101, 109, 137–38, 172; and Barry Goldwater, 101; and higher education critiques, 100, 101–2, 156, 161–62; and John F. Kennedy, 98, 101, 109–10;

Ebert, Roger (*continued*): and Liz Krohne, 97, 171; later life of, 173; and Revilo Oliver, 16, 110, 137–38, 142, 172; and religion, 98, 173; and Rose Bowl, 110; and sex, 46–47, 51; and *Spectator, 80*, 100
Eddy, Edward D., 23
Effort, Beverly, 90
Eisenhower, Dwight, 9, 42, 120, 124
Eisenmann, Linda, 44–45
Elliott, Rambling Jack, 95
Emerson, Thomas I., 81
Evans, M. Stanton, 96
extramural speech. *See* academic freedom; Statement on Extramural Utterances

Fair Play campaign (Champaign-Urbana, IL), 56, 59, 90–91
Fass, Paula S., 44, 53
Finkin, Matthew W., 4, 5
Fish, Stanley, 4
fluoridation protests, 15, 119–20, 121
Flynn, Charles, 136
folk music, 36, 95–96, 100
Forum for Dissent (Urbana, IL), 103, 106
Frank, Rudy, 107
Frankfurter, Felix, 128
Freedom Summer, 16, 155, 170. *See also* civil rights movement
Freeman, Wade, 103
free speech: academic freedom versus, 4–8, 163–69; and conspiracism, 163–69; and *Daily Illini*, 103, 108–9, 137–40, 162, 172; and Roger Ebert, 101, 109, 137–38, 172; and Free Speech Movement, 8, 16, 74, 140, 155–56; and higher education, 1–2, 4–8, 167–69; and Richard McMullin, 108–9; and Sexual Freedom League, 171; and Strom Thurmond, 108; and University of Illinois picketing, 102, 108. *See also* academic freedom; Koch, Leo; Oliver, Revilo
Free Speech Movement, 8, 16, 74, 140, 155–56
Freitas, Donna, 11–12, 163

Galesburg Register-Mail, 121
Geiger, Roger L., 25
gender roles, 10, 11–12, 14, 58, 106; and higher education, 44–45, 50–55, 169–70; and marriage, 44–45, 53–55. *See also* sex
general studies movement, 40–41
God and Man at Yale (Buckley), 118
Goldwater, Barry, 96, 127, 149, 172; and Roger Ebert, 101; presidential campaign of, 156–57
Goodman, Paul, 98, 100
Gove, Samuel, 136
Graebner, Norman, 36
Grange, Red, 19
Graves, Reverend J. E., 91
Great Debates (University of Illinois), 96–97, 100, 103, 127
Greene, Gael, 47, 48–49, 51, 55
Gregory, John Milton, 44
Griffith, Coleman, 79
Grigoriadis, Vanessa, 11
Growing Up Absurd (Goodman), 98, 100

Hargis, Billy James, 128
Harper, Robert and Frances, 55
Hartman, Andrew, 12
Harvard Crimson, 74
Harvard University, 74, 98, 104, 126
Hawley, George, 12–13, 165
Hefner, Hugh, 56
Heller, John L., *151*; and Revilo Oliver, 115, 122–25, 128–29, 136, 150–52; University of Illinois's hiring of, 115
Henry, David Dodds, 14–16, *20*, 50, 51, 95; and bond issue campaigns, 14, 24–30, 70–73, 79; early life of, 13, 19–20, 67; on higher education, 1–2, 5, 8–9, 104–5, 159–61; and Leo Koch, 43, 66–79, 82–83, 85, 134; later life and career of, 169; and New York University, 20–21; and Revilo Oliver, 121–25, 134, 136–43, 153–54; and Pennsylvania State University, 19; and picketing, 102; and red-baiting, 21, 36, 67; and Reserve Officers' Training Corps (ROTC), 93; and State of the University of Illinois reports, 104–5, 159–61; University of Illinois's hiring of, 20–21, 22, 24, 67; and Wayne State University, 20–21
Henry, Don, 94–95

higher education: and baby boom generation, 2, 14, 21, 24–30, 159–62; conservative critique of, 1, 6–7, 161, 168; current problems of, 1–2, 160–61, 167–69, 173; and free speech, 1–2, 4–8, 167–69; and gender roles, 44–45, 50–55, 169–70; and nostalgia for past, 8–10, 173; as public good, 8–9, 167; and silent generation, 2, 14, 21–24, 101, 161–62. *See also* academic freedom; college students; Free Speech Movement; in loco parentis
Hine, Reverend James, 63–64
Hirsch, Jennifer S., 163
Hofstadter, Richard, 15, 126, 129–30, 132
Holmes, Oliver Wendell, 81
Holocaust Museum (Washington, DC), 13, 152
Hoover, Herbert, 148
Hutchison, Dick, 57–60

Icen, Dick, 123
Illini Theater (Champaign, IL), 56
Illini Theater Guild, 114
Illinois Agricultural Association, 29, 30
Illinois Supreme Court, 33, 34, 35, 85
Illio, 71, *99*, 109
Imperium (Yockey), 129
in loco parentis, 10, 50–55, 103–6, 154–55, 160–62. *See also* sex
Institute of Economic Policy (Chicago), 33
International Foundation for Advanced Study, 39
Iowa Regular Baptists, 87

Jacob, Philip E., 22–23
JBS. *See* John Birch Society
J. C. Penney's (Champaign, IL), 91, *92*, 100, 102
Jenner, Albert, 148
John Birch Society (JBS), 12, 15–16; and William F. Buckley, 127, 129, 150; criticisms of, 120, 124–30, 135–36, 166; founding of, 120; and John F. Kennedy, 124–25, 130–36, 143–47; and Revilo Oliver, 120, 124–36, 143–54, 166; and politics today, 166
John Marshall Law School (Chicago), 31
Johnson, John, 139–40, 149

Johnson, Lyndon, 9, 156–57
Johnson, Nora, 46, 48
Johnston, Wayne, 65–67
Journal of Historical Review, 152
Jung, Robert, 16, 139

Kaeser "K" Room (University of Illinois), 97–98
Kalb, Bess, 165
Kay v. Board of Higher Education, 78
Kendall, Willmoore, 118–19, 150
Kennedy, John F., 2, 15, *88*, *89*, *131*; assassination of, 109–10, 130–31; and civil rights, 97; and Cuba, 94–95; and Roger Ebert, 98, 101, 109–10; historical assessments of, 3, 8–9; and Revilo Oliver, 110, 124–25, 131–36, 142–50, 164–65; and Peace Corps, 93; public opinion toward, 3, 164; University of Illinois 1960 visit of, 87–89, 109
Kennedy, Robert, 146
Kerner, Otto, 28
Kerner Commission, 172
Kerr, Clark, 9, 104–5, 155–56, 161
Khan, Shamus, 163
Khrushchev, Nikita, 30, 133
King, Martin Luther, Jr., 21, 106–7, 133. *See also* civil rights movement
Kinsey, Albert, 53, 54, 60, 85
Kinsey reports, 45–46, 54, 85
Kirk, Russell, 120, 149–50
Kirkendall, Lester A., 55
Klatch, Rebecca E., 10–11
Knudson, Charles A., 105
Koch, Leo, *41*, 77, 97, 134, 161; and academic freedom, 1–16, 64–86, 122, 163–69; and American Association of University Professors (AAUP), 76, 80–84; and Camp Summerlane, 85; and Committee for Leo Koch, 84; early life and career of, 39–40; editorials against, 72–73; and David Henry, 43, 66–79, 82–83, 85, 134; and humanism, 12, 39–43, 59, 63–64, 165; later life of, 85–86, 171; and Ira Latimer, 37–38, 64–66, 70–73, 123, 130; and lawsuits against the University of Illinois, 84–85; and Leo F. Koch Fund, 84; letter campaign against, 65–66;

Koch, Leo (*continued*): letters to the editor by, 2–3, 11, 14, 42–43, 57–64; and LSD, 39, 85; Revilo Oliver comparisons with, 1–16, 136–43, 149, 163–67; and nudism, 12, 39, 85, 171; rally for, 71, 72, 80; and religion, 3, 42–43, 58–60, 165; sex views of, 58–61, 74, 85–86, 163–65, 171; and Sexual Freedom League, 12, 39, 85, 171; as teacher, 40–43, 68, 74, 164–65; at University of Illinois, 40–44, 58–78
Koch, Shirley, 40, 60–61, 77, 171
Konda, Thomas Milan, 13, 166, 167
Krohne, Liz, 97, 106, 140, 155, 170–71
Kronhausen, Phyllis and Eberhard, 49
Kugler, Otto, 41–43, 67–68

Labaree, David F., 8, 9
Ladies' Home Journal, 54
Lanier, Lyle, 68–70, 74, 122–23
Latimer, Ira, 12, 14–15, *31*, 75, 110; and anticommunism, 32–38, 64–67, 123; bar application of, 32–33, 35; early life of, 30–31; and Leo Koch, 37–38, 64–66, 70–73, 123, 130; later life of, 171–72; and left-liberal causes, 32, 36–37, 172; and Revilo and Grace Oliver, 14, 33–37, 64–65, 123, 172; and religion, 31–32, 33–35, 65; and University of Illinois, 32, 34–38, 61, 64–67, 70–73
League for Moral Responsibility (Illinois), 65, 73
Lesemann, Ralph, 77–78
Levine, Milton I., 55
Lewis, Oscar, 94
Liberal Discussion Group (University of Illinois), 140
Liberty Bell (magazine), 152
Lincoln, Abraham, 15, 89, 114
Little Clay Cart, The, 114
Lodge, Henry Cabot, Jr., 87
Los Angeles Times, 124
Lucas, Karen, 106

Mademoiselle, 10, 101–2
Madhubuti, Safisha. *See* Easton, Carol
Manchester, William, 21–22
March on the Pentagon, 171. *See also* Vietnam War

March on Washington, 106–7. *See also* civil rights movement
Marcovich, Miroslav, 153
Martin, Eden, 104
Martin, Philip, 104–6
"Marxmanship in Dallas" (Oliver), 132–47, 154, 165–66, 172
Mason, Ruby, 51
Matsuda, Mari J., 6
Mautz, James, 49–50
McCarthy, Joseph, 21, 22, 33, 117, 118
McCarthyism, 18–19, 21, 67, 70, 83
McCollum, Vashti, 32
McCrimmon, James, 41–43, 67–68
McGuire, Patricia, 4
McMullin, Richard, 108–9
McPherson, Aimee Semple, 113
McVeigh, Timothy, 152
McWilliams, Carey, Jr., 97, 100
Mead, Margaret, 54–55
Mehler, Barry, 153
Metz, Michael V., 10, 17
Mikesell, R. D., 35
Miller, Henry, 100
Mintz, Frank P., 147
Mississippi Free Press, 155
Modern Age, 120–21, 149
Moore, Donald, 77, 78
Morantz, Regina Markell, 54
Morey, Lloyd, 19
Morrow, Charles, 121
Morrow, Kelly, 51
Mount, Eloise, 65, 73, 123
Mueller, Kate Hevner, 54
multiversity, 104–5

NAACP: and civil rights campaigns, 12, 56, 90–91, 107; right-wing attacks against, 35, 149
Nack, Bill, 106
National Association of Manufacturers, 120
National Association of Real Estate Boards, 155
National Review, 96, 150; founding of, 119; and John Birch Society, 127, 133; and Ira Latimer, 33; Revilo Oliver as contributor, 12, 15, 33, 116–19, 150; Revilo Oliver expelled by, 127

National Youth Alliance, 152
New England Rally for God, Family, and Country, 152
Newfield, Christopher, 167
News-Gazette, The (Champaign, IL), 18, 34, 42, 98, 109
Newsweek, 73, 135
New Voice (University of Illinois), 96, 97
New York Times, 23, 135, 169
New York University, 20–21, 52
1960s: significance of, 8–13
Nixon, Richard, 42, 87, 156–57
Northwestern University, 90, 108, 170
Nossel, Suzanne, 164, 168
Not All Dead White Men (Zuckerberg), 165
Novak, Robert, 96
Nowlan, Jim, 96, 149

Odetta, 95
Ohio State University, 30–31
Oldfather, William Abbott, 114–15, 116–17
Oliver, Flora Lang, 112–13
Oliver, Franklin, 111–12
Oliver, Grace Needham, 114, *116*, 135, 143, 153; and Ira Latimer, 14, 33–37, 64–65, 123, 172
Oliver, Revilo, *116*, *145*, *147*; academic honors of, 115–16, 125; and *American Opinion*, 124, 129, 132–34, 142, 143–44; anti-Semitism and racism of, 1–16, 117, 127–29, 133, 147–54, 164–67; and William F. Buckley Jr., 12–15, 33, 118–19, 127–29, 150; and Christianity, 119, 144, 165; and *Daily Illini* 1964 and later, 2, 16, 135–40, 149, 162; and *Daily Illini* pre-1964, 114, 125, 149; and devotion to classics, 115, 117; early life of, 113–15, 195n4; family of, 111–14; and fluoridation, 15, 119–20, 121; and John L. Heller, 115, 122–25, 128–29, 136, 150–52; and John Birch Society, 120, 124–36, 143–54, 166; and Willmoore Kendall, 118–19, 150; and John F. Kennedy, 110, 124–25, 131–36, 142–50, 164–65; and Russell Kirk, 120, 149–50; Leo Koch comparisons with, 1–16, 136–43, 149, 163–67; later life of, 172; and Ira Latimer 14, 33–37, 64–65, 123, 172; and Miroslav Marcovich, 153; and "Marxmanship in Dallas," 132–47, 154, 165–66, 172; and Joseph McCarthy, 117, 118; and *Modern Age*, 120–21, 149; as *National Review* contributor, 12, 15, 33, 116–19, 150; and *National Review* expulsion, 127; and neo-Nazism, 12, 116–17, 152–54, 164–67; and William Abbott Oldfather, 114–15, 116–17; and pragmatism, 12, 120–21; public complaints against, 121–22, 128, 135–37, 145–46, 153–54; and Franklin D. Roosevelt, 115, 117, 124; and Richard Scanlan, 153; scholarly output of, 115–16, 117–19, 151, 153, 167; speeches of, 119–21, 127–29, 144–48, 152; as teacher, 122, 149, 151; at University of Illinois, 113–54; and Warren Commission, 3, 132, 146, 148; and Robert Welch, 12, 15, 127, 135, 152; and World War II, 115, 117
Oliver, Revilo (father of professor), 112–13, 115, 117, 172
Osgood, Charles, 94
Oswald, Lee Harvey, 109–10, 130–33, 143–46, 148
Overton window, 163
Oxford University, 129, 130

pacifism, 92–95, 102
Paquette, Gabriel, 161
"Paranoid Style in American Politics, The" (Hofstadter), 129–30, 132
Parent Trap, The (1961), 100
parietals. *See* in loco parentis; sex
Peace Corps, 11, 93
Peltason, Jack, 36, 50, 128–29, 136, 141
Pennsylvania State University, 19
Perlongo, Bob, 22–23
Peter, Paul, and Mary, 95
Peters, John Durham, 6, 168
Pharos (online platform), 152–53, 165, 167
Philbrick, Herbert, 35–36, 37
Pierce, William, 152
Pines, Maya, 55
Playboy, 56
Pogue, Harold, 142
Poland, Jefferson, 85
Pomona College, 113
Porter, Gary, 108, 138, 156–57

Port Huron Statement, 97–98
Post, Robert C., 4, 5
Prairie Post (Maroa, IL), 145–46
"Primer Lesson" (Sandburg), 160

QAnon, 166
Quirk, John, 156, 157

Rabinowitch, Eugene, 94
radical right, 15, 125, *126*, *131*, 169. *See also* John Birch Society; "Marxmanship in Dallas"; "Paranoid Style in American Politics, The"
Ray, Gordon, 43, 122, 124, 134
Reagan, Ronald, 172
Reichman, Henry, 4, 7, 168–69
Reserve Officers' Training Corps (ROTC), 92–93, 102, 109
Revolt on the Campus (Evans), 96
Reynolds, Colin E., 120
Riddle, Oscar, 43, 70–71
Rockland County (NY), 171
Rockwell, George Lincoln, 103
Rolison, Connie, 90, 155, 170
Roosevelt, Franklin D., 115, 117, 124
Rose Bowl (1964 football game), 110
Rosin, Hanna, 11
ROTC. *See* Reserve Officers' Training Corps
Ruby, Jack, 109, 110, 131, 133, 146
Rule, John T., 55
Russell, Bertrand, 78

Sachar, Abram L., 159–61, 166–67
Salaita, Steven, 6, 167
Salisbury, Glenn, 75
Sandburg, Carl, 160
Saturday Evening Post, 10, 102
Saunders, Eleanor, 107, 170
Scanlan, Richard, 153
Scholz, Dale, 144–45
Schrecker, Ellen W., 6, 18, 21
Schwarzlose, Richard, 108
Science (magazine), 43
Scott, Joan Wallach, 4–5, 7, 8, 83, 163–64
sex, 1–3, 10, 13–14; calls for conversation about, 54–55, 162–63; and contraception, 46, 48–49, 54–55, 60, 68; and double standard, 14, 47, 74, 154; and "hookup culture," 11–12, 163; ignorance about, 48–49, 54, 59–60; and in loco parentis, 10, 50–55, 103–4, 154–55, 162; and Kinsey reports, 45–46, 54, 85; Leo Koch's views toward, 58–61, 74, 85–86, 163–65, 171; and LGBTQ+ identities, 11, 45, 51, 163; and petting, 46–47, 54, 57–61, 74; and popular culture, 47–48, 73; and pregnancy, 46, 47, 48–49, 54–55; and "Sex Ritualized," 11, 14, 43–44, 57–61, 77–78; and sexual assault, 1, 11, 47–50, 163; and Sexual Freedom League, 12, 39, 85, 171, 206n33; and sexual revolution, 8–9, 45, 55, 158, 162–63; and "three-foot rule," 51. *See also* gender roles
"Sex Ritualized" (Hutchinson and Bures), 11, 14, 43–44, 57–61, 77–78. *See also* sex
Sexual Freedom League (New York City League for Sexual Freedom), 12, 39, 85, 171, 206n33. *See also* sex
Sharon Statement, 96
Sheehy, Gail, 21–22, 23–24
Shelden, Miriam, 10, 36, *52*; and civil rights, 106–7, 162, 170; and in loco parentis, 53–54, 160, 162; life and career of, 52, 169–70; and universities' role, 16, 53, 160, 163, 173; and women, 52–53, 107, 160, 169–70. *See also* deans of students
Sheridan, Si, 100
Shirah, Betsy. *See* Krohne, Liz
Shirelles, The, 47
silent generation, 2, 14, 21–24, 101, 161–62
Siskel, Gene, 173
Smythe, Dallas, 93–95
snoot boot, 95
Solomon, Barbara Miller, 44
Spectator (Champaign-Urbana, IL), *80*, 100
Spencer, Richard, 13
sphere of legitimate controversy, 163
Springfield Leader and Press (MO), 125
Sputnik, 9, 25
Statement of Principles on Academic Freedom and Tenure, 69, 75, 81, 83. *See also* academic freedom
Statement on Extramural Utterances, 83. *See also* academic freedom
Steinem, Gloria, 21, 46, 55
Steward, Cliff, 104

St. Louis Post-Dispatch, 105, 138
Stoddard, George, 17–19, 21, 67, 79, 179n6
Stone, Victor, 34–36, 75, 83
Stout, Susan, 49–50
Stratton, William, 26–28
Student Nonviolent Coordinating Committee, 155, 170
students. *See* college students
Students for a Democratic Society, 10, 97–98, 102, 155, 157
Szoke, Ron, 103, 106

talkathons, 95
Taxis of the Marne, The (Dutourd), 119
Taylor, Warren, 82
Thelin, John R., 7, 9, 11, 102, 167
Thomas, Norman, 64–65
Thurmond, Strom, 108, 135, 144
Tiebout, Harry, 36; and civil rights, 12, 56, 91, 100; and Leo Koch, 12, 43, 74, 164
Tiede, Hans-Joerg, 83
Time, 21, 73, 96
Times v. Sullivan, 5–6
Tippit, J. D., 146
Treichler, Paula A., 44, 50–51
Tropic of Cancer (Miller), 100
Trump, Donald, 166
Tuchinsky, Joe, 93
Tucker, William H., 153
Tulane University, 40
Turner, Fred, 18, 51–52, 56. *See also* deans of students
Turner Diaries, The (Pierce), 152
twist (dance), 95

Unitarian-Universalist church (Urbana, IL), 85, 103
United Press International, 72, 135
University of California, 9, 40, 104, 161; and Free Speech Movement, 8, 16, 74, 140, 155–56
University of Colorado, 101
University of Illinois: academic freedom committee, 15–16, 34, 75–76, 82, 137–43; academic reputation of, in 1950s, 17, 24; and African Americans, 56–57, 90–92, 106–7, 155, 170; Alumni Association, 136; Assembly Hall, 27, 109, 159; auditorium, 87, 88, 95, 107, 157; and baby boom, 2, 14, 24–30, 159, 161–62; and bond issue referendums, 2, 14–15, 26–30, 79, 161; and William F. Buckley Jr., 97, 100, 127; Chicago campus, 24, 79, 82, 180n22; and civil rights movement, 11–15, 56–57, 90–92, *92*, 106–8, 155; and Clabaugh Act, 18–19, 102–3, 118; classics department, 114–16, 122, 125, 128–29, 150–53; College of Education, 26; College of Liberal Arts and Sciences (LAS), 68–70, 74, 122–23, 128–29; Committee on Student Affairs (CSA), 91; Dads Association, 28, 37, 65, 73; Division of General Studies (DGS), 40–43, 67–68, 165, 182n4; elm trees, 26, 27, 180n27; fraternities and sororities, 55–61, 90–91, 99, 102, 170; Humanist Society, 43, 63, 64; Illini Union, 26–27, 76–77, 90, 108–9; and in loco parentis, 50–54, 103–6, 154–55, 160, 162; and John F. Kennedy 1960 visit, 87, *88*, *89*, 109; and Leo Koch, 40–44, 58–78; and Ira Latimer, 32, 34–38, 61, 64–67, 70–73; law school, 75, 83, 137, 141; and McCarthyism, 18–19, 21, 67; and Richard McMullin, 108–9; Moms Association, 28, 73; and new buildings, 26–30, 79; and Revilo Oliver, 113–54; and pacifism, 92–95, 102; and picketing, 102, 108; and Reserve Officers' Training Corps (ROTC), 92–93, 102, 109; School of Social Work, 25–26; and space shortages, 25–27, 34; statutes of, 69–70, 76, 82–84, 124, 136–41; and George Stoddard, 17–19, 21, 67, 79, 179n6; and student activism and discontent, 56–57, 102–9, 154–58; and student fads, 95–96; student senate, 28, 56, 72, 93–97, 103–8; and Strom Thurmond, 108, 135, 144; and visiting speakers, 18–19, 87–89, 96–97, 102–3, 118; and water fights, 56, 71, 95; and women, 44, 49–61, 107, 160, 169–70; and YMCA/YWCA, 36, 57, 71, 96–98
University of Illinois Board of Trustees, 13, 91, 123; and David Henry's hiring, 21, 67; and Leo Koch, 14–16, 65–70, 75–82, 85, 97; and Revilo Oliver, 16, 137, 139, 142–45; and George Stoddard, 19, 67, 79, 179n6

University of Illinois Press, 114
University of Iowa, 74
University of Michigan, 40, 74
University of Wisconsin-Madison, 155
University of Wisconsin-Milwaukee, 168
Unleashing of Evolutionary Thought, The (Riddle), 43, 70–71
Unsilent Generation, The (Butz), 22
U of I. *See* University of Illinois

Vietnam War, 16, 22; and *Daily Illini*, 107–8, 156–58; protests against, 5, 12, 94, 103, 171
von Brunn, James, 152

Walker, Edwin, 127, 130–31, 132–33, 146
Wall Street Journal, The, 96
Ward, Brian, 8, 9
Warren, Earl, 120
Warren Commission, 3, 132, 146, 148
Watkins, Frances Best, 66–67
Wayne State University, 20–21
Weiss, Jessica, 45
Welch, Robert, 120, 124–27, 166; and Revilo Oliver, 12, 15, 127, 135, 152. *See also* John Birch Society
Welsh, Robert, 157
Westin, Alan F., 125–26

Where the Boys Are (novel and 1960 movie), 47, 48
White, Josh, 95
white supremacy, 1–2, 12–13, 152, 165–67. *See also* alt-right; Oliver, Revilo
Whittington, Keith E., 168
Willard, Arthur, 32
"Will You Love Me Tomorrow" (Shirelles), 47
Wilson, Bob, 145–46
Wilson, John K., 5–7, 80, 83
women. *See* college students; gender roles; sex; University of Illinois
Woodstock festival, 12, 171
Wordlaw, Earl, 107

Yale University, 81, 118
Yellin, Edward, 36, 65–66
YMCA-YWCA (University of Illinois), 36, 57, 71, 96–98
Yockey, Francis Parker, 129
Young, David, 96
Young Americans for Freedom, 10, 96, 97, 102, 156, 157
Young Democrats, 156, 157
Young Republicans, 156

Zuckerberg, Donna, 117, 165

MATTHEW C. EHRLICH is Professor Emeritus of Journalism at the University of Illinois. His books include *Kansas City vs. Oakland: The Bitter Sports Rivalry That Defined an Era* and *Radio Utopia: Postwar Audio Documentary in the Public Interest*, winner of the James W. Tankard Book Award.

The University of Illinois Press
is a founding member of the
Association of University Presses.

University of Illinois Press
1325 South Oak Street
Champaign, IL 61820-6903
www.press.uillinois.edu